ESCAPING THE JOURNEY TO NOWHERE

ESCAPING THE JOURNEY TO NOWHERE
The Psychology of Alcohol and Other Drug Abuse

Glenn D. Walters, Ph.D.

Taylor & Francis
Publishers since 1798

USA	Publishing Office:	Taylor & Francis
		1101 Vermont Avenue, N.W., Suite 200
		Washington, DC 20005-3521
		Tel: (202) 289-2174
		Fax: (202) 289-3665
	Distribution Center:	Taylor & Francis
		1900 Frost Road, Suite 101
		Bristol, PA 19007-1598
		Tel: (215) 785-5800
		Fax: (215) 785-5515
UK		Taylor & Francis Ltd.
		4 John St.
		London WC1N 2ET
		Tel: 071 405 2237
		Fax: 071 831 2035

ESCAPING THE JOURNEY TO NOWHERE: The Psychology of Alcohol and Other Drug Abuse

1 2 3 4 5 6 7 8 9 0   B R B R   9 8 7 6 5 4

This book was set in Times Roman by EPS Group Inc. The editors were Margaret Chang and Caroline Schweiter; the production supervisor was Peggy M. Rote. Cover design by Michelle Fleitz. Printing and binding by Braun-Brumfield, Inc.

A CIP catalog record for this book is available from the British Library.
∞ The paper in this publication meets the requirements of the ANSI Standard Z39.48-1984 (Permanence of Paper)

Library of Congress Cataloging-in-Publication Data

Walters, Glenn D.
   Escaping the journey to nowhere: the psychology of alcohol and
other drug abuse / Glenn D. Walters.
      p.   cm.
   Includes bibliographical references (p.) and index.

   1. Drug abuse—United States—Psychological aspects.
2. Alcoholism—United States—Psychological aspects. 3. Narcotic
addicts—Rehabilitation—United States. 4. Alcoholics—
Rehabilitation—United States. I. Title.
HV5825.W38127 1994
616.86—dc20   94-5567
ISBN 1-56032-318-3 (cloth)   CIP
ISBN 1-56032-319-1 (paperback)

*I dedicate this book to my parents, Richard and Joan Walters,
and my parents-in-law, Robert and Miriam Boyle, whose love, support,
and knowledge have inspired me to look beyond what is and
consider what may be.*

Contents

PART 2: DEVELOPMENT

PART 3: TREATMENT

Preface

Given the number of books and articles written each year on the topic of substance abuse and substance abuse treatment, one might be prompted to ask what the present work has to offer that has not been covered in previous publications. The answer is revealed in this book's advocacy of a viewpoint radically different from that contained in traditional explanations of substance abuse development and treatment. The lifestyle perspective presented here, in fact, deviates so widely from established views on substance abuse that some readers may be tempted to abandon reading it before they have completed the first chapter.

The uncomfortable emotions this book may arouse in persons committed to a more traditional view of drug abuse and drug abuse treatment are signs of intellectual conflict; and it should be kept in mind that intellectual conflict stimulates personal growth and innovation. For this reason, such conflict serves as the primary focus of lifestyle intervention and change. In order to be liberated from the chains that define lifestyle living, whether the lifestyle involves dependency on drugs or dependency on traditional drug treatment philosophies, the individual is encouraged to use intellectual conflict to refine his or her own personal view of the world.

Lifestyle theory views intellectual conflict as one avenue through which growth may be realized, whereas complacency is thought to breed intellectual and emotional stagnation. Intellectual conflict achieves its growth-promoting effect by expanding the scope of current knowledge and allowing for the prospect of adaptive living. Adaptability entails the development of personal resources through interaction with one's wider social and physical environment. The key to change, according to lifestyle theory, is using adaptive skills to find innovative solutions to life's problems.

A lifestyle, on the other hand, provides roles, rules, relationships, and explicit criteria for success and failure. It supplies short-term solutions to a problem but ignores pivotal long-term issues. In order to break free of the mesmerizing influence of a drug or other lifestyle, individuals must be receptive to new information from which they can derive their own conclusions, rather than rely on lifestyle-based rituals and activities.

This book provides new information in the form of a perspective on drug abuse that stems from the author's earlier work with criminal offenders. Hence, the book may not be relevant to all forms of substance abuse but is an alternative that clearly warrants further study. After all, research suggests that early antisocial behavior is often the single best predictor of future substance abuse difficulties (Nathan, 1988).

In the pages that follow, a lifestyle interpretation of drug use behavior will be presented. Some readers will view it with interest, others with suspicion. Such a difference of opinion, however, speaks to the value of this book and of the viewpoint it represents. The lifestyle approach to drug-seeking behavior may not be applicable to all substance abuse problems or populations, and it may be more appropriate in some settings than others; however, it does seem capable of promoting intellectual conflict. Thus it may stimulate growth in a field that has too long depended on the disease and traditional social work models to conceptualize the drug-seeking behavior of its clients. The challenge for readers of this book is to comprehend and reflect on lifestyle theory, in its entirety, before arriving at a conclusion about the value of the overall model for their own academic, clinical, or professional purposes. In *Escaping the Journey to Nowhere*, the reader will be introduced to the lifestyle model's interpretation of drug-seeking behavior, divided into three basic sections: origins, development, and treatment.

Glenn D. Walters

Part 1

Origins

Chapter 1

Of Pebbles, Ponds, and Ripples

INTRODUCTION

A pebble thrown into a pond gives rise to a ripple that reaches out symmetrically toward shore until it is interrupted by a jutting rock or tree branch. Several pebbles tossed into a pond create multiple circular patterns, many of which form overlapping or interacting ripples. If these pebbles are used allegorically to describe the development of a drug lifestyle, they symbolize sundry internal and external conditions, whereas the pond represents the life space of the individual. It can be inferred from this analogy that even though numerous influences impinge on a person's life space, their primary effect is communicated through their interactions with other influences. The ripples that blanket the surface of a lake or pond may have wide-ranging consequences not only for the individual but for others as well. Humans are, by nature, social animals who seek the company of other human beings. Consequently, the ripples that define one person's life space frequently spill over to affect the life spaces of people with whom the subject comes into contact, represented in the pebble analogy by adjacent or linking pools of influence.

Although the ponds used to symbolize the life spaces of individual subjects may differ in shape, size, and depth, their most discriminating features are the unique panoply of ripples each pond displays in response to the pebbles that pummel its surface. Each pond exhibits its own pattern of ripples, representative of the singular nature of each person's life space, and, like fingerprints, no two patterns are exactly alike. Moreover, individuals seek to amplify certain ripples while resisting others in an effort to accentuate specific features of their life space and downplay others.

Traditional explanations of drug use behavior, for the most part, have focused on classes and categories of pebbles (or conditions), based on the assumption that understanding the shape, size, or nature of such influences will provide insight into the development and treatment of drug-seeking behavior. Lifestyle theory, on the other hand, contends that understanding the *ripples* and the manner in which individuals attempt to amplify or limit these ripples will ameliorate the problem of substance abuse. Still, the pebbles are clearly not to be ignored. Before examining the major categories of pebbles that underlie an understanding of the origins of a drug lifestyle, certain definitional issues must be addressed.

DEFINITIONAL ISSUES

Most definitions hold that a drug is any chemical substance other than food that affects the structure or function of the body. The investigation presented here confines itself to chemical compounds—alcohol, marijuana, cocaine, and heroin, among others—that alter a person's mood or subjective emotional state. Whether a drug is legal or illegal, manufactured or harvested, injected or swallowed, the critical issue from the standpoint of this book is that the drug lends itself to widespread misuse because of its mood-altering properties. Drug abuse is defined here as an individual's regular ingestion of a mood-altering substance to the point where his or her physical, emotional, or social well-being is compromised. There is a distinct developmental progression to drug abuse that is not lost on lifestyle theory: namely, that dependence on and preoccupation with drug use and drug-related activities escalate as one's involvement with drugs widens. These issues will be scrutinized in the middle section of this book. With drugs and drug abuse briefly defined, the next order of business is to identify and discuss traditional perspectives on drug-seeking behavior.

TRADITIONAL PERSPECTIVES ON DRUG ABUSE

A plethora of perspectives designed to unravel the mysteries of substance abuse has been proposed. Most, however, are concerned principally with a narrow range of factors or etiological agents. These factors generally fall into one of three general categories: biological agents, psychological agents, and sociological agents. With these categories as an organizing framework, the major theories of drug abuse can be grouped into three primary clusters, as illustrated in Table 1-1. Each of the major perspectives on drug abuse will receive cursory attention here, to be followed by a more comprehensive examination in subsequent chapters of this book.

Biological Perspective

Biology-based theories of drug-seeking behavior emphasize the genetic and physiological correlates of substance abuse and drug dependency. Scholars who profess allegiance to a genetic interpretation of drug-seeking behavior contend that certain individuals are genetically predisposed to engage in drug-seeking behavior (Schuckit, 1987). The inherited quality that predisposes a person to such activities is still open to debate, although it has been speculated that genetic factors may affect future drug use outcomes by influencing the manner in which the brain and central nervous system process alcohol and other drugs (Wilson & Plomin, 1985).

The disease model of addiction, as advocated by the American Medical Association (AMA) and such popular self-help groups as Alcoholics Anonymous (AA), maintains that biological factors are of prime etiological significance in the formation of drug-seeking patterns of behavior. This model holds that alcohol abuse and other chemical dependencies are incurable, progressive, and potentially fatal diseases that can only be arrested through adherence to a goal of total abstinence (Miller & Gold, 1990). The ultimate validity of this perspective rests on its ability to conceptualize

Table 1-1   Major Perspectives on Drug Abuse

Variables emphasized	Model of drug abuse
Biological	
Heredity	Genetic approach
Other	Disease model
Psychological	
Learning	Opponent-process
	Operant studies
	Social learning theory
Personality	Addictive personality
Psychological disorder	Self-medication hypothesis
Sociological	
Sociocultural	Sociocultural perspective
Familial	Parental rejection
Peers	Differential association

drug-seeking behavior usefully and to supply practical procedures for intervention—topics discussed in Chapters 2 and 10.

Psychological Perspective

Psychological perspectives on drug use behavior rely on three primary types of putative etiological agents: learning, personality, and psychological disorder. Learning theories of drug-seeking behavior emphasize classical, operant, or social learning models of behavior acquisition in which, respectively, environmental cues elicit a drug-seeking response, a subject pursues drugs because of their immediately reinforcing value, or other individuals serve as models for drug use behavior. Shephard Siegel's (1988) opponent-process learning model of drug-seeking behavior, for instance, takes a classical conditioning approach to the question of drug tolerance, withdrawal, and craving.

The second set of psychological conditions implicated in the development of drug-seeking behavior revolves around the personality of the user. Some theorists propose an addictive personality model of drug abuse vulnerability (Nakken, 1988), in which the individual is seen as engaging in a self-defeating pattern of activity as a consequence of various character flaws.

A third theme sounded by psychology-oriented models of drug-seeking behavior is that substance abuse may exist as a symptom of some underlying psychological disorder. This theme finds expression in the self-medication hypothesis, in which substance abuse is interpreted as an attempt by the individual to eliminate, quell, or diminish uncomfortable feelings of depression, anger, or isolation (Khantzian, 1985). The validity of these psychological perspectives on drug abuse is examined in Chapter 3.

Sociological Perspective

The domain of sociological etiological agents relevant to the initiation of drug-seeking behavior encompasses both wide-spectrum (sociocultural) and narrow-band (familial and peer) influences. The sociocultural perspective maintains that the cultural context of human behavior must be taken into account when investigating an activity like substance abuse. MacAndrew and Edgerton (1969), for example, note that changes in behaviors attributable to the use of alcohol are widely influenced by sociocultural beliefs, values, and practices.

The role of the family in promoting future drug activity is succinctly summarized in Simons, Conger, and Whitbeck's (1988) family model of juvenile substance abuse, in which parental rejection and maternal/paternal drinking behavior are perceived to exert both a direct and an indirect (through the intermediary action of aggression, peer associations, self-esteem, and coping style) effect on future substance abuse difficulties. Peers are also viewed as a powerful narrow-band source of motivation for adolescent substance abuse, as epitomized in Sutherland's differential association theory of deviant behavior (Sutherland & Cressey, 1978) and substantiated in a recent study on marijuana use among college students (Orcutt, 1987). These sociological explanations of drug use behavior, and the data on which they are based, are elaborated in Chapter 4.

A TWO-TRACK MODEL

Lifestyle theory affords researchers and clinicians an alternative view of drug-seeking behavior by emphasizing the lifestyle that grows up around a person's use of chemical substances. Although lifestyle theory does not discount the influence of conditions on future and concurrent criminal outcomes, it holds that such conditions are simply one factor in a more comprehensive equation that expounds the nature of a drug lifestyle. The other two major elements of the equation are choice and cognition. However, conditions, choice, and cognition taken together do not account for lifestyle theory in its entirety; the lifestyle approach operates along two tracks, and each must be considered in forming a comprehensive understanding of drug-seeking behavior. These two tracks are actually different divisions of the same model; they overlap, intersect, and eventually merge. The tracks, known as the *structural* and *functional* divisions of lifestyle theory, provide a richer source of information and hypotheses than is possible in the traditional single-track approach to studying drug-seeking behavior.

The structural, or content, track of lifestyle theory spotlights the conditions, choices, and cognitions that form the nucleus of a drug lifestyle. *Conditions* are those internal or external factors that contribute to future and concurrent drug use outcomes by augmenting or abating a person's options in life. *Choices* are decisions individuals make with respect to the use of drugs, and *cognitions* are the thinking patterns employed by individuals to justify and rationalize such use and to minimize the seriousness of any negative long-term consequences such use may create. These three factors constitute an interlocking network of influences that define the structural features of a drug or other lifestyle. The structural model, therefore, provides a blueprint of lifestyle content with which the component features and defining characteristics of a drug lifestyle can be identified, examined, and modified.

The functional track of lifestyle theory outlines the process of lifestyle development and change. Here, the emphasis is on existential fear and the subject's reaction to this fear. The theory advocates adaptation as the optimal response to existential fear, because adaptation maximizes opportunities for long-term success. Lifestyle behavior, on the other hand, is the antithesis of successful adaptation. Bruce Alexander (1990) has advanced the hypothesis that addiction is adaptation in the face of "integration failure." Lifestyle theorists prefer to view substance abuse as faulty adaptation in the face of existential fear. Although there are features of drug abuse and crime that are clearly adaptive, the drug lifestyle is construed by the functional track of lifestyle theory to be the reverse of adaptation, in that it exists as a short-term repetitive solution to a series of long-term problems. Adaptation, in contrast, epitomizes innovation, as represented by the act of changing one's behavior to suit changing environmental conditions in an effort to balance short- and long-term goals and expectations.

Few people embrace a lifestyle in its entirety, and even fewer achieve consummate adaptation. It is imperative that the reader appreciate the fact that the drug lifestyle serves as a caricature that few people fit in the absolute. The objective of the functional track of lifestyle theory is not to determine whether individuals reflect all aspects of this caricature, but to measure how closely they approximate this hypothetical entity at a particular point in time. For diagnostic purposes, lifestyle theory draws an arbitrary circle around the caricature (using information gathered through sources such as the Drug Lifestyle Screening Interview described in Chapter 8) and classifies everyone who falls inside the circle as significantly committed to the drug lifestyle ideal. Because adaptation and the drug lifestyle are two extreme points on a continuum of human experience, most actions that people take are a combination of the extremes. The goal of lifestyle intervention is to enhance subjects' adaptive resources while minimizing their reliance on lifestyle activities.

THE PURPOSE OF THIS BOOK

The overriding purpose of this book is to provide an alternative view of drug-seeking behavior that is capable of supplementing or replacing traditional perspectives on substance abuse. Lifestyle theory looks beyond the physiological action of the drug and challenges traditional notions about "disease" and addiction. It de-emphasizes—but does not ignore—the psychological and social conditions that give rise to a person's initial involvement with drugs, choosing instead to concentrate on the lifestyle that forms from continued involvement in drug-related activities. This shift in focus gives birth to a theory in which concepts such as drug of choice and addiction are discarded in favor of a perspective in which habitual drug use is seen as a response to existential fear, the expression of which is a complex function of the conditions, choices, and cognitions that define a person's life space.

This book begins with the pebbles, or conditions, that initially give rise to the ripples, or behavioral patterns, of a drug lifestyle. It then moves into a discussion of the developmental and treatment implications of lifestyle theory, topics that speak to the potential integration of the structural and functional tracks of lifestyle theory.

Chapter 2

Biological Factors

INTRODUCTION

The biological perspective on drug-seeking behavior holds that heredity and physiology play a major role in the etiology of alcoholism and drug abuse. The first of these two factors, heredity, is grounded in genes, microscopic collections of nucleotides organized along a section of DNA. There are several millions of these tiny structures distributed throughout the human body; their job is to code for the production of certain proteins or control other genetic material in the development of specific physical attributes (e.g., eye color) and behavioral predispositions. Physiological investigations are included in a biological study of substance abuse, first, because they offer a method by which putative genetic effects may be identified and explained, and, second, because they help identify potential sources of biology-environment interaction. This chapter scrutinizes the biological roots of substance abuse in an effort to determine whether genetic and physiological factors are significantly involved in the formation of a drug lifestyle.

GENETIC STUDIES

Three primary methodologies have been used to explore the heritability of alcoholism and drug abuse: family studies, twin studies, and adoption studies.

Family Studies

Family studies document substance abuse problems in the biological relatives of known alcoholics and drug addicts as a means of investigating the possibility of a familial link in substance abuse. The results of such studies indicate that the incidence and prevalence of alcoholism are significantly higher in the first- and second-degree relatives of alcoholics than in the first- and second-degree relatives of nonalcoholics (Hesselbrock et al., 1982; Moskalenko, Vanyukov, Solovyova, Rakhmanova, & Vladimirsky, 1992). A family study carried out by Lewis, Rice, and Helzer (1983) found alcoholism to be 1½ to 2 times more prevalent among subjects reporting a family history of alcoholism. Stabenau and Hesselbrock (1984) found that 89% of a group of 321 male and female inpatients with DSM-III diagnoses of alcohol dependence acknowledged a history of alcohol abuse in a parent, aunt, or uncle. Using a community-based rather than clinic-based sample of adolescents and young adults, Pandina and Johnson (1990) observed that subjects reporting a prior history of familial alcohol abuse were twice as likely to recount personal problems with alcohol or other drugs than subjects with no family history of alcohol abuse, although there were no group differences with respect to the severity of substance abuse symptomatology.

On the grounds that research shows a genetic link for primary affective disorder (McNeal & Cimbolic, 1986), it has been speculated that clinical depression and other manifestations of primary affective disorder may be responsible for the relationship observed between drug abuse and indexes of genetic influence. However, a family study of 160 substance abusers (over half of whom listed opiates as their primary drug of abuse) consecutively admitted to a hospital-based drug treatment program failed to enlist support for this hypothesis (Mirin, Weiss, Sollogub, & Michael, 1984). Penick and colleagues at the Kansas University Medical Center, on the other hand, determined that male alcoholics who acknowledged a family history-positive for alcohol abuse were significantly more likely to report that one or more family members suffered signs of clinical depression than male alcoholics with no known history of familial alcohol abuse (Penick et al., 1987). The issue of whether a family history of clinical depression accounts for the gene-drug abuse connection observed in family studies awaits further study with the aid of longitudinal data.

High risk research studies investigate the subclinical features of sub-stance abuse in persons thought to be at risk for addictive problems by virtue of their having an alcoholic or drug-abusing biological parent. Em-ploying this methodology with data collected from a large group of college students, researchers under the direction of McCaul (McCaul, Svikis, Turk-kan, Bigelow, & Cromwell, 1990) determined that a history of alcohol abuse problems in the first-degree relatives of these students predicted the student's first use of alcohol, number of self-reported drinks per month, first use of marijuana, and lifetime use of marijuana. Lifetime use of cocaine, hallucinogens, and sedatives in this sample also correlated with a family history of alcoholism, as did self-reported problems with drug use. Other high risk studies show that the sons of alcoholics are often rated by teachers (Aronson & Gilbert, 1963) and significant others (Lund & Landesmann-Dwyer, 1979) as more sensitive and less emotionally con-trolled than the sons of nonalcoholics. High risk studies, however, have not always produced results commensurate with the genetic hypothesis: de Wit and McCracken (1990), for instance, failed to discern a relationship between a family history of alcoholism and preference for and subjective response to alcohol in a group of young adults.

Explaining the relationship known to exist between a family history of alcoholism and a subject's own use of alcohol and/or other drugs is problematic, because the results may denote the influence of heredity, family environment, or both. Environmental interpretations of these find-ings hold that children imitate the drinking behavior of their parents—a supposition that finds support in several preliminary reports surveying the activities of children exposed to alcohol-abusing parental role models (cf. Cahalan, Cisin, & Crossley, 1969). However, parental alcohol abuse may also inspire an antidrug or drug-aversion response on the part of the af-fected child. Hence, the results of a recent investigation on this issue signify that the offspring of high-volume drinking mothers and fathers fall into two groups in their approach to alcohol: a large group of abstainers, fol-lowed by a much smaller group of high-volume drinkers (Harburg, Di-Franceisco, Webster, Gleiberman, & Schork, 1990). A subject's aversion to alcohol was strongest, according to the results of this study, when the opposite-sex parent had a drinking problem the subject could neither deny nor rationalize. This finding suggests that, instead of being the passive victims of their parents' drinking histories, many children of alcoholics are active decision makers capable of learning to avoid future substance abuse problems by psychologically distancing themselves from the pathological drinking behavior of their parents.

The results of family studies imply that drug abuse generally follows along family lines. In partial support of a genetic interpretation of this effect, Stabenau (1986) ascertained that alcoholics with histories of alcohol abuse on both sides of their family trees experienced more difficulty controlling their intake of alcohol and encountered a greater number of alcohol-related physical problems than alcoholics with no familial history of alcohol abuse or with alcohol abuse on only one side. There is even incipient support for the supposition that this family effect is specific, to the extent that opiate addicts have a much higher rate of familial opiate abuse than familial alcohol abuse, whereas alcoholics exhibit a converse pattern (Robins, West, & Herjanic, 1975).

Like the high risk strategy and traditional family pedigree studies, investigations utilizing a half-sibling methodology also reveal a significant family effect for both alcohol abuse and other forms of drug involvement (Schuckit, Goodwin, & Winokur, 1972). However, because it is difficult to discern the individual contributions of heredity and environment from the results of family pedigree studies, alternate investigative strategies have been proposed. One such approach is the twin method.

Twin Studies

There are two categories of twins: monozygotic (one-egg) and dizygotic (two-egg), commonly referred to as identical and fraternal twins, respectively. This distinction underlies the logic of the twin method for investigating the heritability of traits and behaviors: Proponents of the method argue that because monozygotic twins possess identical genetic backgrounds and dizygotic twins share only half their genes in common, characteristics and behaviors for which monozygotic twins display greater concordance (agreement) than dizygotic twins must be genetically influenced. Although the twin method has proven itself effective in delineating genetic patterns for such physical characteristics as hair color and height, it runs into problems when used to investigate complex human behaviors like alcoholism and drug abuse, because its ultimate validity rests on the feasibility of the equal environments assumption.

The equal environments assumption holds that there are no major variations between the early environments of monozygotic and dizygotic twins capable of explaining a higher rate of concordance in the monozygotic group. Phenomena such as twinning, where identical or monozygotic twins are treated more similarly than fraternal or dizygotic twins, however, bring this assumption into question. Furthermore, in one of the more rigorously designed twin studies on crime, Dalgard and Kringlen (1976) found that monozygotic twins reported greater similarity in how they were treated by significant adults and a stronger sense of mutual identity with their co-twins than did dizygotic twins. Given that monozygotic twins may grow up under more similar environmental conditions than dizygotic twins, twin research may be less than ideal for the purpose of distinguishing between the contributions of nature and nurture to development of complex human behaviors like substance abuse and crime.

Twin studies in which the concordance rates for alcoholism and drug abuse are compared for monozygotic and dizygotic twins have produced mixed results, although the weight of evidence suggests that the concordance for substance abuse may be higher in monozygotic twins, at least where males are concerned (see Table 2-1). The results of studies inspecting drug abuse patterns in females, on the other hand, have fairly consistently demonstrated that there is little difference in concordance for alcoholism and drug abuse between female monozygotic and dizygotic twins. One point worth noting is that Kaij (1960) determined that the monozygotic-dizygotic differentiation was strongest when the level of alcoholism was most severe. It can be argued on the basis of Kaij's data that heredity exerts its most potent effect on the more serious forms of substance abuse, although this hypothesis awaits further study and empirical verification.

Adoption Studies

In response to the problems associated with the use of family and twin data, adoption studies have become the method of choice for many researchers investigating the genetic roots of human behavior. Scientists utilizing this method of data collection probe the behavioral outcomes of persons adopted away from their biological homes at an early age. A genetic interpretation of an adoption study finding is suggested when greater concordance is recorded between biological parents and their adopted-away offspring than between adoptive parents and these same children. Like studies comparing monozygotic and dizygotic twins, early adoption studies showed evidence of a genetic link for drug abuse in males but not females (Goodwin, Schulsinger, Hermansen, Guze, & Winokur, 1973). In line with outcomes observed in high risk family studies, the adopted-away offspring of alcoholic biological parents were found to be more hypersensitive, insecure, and quick-tempered than the progeny of nonalcoholic biological parents (Goodwin, Schulsinger, Hermansen, Guze, & Winokur, 1975).

Bohman, Cloninger, and their colleagues (Bohman, Sigvardsson, & Cloninger, 1981; Cloninger, Bohman, & Sigvardsson, 1981) have conducted one of the more extensive series of adoption studies on drug abuse. Taking 862 males and 913 females born to single women in Stockholm, Sweden, between 1930 and 1949 and adopted by nonrelatives during the first 3 years of life, Bohman and Cloninger set out to plumb the depths of the putative gene–drug abuse relationship. Results indicated that the biological fathers and mothers of problem-drinking male offspring recorded higher levels of alcoholism than the biological parents of non-alcohol-registered sons. For females, however, only the biological mother–daughter

Table 2-1 Twin Studies on Drug Abuse

Study	Country	Criterion diagnosis	Monozygotic			Dizygotic		
			N	Sex	Concord	N	Sex	Concord
Kaij (1960)	Sweden	Alcohol abuse	58	M	.54	138	M	.28
		Chronic alcoholism	27	M	.71	60	M	.32
Partanen et al. (1966)	Finland	Alcoholism	172	M	.26	557	M	.12
		Heavy alcohol use	198	M	.75	641	M	.63
		Heavy tobacco use	198	M	.73	640	M	.68
		Heavy caffeine use	198	M	.70	641	M	.60
Jonsson & Nilsson (1968)	Sweden	Alcoholism	15	M&F	.22		M&F	.16
Gurling et al. (1981)	United Kingdom	Alcoholism	13	M	.33	20	M	.30
				F	.08	8	F	.13
Hrubec & Omenn (1981)	United States	Alcoholism	271	M	.26	444	M	.12
Pedersen (1981)	Sweden	Tranquilizer use	39	M	.26	32	M	.12
			36	F	.28	30	F	.17
Kaprio et al. (1987)	Finland	Beer consumption	841	M	.41	1885	M	.22
		Spirits consumption	841	M	.32	1885	M	.13
Pickens & Svikis (1988)	United States	Alcoholism	40	M	.70	53	M	.43
			24	F	.29	22	F	.36
		Problematic drug use	22	M	.55	47	M	.31
			15	F	.27	13	F	.23

Note. N = Number of twin pairs; Concord = simple concordance (present/absent) of criterion diagnosis except for Pedersen (1981) and Kaprio et al. (1987) studies, in which intraclass correlations were used.

relationship was significant. Interestingly, there was no association between adopted parent and adoptee alcoholism for either males or females. A discriminant analysis of these data revealed the presence of two types of alcoholism, one of which (male-limited) appeared to be more strongly associated with genetic factors than the other (milieu-limited). Table 2-2 outlines the major adoption studies conducted on drug abuse.

Adoption studies gauging the heritability of drug abuse and chemical dependency reveal moderately strong concordance between biological parents' drug abuse and chemical abuse problems in their adopted-away offspring. Although not immune to problems of analysis, exposition, and interpretation (see Walters & White, 1989), the adoption method of data collection nonetheless offers the best hope of separating out the individual contributions of nature and nurture in the evolution of a drug lifestyle. Efforts to integrate the adoption model with other strategies (e.g., comparing twins separated at birth or contrasting siblings and half-siblings adopted by different families) offer the most promise of clarifying the pertinent issues on this subject and expanding current knowledge on the gene–drug abuse relationship. However, enthusiasm for this method must be tempered with a resolve to avoid the criticisms of biased sampling and inaccurate self-reporting that have been levied against the so-called Minnesota twin studies, in which monozygotic twins separated at birth and reunited, allegedly for the first time, were interviewed and psychologically tested by a team of researchers (Horgan, 1993).

Genetic Correlates of Drug Abuse

Genetic theories of drug-seeking behavior were granted a certain degree of credibility by the popular media after a group of investigators from the Texas Health Science Center in San Antonio reported having identified a genetic marker for alcoholism, labeled the A1 allele, on the arm of the D_2 dopamine receptor gene (Blum et al., 1990). This finding was hailed as a major breakthrough in the war on alcoholism and drug abuse. However, a recent review of research conducted on the A1 allele unearthed little evidence in support of the claim that this allele serves as a genetic marker for alcoholism. Although the original Blum study yielded A1 allele prevalence rates of 37% and 13% for alcoholics and control subjects, respectively, a compilation of data from nine studies conducted independent of the Blum group revealed A1 allele prevalences of 18% for both alcoholic ($N = 378$) and control ($N = 427$) subjects (Gelernter, Goldman, & Risch, 1993). These data do not, however, rule out the possibility that genetic factors may contribute to substance abuse susceptibility, although it is more likely that the effect, if it exists, operates along polygenetic lines and is responsive to a number of environmental influences.

Table 2-2 Adoption Studies on Drug Abuse

Study	Country	Criterion diagnosis	Index adoptees			Control adoptees		
			N	Sex	Percent	N	Sex	Percent
Roe & Burks (1945)	United States	Alcohol abuse	27	M&F	3.7	22	M&F	4.5
Schuckit et al. (1972)	United States	Alcohol abuse	22	M&F	50.0	104	M&F	7.7
Goodwin et al. (1973)	Denmark	Alcoholism	55	M	18.0	78	M	5.0
		Drug abuse	55	M	9.0	78	M	2.0
Bohman (1978)	Sweden	Alcohol abuse	89	M	39.4	892	M	13.1
			197	F	2.5	1988	F	2.3
Cadoret & Gath (1978)	United States	Primary alcoholism	6	M&F	33.3	78	M&F	1.3
Bohman et al. (1981)	Sweden	Alcohol abuse	172	F	7.0	741	F	2.6
Cloninger et al. (1981)	Sweden	Severe alcohol abuse	307	M	7.8	555	M	4.9
Cadoret et al. (1986)	United States	Alcohol abuse	39	M&F	48.7	404	M&F	13.9
		Drug abuse	39	M&F	25.6	404	M&F	7.4

Note. Index adoptees are subjects with a family history positive for substance abuse; control adoptees are subjects without a reported family history of substance abuse. Percent represents the percentage of adoptees in each group who satisfied the criterion diagnosis for substance abuse.

Demonstrating that a relationship exists between heredity and drug abuse is one thing; explicating this relationship is quite another. One possible interpretation of the gene-drug relationship is that a biology-based idiosyncratic response to alcohol may serve as a risk factor for future substance abuse difficulties. Three laboratories, two in the United States (O'Malley & Maisto, 1985; Schuckit, 1984) and one in Denmark (Mednick, 1983), have uncovered results suggesting that sons of alcoholics demonstrate fewer signs of intoxication after consuming a low-moderate dose of ethanol than sons of nonalcoholics. This effect occurs even after controlling for differences in psychological expectations of alcohol and physical blood-alcohol concentrations. It has been speculated that such genetically influenced characteristics as reduced sensitivity to or increased tolerance for alcohol may elevate a subject's risk of alcohol-related problems by interfering with his or her ability to detect impending inebriation. They may also increase the likelihood that such a subject will be able to avert the negative short-term effects of ethanol that instinctively limit excessive drinking in persons who characteristically experience nausea and disorientation in response to high-moderate doses of alcohol (Wilson & Plomin, 1985).

It is possible, then, that genetic variables may act to increase the risk of drug involvement by making a person less sensitive to the short-term negative effects of alcohol and by bolstering his or her ability to tolerate larger than average doses of alcohol or other mood-altering substances. Genetic factors may also protect other subjects against future drug involvement by enhancing their sensitivity to alcohol and other drugs. Take, for instance, the fact that two thirds to three quarters of the world's Asian population experiences an unpleasant reaction to alcohol characterized by a flushed face and upper body, queasiness, and an increased heart rate (Wolff, 1972), along with the observation that persons of Japanese and Chinese ancestry living in the United States enjoy a low rate of alcohol abuse (Suwaki & Ohara, 1985). The so-called "oriental flush" response may limit the use of alcohol by promoting a mild aversive reaction in the presence of an intoxicating beverage. Additional research has demonstrated that a fast flushing response is significantly more effective than a slow flushing response (Park et al., 1984) and that a partial or unpredictable flushing response is less effective than no response at all (Higuchi, Parrish, Dufour, Towle, & Harford, 1992) in preventing future alcohol abuse problems.

Common sense dictates that the genetic features of drug dependency and abuse should not be considered independent of environmental factors. As has been observed with disquieting regularity, the appearance of an oriental flush has not protected groups like Native Americans and Alaskan Inuits from experiencing some of the highest rates of alcoholism in the United States, if not the world (Peele, 1986). Furthermore, a survey of men and women of Japanese heritage living in Japan, Hawaii, and California (Kitano, Chi, Rhee, Law, & Lubben, 1992) revealed a relationship between sociocultural milieu and alcohol consumption practices. Although the three groups were roughly equivalent in terms of their ability to generate a flushing response to alcohol, the volume of alcohol imbibed varied according to the social acceptability of alcohol use within each specific subculture. The gene-based flushing response, therefore, may be effective in preventing alcohol abuse problems only when it is rapid and consistent, and occurs in a climate conducive to moderate social drinking or abstinence.

Additional sociological and environmental factors may moderate the gene–drug abuse relationship. Heath, Jardine, and Martin (1989), in a study conducted on Australian twins, established that heredity, as measured by differences in concordance for monozygotic and dizygotic twins, accounted for 60% of the variance in alcohol consumption in unmarried females, but only 31% of the variance in married females. Because Heath et al. ascertained that females thought to be genetically predisposed to heavy drinking were no less likely to get married than nongenetically predisposed females, they speculated that marital status may serve a protective function for otherwise high-risk females. This finding, again, suggests that genetic research cannot be considered independent of environmental factors. The gene–environment interaction hypothesis warrants a great deal more attention than it has so far received. One way to achieve this goal is through a review of studies on the physiology of drug abuse.

PHYSIOLOGICAL STUDIES

It has been noted that animals will self-inject drugs commonly misused by humans (Griffiths, Bigelow, & Henningfield, 1980) and that preference for alcohol (Deitrich & Spuhler, 1984) and morphine (Nichols & Hsiao, 1967) can be bred in both rats and mice. Consequently, many researchers interested in a comprehensive understanding of the physiology of human drug use and abuse have employed animal models of investigation. Although the generalization of results from research on laboratory mice, rats, and monkeys to human behavioral problems like alcohol abuse can be problematic, animal studies provide an opportunity to examine the physiological underpinnings of drug use in ways that are unavailable in fields where no commonly accepted animal models exist (e.g., criminology). The following sections discuss the physiological correlates of drug abuse in terms of the central nervous system, the autonomic nervous system, biogenic amines, and abnormal metabolites.

Central Nervous System

The central nervous system (CNS) is made up of the brain and spinal cord. The basic unit of the CNS is the neuron or nerve cell, a microscopic entity with a nucleus, an axon, and branchlike appendages called dendrites. Neurons communicate with one another through an electrochemical process. The electrical potential or activity of the CNS has been studied using several different methods and procedures; the electroencephalograph (EEG) is perhaps the most popular technique currently available to researchers and clinicians interested in a general estimate of neuroelectrical activity. The EEG patterns of adult subjects administered low and intermediate doses of marijuana, ethanol, cocaine, and morphine show an increased level of alpha wave activity that corresponds with subjective reports of euphoria and well-being (Lukas, Mendelson, Amass, & Benedikt, 1990). It has also been noted that non-alcohol-abusing subjects with family histories of alcoholism demonstrate accentuated slow alpha wave activity and reduced fast alpha wave activity after ingesting alcohol compared with non-alcohol-abusing subjects without family histories of alcoholism (Pollock et al., 1983).

EEG studies on alcoholism and drug abuse reveal the presence of abnormal EEG readings in currently abstinent persons with personal histories of alcoholism or drug abuse, although gender effects have been reported. Gabrielli et al. (1982) observed excessive beta wave activity in EEGs produced by female offspring of alcoholics but not in the EEGs of similarly predisposed male offspring, whereas Propping, Kruger, and Norbert (1981) witnessed increased beta wave activity and decreased alpha wave activity in female, but not male, alcoholics and their relatives. Studies investigating evoked or event-related potentials in alcohol abusers note a wavelength of decreased amplitude and increased latency in currently abstinent subjects (Propping, Kruger, & Janah, 1980). The event-related potentials of sons of alcoholics also show reduced amplitudes of both positive and negative waves relative to those of sons of nonalcoholics (Begleiter, Porjesz, Bihari, & Kissin, 1984). It has been argued that these results portend the significance of attentional deficits in the development of subsequent chemical dependencies (Schuckit, 1985). However, these studies provide contradictory evidence as to the precise pattern of electroencephalographic response that allegedly denotes an increased risk for substance abuse (Peele, 1986).

Cloninger (1987) speculates that different patterns of substance abuse (Type I vs. Type II) may account for the lack of congruence in research on its EEG correlates. Research indicates that an abstinent Type I alcohol abuser (hypervigilant, worrisome) exhibits a reducing pattern of resting EEG activity (i.e., low alpha wave activity and high beta wave activity), whereas an abstinent Type II alcohol abuser (hypovigilant, impulsive) demonstrates an augmenting pattern of resting EEG response (i.e., increasing amplitude of EEG potentials). The EEGs of Type I alcohol abusers show increased alpha wave activity following the introduction of alcohol, corresponding with reports that Type I abusers experience a growing sense of calm alertness and reduced tension while drinking (Propping et al., 1980). Type II alcohol abusers, on the other hand, demonstrate lower levels of augmentation or reduced perceptual reactance after ingesting alcohol (O'Connor, Hesselbrock, & Tasman, 1986). Accordingly, alcohol may serve to compensate for preexisting idiosyncracies in the cortical function of persons at increased risk for development of divergent patterns of alcohol abuse. When interpreting these results, however, it is necessary to keep in mind that the EEG is only about 60% accurate (Filskov & Goldstein, 1974) and produces abnormal readings in 15% to 20% of persons with no known neurological disorder (Mayo Clinic, 1976).

Other measures of central nervous system activity and well-being have also been applied to groups of alcoholics and drug addicts. Using a high-risk methodology and data generated from the Danish birth registry, Knop, Goodwin, Teasdale, Mikkelsen, & Schulsinger (1984) found higher Category Test scores (indicating decreased cerebral efficiency and problem-solving ability) in 134 males with at least one alcoholic parent compared with 70 control males without any history of parental alcohol abuse. Hesselbrock, Stabenau, and Hesselbrock (1985), on the other hand, were unable to uncover any significant discrepancies between alcohol-abusing and nonabusing college students or between students with and without a family history of alcoholism on a series of neurocognitive measures (Category Test, Trailmaking Test, Tactual Performance Test, Wechsler Adult Intelligence Scale). Although there appear to be certain functional abnormalities of the central nervous system associated with drug and alcohol abuse, it is difficult to determine with any degree of certainty whether they are a cause of substance misuse or simply an effect of chronic use of psychoactive substances.

Autonomic Nervous System

The autonomic nervous system (ANS) regulates smooth muscle, cardiac muscle, and glands through two anatomically distinct divisions known as the sympathetic and parasympathetic branches. The sympathetic branch of the ANS is concerned with the release of stored energy, whereas the parasympathetic branch is designed to enhance the body's supply of stored energy. Sympathetic activity causes increased heart rate, piloerection, slowing of the digestive tract, and preparation of the organism for emergencies (the so-called "fight or flight" response). Parasympathetic activity, on the other hand, lowers heart rate and blood pressure, increases the motility of the digestive tract, and promotes a general state of bodily relaxation. Although it is commonly believed that CNS stimulants like cocaine increase sympathetic activity, whereas CNS depressants like alcohol elicit the parasympathetic response, research indicates that the effect of various drugs on ANS functioning may be substantially more complicated.

An early investigation examining the influence of alcohol on ANS functioning revealed the presence of a "normalizing" effect, in which the consumption of ethanol led to increased sympathetic activity on the part of persons possessing lower initial resting levels of sympathetic activity and decreased sympathetic activity in subjects expressing higher resting levels of sympathetic response (Kissin, Schenker, & Schenker, 1959). Along similar lines, a stress-dampening or analgesic effect has been observed in persons at elevated risk for alcohol-related problems (Sher & Levenson, 1982), as well as in those who consume high volumes of alcohol (Cutter, Maloof, Kurtz, & Jones, 1976). There are also data to suggest that high-risk persons experience a more positively reinforcing or less negatively punishing effect after initial and subsequent ingestion of mood-altering chemical substances (Schuckit, 1984). These findings may, in fact, help clarify the relationship between heredity and substance abuse observed in research on the genetic correlates of risk-taking behavior, in the sense that inherited ANS anomalies may place an individual at increased risk for future drug abuse.

Two psychologists affiliated with McGill University in Montreal conducted a high risk study of the autonomic precursors of drug-seeking behavior. Finn and Pihl (1987) formed three groups of male subjects on the basis of a self-reported history of alcohol abuse in two generations of relatives. High-risk subjects were identified by the presence of alcohol abuse in their father, grandfather, and at least one other male relative. Moderate-risk subjects had alcohol abuse in one parent but in no other relative, and low-risk subjects had no recorded history of familial alcohol abuse. Sober high-risk subjects displayed greater cardiovascular response (increased blood volume and heart rate) in anticipation of a mild electrical shock than sober moderate-risk and low-risk subjects. Alcohol consumption led to decreased physiological reactivity in high-risk subjects, but a converse effect was observed in moderate- and low-risk subjects. Finn and Pihl concluded that persons at risk for alcohol abuse have an inherited hypersensitivity to stress that may make them more responsive to the inebriating effects of alcohol than persons who are not genetically predisposed to substance abuse.

Biogenic Amines

The brain is the primary target of drug effects. Alcohol, heroin, cocaine, and other psychoactive substances influence human behavior and experience by interacting with the biogenic amines, which are distributed throughout the central nervous system but find their heaviest concentration in the brain. These biogenic amines, many of which come under the classification of neurotransmitters, control behavior by providing a communication network of chemical substances that act on the receptor sites of individual brain cells. Each amine exerts either an excitatory or inhibitory action on neighboring cells by means of an electrochemical process, discussed previously in the section on central nervous system correlates of drug abuse. Serotonin, dopamine, and norepinephrine are the biogenic amines that have generated the greatest investigative fervor on the biophysiology of drug abuse. These, along with several other biogenic amine neurotransmitters, are discussed below.

Serotonin Brain serotonin, or 5-hydroxytryptamine (5-HT), is distributed in the cells of the midline or raphe region of the pons and upper brain stem, as well as in portions of the higher brain and cerebral cortex. Decreased levels of serotonin have been noted in the cerebral cortex, thalamus, hypothalamus, hippocampus (Murphy, McBride, Lumeng, & Li, 1982), frontal cortex, anterior striatum, and nucleus accumbens (Murphy, McBride, Lumeng, & Li, 1987) of alcohol-preferring rats. When 5-hydroxytryptophan (5-HTP), the precursor of 5-HT, is infused into the ventricles of laboratory rats, a noticeable decrease in alcohol intake occurs (Hill, 1974), whereas injections of serotonin uptake inhibitors in humans lead to decreased desire for and consumption of ethanol in problem drinkers (Kranzler & Orrok, 1989). Conversely, administration of 5,6-dihydroxytryptamine (5,6-DHT), a 5-HT antagonist, has been shown to increase alcohol consumption in some strains of rats (Myers & Melchior, 1975), although other strains of rats show no such effect in response to 5,6-DHT administration (Kiianmaa, 1976). It has been speculated that the gene for tryptophan pyrrolase may be overactive in alcoholics, resulting in an abundance of kyurenine and an undersupply of serotonin (Goodwin, 1989), although this hypothesis requires critical review.

Cocaine tends to abate the synthesis, release, and activity of 5-HT in specific regions of the central nervous system. Dackis and Gold (1988) have argued that the antiserotonergic effect of cocaine may explain the insomnia often associated with cocaine intoxication and the hypersomnia and general lack of energy that commonly result from cocaine withdrawal. There appears to be some evidence that serotonin is sensitive to both alcohol and cocaine, which may explain several of the acute and chronic symptoms associated with the abuse of each substance. On the other hand, the role of seratonin as a principal cause of drug abuse has yet to be established, although the fact that certain serotonin–drug effects may be strain-specific implies that a genetic predisposition to drug abuse may exist, in part, by way of indoleamine-rich pathways that project to upper regions of the forebrain. To complicate matters, it has been speculated that the serotonin–drug abuse relationship may vary by critical site (Myers, 1978).

Catecholamines. The catecholamine chain of monoamines yields dopamine (DA) and norepinephrine (NE). Dopamine is scattered throughout the central nervous system but is most heavily concentrated in the limbic and mesolimbic regions of the brain. Norepinephrine, on the other hand, forms two major fiber systems, one centered in the locus coeruleus and the other tied loosely into the lateral ventral tegmental fields. Dopamine diminutions of up to 25% were observed when the cells of the nucleus accumbens of alcohol-preferring rats were biopsied (Murphy et al., 1987); however, infusion of a dopamine neurotoxin into the cerebral ventricles of laboratory rats led to diminished levels of alcohol imbibition in two strains of rats, but had no effect on two other strains (Myers, 1978). Inhibition of dopamine-β-hydroxylase (DBH), the enzyme responsible for converting dopamine into epinephrine, was found to suppress the effect of ethanol in one strain of rats (Amit, Levitan, & Lindros, 1976) but to augment the effect of alcohol in a second strain (Alkana, Parker, Cohen, Birch, & Nobel, 1976).

Cocaine apparently stimulates the dopamine-mediated reward centers of the midbrain by blocking synaptic reuptake of DA and NE, increasing dopaminergic and noradrenergic synthesis and expanding the number of catecholamine binding sites available to free-floating DA and NE (Wise, 1985). The strength of the dopamine–cocaine relationship is supported by studies showing that self-administration of cocaine by laboratory animals is substantially reduced by drugs that block DA at the receptor site (Pickens & Harris, 1968). Of course, chronic cocaine use inevitably depletes the level of DA available systemwide, because repeatedly blocking reuptake prevents dopamine recycling and decreases postsynaptic dopamine receptor availability (Volkow et al., 1990); this physiological effect probably gives rise to the psychological depressions commonly observed in cocaine withdrawal (Dackis & Gold, 1988). Like serotonin, the catecholamines appear to be greatly affected by the action of both alcohol and cocaine, although more research is required to establish the causal order of the catecholamine–drug relationship.

Other Biogenic Amines. It has been speculated that alcohol may stimulate Γ-aminobutyric (GABA) receptor-mediated uptake of chlorine (Cl^-) ions into isolated brain vesicles. Suzdak et al. (1986) ascertained that a drug known to antagonize Cl^- uptake in GABA sites blocked the anticonflict effect of ethanol in rats without interfering with the anticonflict activity of the barbiturate drug pentobarbital. Decreased levels of acetylcholine

(ACh) have been discovered in the brain stem, hippocampus, and caudate nucleus of alcohol-dependent rats undergoing withdrawal (Hunt & Dalton, 1976), whereas systemic application of alcohol is known to suppress ACh levels in the cortex of laboratory rats (Morgan & Phillis, 1975). In addition, prolonged use of alcohol is known to reduce the level of opiate peptides like endorphin and enkephalin in the basal ganglia by interfering with the binding of endogenous opioid peptides with opiate receptor sites in the brain (Myers, 1989). One study, in fact, found the level of enkephalin in alcohol-preferring mice to be significantly lower than that observed in an alcohol-avoiding strain (Gianoulakis & Gupta, 1986).

The opiate peptides have attracted the attention of researchers appraising the effects of morphine, heroin, and other exogenous opioid agents on CNS functioning. It has been shown, for instance, that protracted use of morphine derivatives may inhibit the binding of endogenous opioid agents like endorphin and enkephalin to opioid receptor membranes in the cortex (Bidlack, Frey, Seyed-Mozaffari, & Archer, 1990), while at the same time "upregulating" (increasing the number of) such receptor sites, thereby increasing the subject's sensitivity to pain (Rothman, Long, Bykov, Rice, & Holaday, 1990). Although opiate drugs and the opioid peptides they mimic are classified as inhibitory in their neural activity, the inhibitory–excitatory action of these agents tends to vary as a function of the region of the brain under examination. Hence, whereas the opiate drug normorphine and opioid peptides β-endorphin and Met-enkephalin inhibit the majority of cells in the cerebral cortex, caudate nucleus, thalamus, and brain stem, they exert an excitatory effect on the pyramidal cells of the hippocampus (Collier, 1980). Opiates are also thought to inhibit the locus coeruleus by opening potassium channels (Aghajanian, 1985), and one study found opiate dependence and tolerance to be correlated with a reduced level of activity of a second message system known as cyclic-AMP (Collier, 1980).

Abnormal Metabolites

As depicted in Figure 2-1, alcohol is metabolized into acetaldehyde by the enzyme alcohol dehydrogenase (ADH). Acetaldehyde is then metabolized

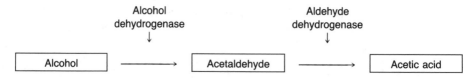

Figure 2-1 Metabolization of ethyl alcohol.

into acetic acid by the enzyme aldehyde dehydrogenase (AldDH), the product of which is converted into carbon dioxide and water through the Krebs cycle. Acetaldehyde and related biogenic aldehydes exert a powerful effect on the nerve cells of the brain and have a strong affinity for several of the brain's neurotransmitters, dopamine and serotonin (5-HT) in particular. Because acetaldehyde and several of these neurotransmitters compete for the same enzyme (AldDH), occasions when the system is overloaded with alcohol can contribute to a buildup of acetaldehyde, neurotransmitters, or both; this buildup in turn promotes the formation of abnormal metabolites, which may then lead to a rise in alcohol intake. Tetroisoquinolones (TIQs) arise from the interaction of aldehyde and the catecholamine DA, whereas tetrahydro-β-carboline (TBC) forms from an interaction of aldehyde and the indoleamine 5-HT. One TIQ metabolite is the biological precursor of morphine, whereas one indoleamine-based TBC has been shown to exhibit a clear predilection for benzodiazepine receptors in the brain (Myers, 1989).

Although it has been speculated that a genetic factor is responsible for the production of abnormal metabolites, to the extent that some people are born with an exceptionally slow rate of acetaldehyde metabolism that puts them at risk for alcohol abuse, only circumscribed support exists for this hypothesis (Goodwin, 1989). There is reasonably strong evidence, however, that the abnormal metabolites that form when aldehyde and neurotransmitters combine promote increased levels of alcohol consumption. Thus, when TIQ or β-carboline metabolites are infused directly into the cerebral ventricles of monkeys and rats, an abnormally high rate of alcohol consumption is recorded (Myers, 1989). Furthermore, TIQs have been identified in the cerebral-spinal fluid of chronic alcoholics even after the acute effects of alcohol intoxication have worn off (Sjoquist, Perdahl, & Winblad, 1983). The introduction of TIQs into the brains of rodents has been shown to augment periods of alcohol-induced sleep (Church, Fuller, & Dudek, 1976) and to magnify withdrawal-related convulsive episodes in mice and rats (Blum, Eubanks, Wallace, Schwertner, & Morgan, 1976). Although TIQs may be important biological markers for drug-seeking behavior, it is uncertain whether they have their basis in a genetic defect or are simply a consequence of a nervous system overloaded with alcohol, some of which is transformed into abnormal metabolites.

CONCLUSION

The results of this review suggest that biological factors can potentially be used to discriminate between those who do and do not abuse drugs. However, biological differences may be largely the consequence, rather than the cause, of substance abuse difficulties; it is clear that regular ingestion of alcohol and other drugs has a bearing on how a biological unit or system functions. Genetically oriented theorists argue that there is at least preliminary support for the position that several of these biological differences may predate an individual's use of drugs. Differences may include the autonomic hyperactivity that has been linked to a family history of substance abuse, which some individuals may attempt to reduce by drinking alcohol, smoking marijuana, or injecting heroin, and the natural underresponsiveness to alcohol that allows an individual to imbibe more alcohol than his or her peers and consequently avoid the negative short-term effects of alcohol that may keep many persons from becoming habitual users. There is, however, no convincing evidence to support the argument that alcoholism and drug abuse operate along the lines of a disease, as has been proposed by groups such as the AMA and Alcoholics Anonymous.

Although biological factors may have a place in a comprehensive theory of drug-seeking behavior, they cannot be considered independent of various psychological and sociological influences. Thus, while it is possible that an inborn underresponsiveness to the inebriating effects of alcohol may place a person at increased risk for substance abuse, psychological, sociological, and situational factors can either exacerbate this risk or reduce it through a combined interactive effect. A decreased sensitivity to the inebriating effects of alcohol may allow an individual the opportunity to consume larger quantities of alcohol than his or her peers, which in turn may promote the formation of TIQs through the interacting influence of both situational (availability of alcohol) and sociological (peer pressure) factors. Likewise, the biological oriental flush response does not operate independent of various sociocultural and psychological influences, as represented by the fact that some groups, like Native Americans, experience this response yet suffer a high rate of alcohol abuse (Peele, 1986). Also, anecdotal evidence from Japan indicates that some oriental males attempt to "drink over" the flush in an effort to prove their masculinity (Weiss, 1992b). These findings suggest that we must look to the interaction of biological and environmental factors to understand drug-seeking behavior—a theme that will be echoed throughout this book, regarding the origins, development, and treatment of a drug lifestyle.

Chapter 3

Psychological Factors

INTRODUCTION

Although psychology-oriented research covers a wide spectrum of issues, from those that are largely academic in nature (e.g., physiological psychology, perception, and sensation) to those that are appreciably more practical (psychological assessment and clinical psychology), these different avenues of psychological inquiry are united by the common goal of acquiring knowledge about individual human behavior. Because there is insufficient space in this chapter to orchestrate a comprehensive review of psychological knowledge applicable to research on drug abuse, the current discussion will focus on three areas of psychological interest that perhaps most clearly represent the scope of psychological research on drugs and drug abuse: learning, personality, and emotional disorder.

LEARNING

Psychologists have long recognized the role of learning in the sequence of events thought to be responsible for human development and behavior.

Countless studies have documented the fact that animal and human behavior is influenced, shaped, and patterned by its consequences. These consequences are of two main types: reinforcers and punishers. A reinforcer is any stimulus or event that by its delivery or removal increases the probability of a response being repeated in the future. A punishing condition, on the other hand, is a stimulus or event that by its delivery or removal decreases the probability of a response being repeated in the future.

Learning also occurs through conditioning and observation. By pairing a neutral stimulus (a bell ringing) with meat powder, Russian physiologist Ivan Pavlov (1927) was able to demonstrate that the natural response of salivation could be elicited even after the meat powder was discontinued and the stimulus was presented alone. Socially, humans learn through example, as shown in studies documenting people's ability to learn by observing and modeling the actions of others (Bandura, 1977). This section considers the three major learning paradigms—operant studies, classical conditioning, and observational learning—in terms of what they can contribute to the understanding of drug-seeking behavior.

Operant Studies

It has been noted that marijuana use does not always produce a subjective high in the previously uninitiated (Becker, 1953), that opiates often provoke feelings of nausea and discomfort in novice users (Beecher, 1959), and that alcohol may stimulate a negative effect in persons imbibing it for the first time (Kuehnle, Anderson, & Chandler, 1974). Such findings suggest that operant learning principles may help explain a person's decision to use drugs, even though there are important individual differences in the subjective reactions of persons exposed to various categories of chemical substance. Haertzen, Kocher, and Miyasato (1983), in fact, propose that high-risk individuals may experience more reinforcing and fewer punishing consequences after initial and subsequent use of alcohol and other drugs than individuals with a lower risk of substance abuse problems. In support of this claim, Kozlowski and Harford (1976) discerned that subjects who found cigarette smoking an initially unpleasant experience were less apt to continue smoking than persons encountering less aversive inaugural effects.

Individual differences in initial liking are important, but so are the pharmacological properties of a drug itself. Different classes of drugs produce divergent preference levels that are reasonably consistent across subjects. Cocaine and heroin, for instance, typically evoke a high degree of liking in first-time users, whereas tobacco, caffeine, and major tranquilizers receive much lower ratings of initial pleasure from novice consumers (Haertzen et al., 1983). Dose-related effects (greater initial liking for higher doses of a drug) have been noted for pentobarbital, diazepam (Griffiths et al., 1984), and cocaine (Fischman, Schuster, & Rajfer, 1983), but not for nicotine (Henningfield & Griffiths, 1980). In an effort to address the reinforcing value of drugs more directly, investigators have turned their attention to drug self-administration studies. A subject's willingness to self-administer drugs and to select one drug over another are, in fact, ways by which the operant features of drug use behavior can be studied.

Self-administration studies explore the degree to which subjects choose or are willing to work for a particular dosage of drug relative to their choice of or willingness to work for another dosage, drug, or substance (placebo, food). Laboratory studies suggest that animals will self-administer a variety of chemicals, including cannabis (Takahashi & Singer, 1979), morphine (Woods & Schuster, 1968), central nervous system (CNS) depressants (Walton & Deutsch, 1978), CNS stimulants (Balster, Kilbey, & Ellinwood, 1976), and the dissociative anesthetic phencyclidine (Balster & Woolverton, 1980). Drugs that have served as reinforcers in self-administration studies on humans include alcohol (de Wit, Uhlenhuth, Pierri, & Johanson, 1987), marijuana (Mendelson & Mello, 1984), cocaine (Fischman & Schuster, 1982), morphine (Jones & Prada, 1975), and nicotine (Henningfield, Chait, & Griffiths, 1983). The principal methodologies used to study drug self-administration are choice and free operant procedures.

Choice Studies Before a subject can choose one drug over another, he or she must be able to discriminate subjectively between different chemical compounds. It has been determined that animals are capable of discriminating between morphine and a saline solution, different classes of opioids, and different dosages of the same opiate (Woods, Young, & Herling, 1982). Drug discrimination studies employing human subjects show that chemical compounds with similar pharmacological properties are perceived as more alike than substances with dissimilar pharmacological properties (Bigelow & Preston, 1989). Although drug discrimination studies are not particularly useful in defining abuse liability, they are invaluable for the purpose of assessing a subject's ability to discriminate between distinct chemical compounds and different dosage levels of the same compound. This knowledge, in turn, allows researchers to invest greater confidence in the outcomes of studies following a choice methodology to investigate the abuse liability and reinforcing value of designated chemical substances.

Based on the results of choice studies with animals, it can be inferred that rats, dogs, and monkeys prefer certain drugs or dosages of a particular drug over other drugs and dosages (Brady & Griffiths, 1977). Data provided by sources following the choice method of investigating drug preference in nonhuman species indicate that under select circumstances, taking a drug may be preferred over access to other pleasurable activities, such as eating or sex. In choice studies probing preference for cocaine, for instance, it has been demonstrated that laboratory animals frequently select cocaine over food or the opportunity for sex, even after being deprived of food or a willing sexual partner for a significant period of time (Schnoll, Daghestani, & Hansen, 1984). As the reader may have already surmised, research on choice behavior in humans is substantially more complex and the results appreciably more equivocal than those obtained with animals.

As was also found in animal studies, human subjects instructed to choose between stimulant drugs and a placebo prefer the former approximately 80% of the time (Johanson & Uhlenhuth, 1980a). Extending this methodology to several classes of depressant medication, however, Johanson and Uhlenhuth (1980b) were unable to discern an overall preference for the sedative drug diazepam when subjects were given a choice between diazepam and an inert substance made to look like diazepam (a diazepam placebo). The researchers did note, however, that diazepam served as a reinforcer for a small group of participants. The issue at hand, then, is to determine the accuracy with which diazepam-preferring individuals can be identified and categorized.

One plausible behavioral marker of diazepam preference is a prior history of alcohol or sedative abuse. Griffiths, Bigelow, Liebson, and Kaliszak (1980) studied persons with backgrounds of sedative abuse and surmised that such individuals preferred both pentobarbital and diazepam to a placebo, and preferred higher to lower dosages of pentobarbital. In another study, de Wit and her colleagues (de Wit, Pierri, & Johanson, 1989) witnessed a clear preference for diazepam in both light and moderate drinkers, but reported that the preference was highest in moderate drinkers. A high initial anxiety level, on the other hand, appears to have little, if any, bearing on preference for anxiolytic drugs (McCraken, de Wit, Uhlenhuth, & Johanson, 1990). It may be that whereas stimulant drugs are reinforcing for most first-time users, sedative drugs like diazepam and pentobarbital are initially reinforcing only for persons with histories of sedative abuse and/or an ongoing pattern of moderate to high alcohol use.

Free-Operant Studies   Operant-level studies explore the degree to which voluntary behavior is established and maintained by certain schedules of reinforcement, using access to an abusable chemical compound as the reinforcing condition. Henningfield and Goldberg (1983) ascertained that the delivery of nicotine on a fixed-ratio schedule led to an increased rate of response in human subjects that extinguished when saline was substituted for nicotine. Marijuana has also been shown to support operant behavior in humans. Mello and Mendelson (1985), for instance, ascertained that subjects were willing to exercise 30 min in exchange for 1 g of marijuana. In fact, both male and female subjects worked longer than required to earn the number of marijuana cigarettes they consumed each day. Alcohol, on the other hand, displays a cyclical pattern of response characterized by alternating periods of high activity/low consumption and low activity/high consumption (Mello & Mendelson, 1972). Further evidence that marijuana may be a more effective reinforcer than alcohol is revealed in the results of a study in which the introduction of marijuana as a competing reinforcing condition in an operant-style learning paradigm led to a reduced level of alcohol consumption, but the introduction of alcohol had no appreciable effect on subjects' use of marijuana (Mello, Mendelson, Kuehnle, & Sellers, 1978).

Self-administration of diazepam and pentobarbital drops dramatically when the cost requirements (Bigelow, Griffiths, & Liebson, 1976) and response–reinforcement interval (Griffiths, Bigelow, & Liebson, 1976) are increased. Dose–response relationships, on the other hand, are formidably complex. Thus, higher dosages of nicotine are associated with decreased levels of operant response (Henningfield & Griffiths, 1980), whereas higher dosages of diazepam (Roache & Griffiths, 1985) and pentobarbital (McLeod & Griffiths, 1983) correlate with an increased rate of operant activity. To complicate matters further, research suggests that there may be no dose–response effect for cocaine (Fischman & Rachlinski, 1989), possibly because cocaine is highly reinforcing even at relatively low levels. Research on the dose-response relationship is confounded further by a literature that is largely equivocal and occasionally contradictory (de Wit, Pierri, & Johanson, 1989; Fischman & Rachlinski, 1989).

The differential reinforcing values of certain classes of chemical substance are another area of concern to investigators probing the operant features of drug-use behavior. A series of animal studies suggests that alcohol may serve a reinforcing function in alcohol-preferring rats but have little reinforcement value for non-alcohol-preferring rats (Ritz, George, de Fiebre, & Meisch, 1986). Differential effects have been identified in human subjects as well. Bigelow et al. (1976), for instance, observed a connection between a history of prior drug abuse and a subject's willingness to work for a sedative drug reinforcer, although this effect was found to attenuate once the response requirements of the task were increased. There is also evidence to suggest that whereas alcohol may reduce tension in persons who do not abuse alcohol, it is reinforcing to abusers for reasons other than tension reduction (Nathan & O'Brien, 1971). The results of at least one study imply that for some subjects alcohol may actually amplify, rather than ease, tension (Klepping, Guilland, Didier, Klepping, & Malval, 1976). Perhaps the reinforcing properties of alcohol and other drugs can be traced to their ability to affect the neural pathways of the medial forebrain bundle where the "pleasure centers" of the brain are presumably located (Wise & Bozarth, 1987).

Classical Conditioning

Abraham Wikler (1948) called attention to the possible link between conditioning and drug relapse after observing inpatients at the Addiction Research Center in Lexington, Kentucky, discussing their past drug experiences. Although detoxified, many of these patients reported experiencing what appeared to be mild signs of opiate withdrawal when reviewing situations and events associated with their past use of drugs. Wikler followed up these observations with a series of animal studies, the results of which indicated that rats exposed to environmental cues previously conditioned to their use of opiates experienced withdrawal-like symptoms (Wikler & Pescor, 1967). This conditioned withdrawal response was thought by Wikler to be responsible for the urges and cravings reported by human drug addicts long after their physical dependence on drugs has worn off. Craving, then, is defined by Wikler and his colleagues as an aversive state created by environmental cues associated with previous attempts to withdraw from drugs (Ludwig & Wikler, 1974). However, less than 30% of the opiate addicts interviewed by McAuliffe (1982) and only 16% of the opiate addicts surveyed by Chaney, Roszell, and Cummings (1982) reported relapse episodes that could be even remotely attributed to a conditioned withdrawal response.

The lack of empirical support for Wikler's conditioned withdrawal interpretation of the subjective craving responses of detoxified drug abusers has led to alternative hypotheses. Shephard Siegel (1988) is the architect of one of the better-substantiated alternative explanations of the association between environmental cues and drug-related withdrawal, tolerance, and craving. Siegel postulates that these phenomena materialize in response to environmental cues that gradually take the form of conditioned stimuli after successive pairings with the drug of abuse and that promote a homeostatic state in the drug user before the actual introduction of the chemical substance. Drugs, according to Siegel, elicit an unconditioned emotional response in the user, whereas environmental cues associated with the preparation and use of drugs promote a conditioned emotional response. This conditioned emotional response encompasses both conditioned druglike responses and conditioned drug-opposite responses, which give rise to craving through an opponent-process mode of innervation. Wikler's conditioned withdrawal and Siegel's opponent-process models of tolerance and withdrawal symptomatology are displayed in Figure 3-1.

Conditioned druglike responses have been observed in studies employing both animal (Eikelboom & Stewart, 1979) and human (Meyer &

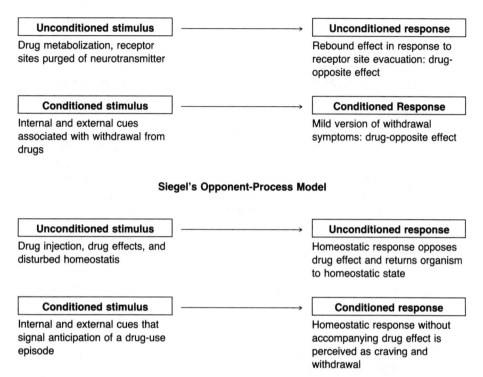

Figure 3-1 Comparison of Wikler's and Siegel's models of tolerance and withdrawal symptomatology. Adapted from O'Brien, C. P., Childress, A. R., McClellan, A. T., Ehrman, R., & Ternies, J. W. (1988). Types of conditioning found in drug-dependent humans. National Institute on Drug Abuse Research Monograph Series, *84,* 44–61.

Mirin, 1979) subjects. The interlinking of drug effects and environmental cues may also explain the evolution of drug-based rituals as persons become increasingly involved in drug lifestyle activities. O'Brien et al. (1980) reported that opiate addicts acknowledged pleasurable feelings after self-injecting saline, but that subsequent injections produced increasingly more unpleasant effects. It may well be that whereas these conditioned environmental stimuli initially produced druglike conditioned responses, repeated exposure to these stimuli in the absence of any drug effect gradually weakened the druglike response while leaving the drug-opposite response intact.

There is always the possibility that individual differences influence a subject's sensitivity to druglike and drug-opposite effects. Meyer and Mirin (1979), for instance, reported that 11 patients receiving naltrexone (an opiate blocker) stopped injecting heroin in less than five trials, whereas another 11 patients injected an average of 16 doses of heroin before desisting. In comparing the 11 rapidly desisting and 11 slowly desisting patients, Meyer and Mirin discerned that the latter group displayed a distinct pattern of autonomic response (changes in heart rate, blood pressure, etc.) during the first three "blocked" trials that mimicked the natural effects of opiate drugs. Moreover, a dissipation of opiatelike autonomic responses coincided with the decision to stop injecting the naltrexone-blocked heroin in this group of slow desisters.

The drug-opposite effects of conditioned environmental stimuli have been used to explain the development of both tolerance and withdrawal. It is argued that environmental cues elicit an anticipatory drug-opposite conditioned response that prepares the organism for the drug effect and protects against overdose. Stimulus-controlled drug-opposite effects therefore shield the individual from the jarring physical consequences of drug ingestion, while simultaneously encouraging the formation of tolerance, whereby larger doses of the drug are required to achieve the same subjective effect. Unfamiliar surroundings fail to supply the environmental cues that normally elicit a drug-opposite effect; as a consequence, the same dosage of drug the individual is able to tolerate in a setting replete with familiar environmental cues may precipitate an overdose if taken in an environment dominated by unfamiliar contextual cues (Siegel & Ellsworth, 1986).

Using an animal model of addiction, Fanselow and German (1982) generated support for Siegel's position on drug-opposite effects by showing that morphine paired with a distinctive environmental cue resulted in conditioned tolerance, although this tolerance dissipated once the drug and cue were presented unpaired. Extending Siegel's opponent-process model of drug tolerance and withdrawal to research on humans, Newlin (1984) observed conditioned compensatory responses for finger pulse amplitude, finger temperature, and heart rate when subjects trained on vodka and tonic were administered tonic only. More recently, Newlin, Pretorius, and Jaffe (1990) recorded autonomic and subjective responses to an opiate placebo in 12 hospitalized heroin addicts that revealed the presence of druglike and drug-opposite conditioned responses after only four trials.

Withdrawal-like symptoms, as Wikler originally observed, can be anticipated when previously addicted patients are exposed to specific drug-related cues. Shephard Siegel (1988) and others argue that conditioned withdrawal occurs because there is no drug effect to counterbalance the drug-opposite effect of the conditioned environmental stimuli. In support of this claim, Sideroff and Jarvick (1980) determined that videotape presentations of drug use (e.g., preparing and then injecting heroin) evoked withdrawal-like reactions in former heroin addicts, but failed to elicit a response in opiate-naive subjects; and Teasdale (1973) discovered that heroin-related slides, but not heroin-unrelated slides, elicited withdrawal-like symptoms in former opiate abusers. Likewise, Ludwig, Cain, Wikler, Taylor, and Bendfeldt (1977) observed signs of withdrawal and increased craving in recovering alcoholics exposed to alcohol-related cues (e.g., a mock bar setup or the smell of liquor). Other studies suggest that conditioned withdrawal can occur in monkeys after as few as 10 trials (Goldberg & Schuster, 1970) and in humans after as few as 12 trials (O'Brien, Testa, O'Brien, Brady, & Wells, 1977).

The results of studies highlighting the effect conditioned tolerance and conditioned withdrawal have on drug-seeking behavior suggest that environmental modification may be an effective means of treatment for drug dependency. Outcomes obtained from formerly addicted Vietnam combat veterans returning to the United States during the late 1960s and early 1970s support such a claim. Despite concerns by social policymakers that servicemen who had abused heroin in Vietnam would continue this behavior upon their return home, research suggests that only about 12% of the previously addicted servicemen who had been detoxified prior to their departure from Vietnam actually relapsed (O'Brien et al., 1980; Robins, Davis, & Goodwin, 1974). This remarkably low rate of relapse can be construed as corroborating the conditioned cue model of tolerance and withdrawal in the sense that these servicemen were returning to an environment in which their surroundings and stimuli differed noticeably from the environmental cues that supported their drug use in Vietnam (Robins et al., 1974). The relapse-dampening effect of geographic relocation on opiate addicts in Detroit, Michigan (Ross, 1973), and San Antonio, Texas (Maddux & Desmond, 1982), lends further credence to a conditioned cue interpretation of tolerance and withdrawal symptomatology.

The classical conditioning model of addictive behavior also holds that extinction can be an effective means of promoting abstinence in previously addicted individuals. Childress, McLellan, Ehrman, and O'Brien (1988) report on the success of a procedure in which craving and conditioned responses to cocaine- and opiate-related stimuli were reduced in groups of cocaine and heroin abusers with the aid of an extinction paradigm. After repeatedly exposing subjects to cocaine- and opiate-related cues in the absence of the unconditioned stimulus (i.e., cocaine or heroin), the researchers observed that the levels of craving and conditioned withdrawal formerly elicited by the drug-related cues fell considerably (Childress et al., 1988). However, as these authors point out, therapeutic interventions need to consider cues that occur early in the stimulus chain (e.g., acquiring money for the drugs, the corner where the subject previously "copped" drugs), as well as cues more proximal to the actual ingestion of the drug (e.g., preparing the syringe, injecting the drug into a vein). In addition, because stimuli in the natural environment are more varied and potent than stimuli reproduced in a treatment setting, interventions should be directed at natural environmental cues (Childress et al., 1988).

Observational Learning

The conditioned withdrawal perspective on craving holds that situations reliably paired with drug withdrawal become conditioned stimuli capable of eliciting withdrawal-like symptomatology (Wikler & Pescor, 1967), whereas the opponent-process or compensatory response model proposes that craving can be attributed to an associational bond between situational cues and drug administration thought to cause homeostatic drug-opposite effects (S. Siegel, 1988). Marlatt's (1985) relapse prevention model also uses learning theory to account for craving, but here the emphasis is on craving as a positive outcome expectancy (anticipation of euphoria and relief from withdrawal) with clear social learning referents. Marlatt's supporters can point to studies denoting correlations of only .38 and .40 between self-reported urges and physiological reactivity and actual drug use, respectively (Tiffany, 1990). These findings illustrate the potential value of a third learning paradigm in understanding the development of drug-seeking behavior: the social or observational learning model of investigation.

Breaking down the observational learning process into its component features, Bandura (1977) makes a clear distinction between behavioral acquisition and performance. Subjects who attend to a modeled behavior, retain or encode their observations, and are motorically capable of reproducing the observed action are said to have acquired that skill or behavior. Whether subjects actually display the skill depends on whether they are reinforced for its performance or anticipate being reinforced at some future point.

Extending this paradigm to the issue of drug use, we note that a child or adolescent may acquire knowledge about drug use deportment by observing the behavior of persons engaged in a drug lifestyle but still not perform these behaviors because of a lack of current or anticipated reinforcement. This example illustrates two critical points. First, drug use can be learned through observation but requires reinforcement to be performed. Second, many factors, among them individual differences, enter into a person's decision to use or not use drugs. The social learning features of drug use behavior will be examined further in Chapter 4; the effect of individual differences in personality on subsequent drug use behavior is discussed in the section that follows.

PERSONALITY

Personality correlates of drug abuse will be discussed under two headings: personality as a predictor of substance abuse, and the clinical assessment of personality and adjustment.

Personality as a Predictor of Substance Abuse

If the intent is to predict future behavior, then the age at which stable predictors of human behavior appear must first be determined. Rutter and Giller (1984) estimate that replicable correlates of delinquent behavior and drug misuse begin to emerge around the time a child enters school. Although it is doubtful that behavioral consistency is established by the time a child enrolls in kindergarten, this period serves as a general developmental marker for the appearance of the gradually evolving sense of behavioral stability that some call personality. Even those scholars who take issue with the concept of personality (see Mischel, 1969) recognize the necessity of incorporating the prospect of relatively enduring patterns of behavior into their theories. With the many complex and competing issues that confront the study of personality in mind, the behavioral precursors and personality characteristics of potential significance to a comprehensive theory of drug-seeking behavior are discussed next.

Early and frequent use of chemicals has been shown to correlate with prepubescent and juvenile rebelliousness (Bachman, Johnston, & O'Malley, 1981), nonconformity (Jessor & Jessor, 1977), and resistance (Goldstein & Sappington, 1977). Kellam and Brown (1982) employed a longitudinal research design to demonstrate that aggression in a group of black male first graders, particularly when it was accompanied by shyness, predicted a high rate of drug use some 10 years later. Cross-sectional studies have revealed that drug abusers score low on measures of personal competence and social responsibility (Smith & Fogg, 1978), and high on measures of aggression and interpersonal conflict (Rydelius, 1983).

Labouvie and McGee (1986), on the other hand, were unable to confirm the presence of a nexus between self-esteem and substance abuse in a longitudinal study of adolescent respondents. They were, however, able to detect a relationship between substance abuse and several other personality measures, with heavy drug-consuming youth registering higher scores on measures of affiliation, autonomy, impulsivity, and exhibitionism and lower scores on measures of achievement orientation, cognitive structure, and harm avoidance than moderate drug-consuming youth. As could be anticipated, early substance use often foreshadows later substance use and is an empirically verifiable precursor of future drug-related problems (Robins & Przybeck, 1985).

Early and rapid onset of substance use aside, the most consistent predictor of future drug involvement may be a history of conduct problems in childhood and early adolescence. Studies have found childhood conduct disorder and juvenile delinquency to be associated with later displays of substance misuse (Hagnell, Lanke, Rorsman, & Ohman, 1986). Jones (1968) observed that future alcoholics were often described by others as having been rebellious, poorly controlled, and overtly hostile as children. The predictive status of antisocial behavior is verified by research depicting the direction of the relationship between antisocial behavior and substance use as flowing from delinquency to drug use rather than from drug use to delinquency (Elliott, Huizinga, & Ageton, 1985). However, the recency of antisocial behavior is also a key discriminating factor; it has been noted that adolescent antisocial activity is more predictive of adult antisocial behavior and substance abuse than antisocial behavior recorded during the preadolescent years (Hawkins, Lishner, & Catalano, 1985).

Other research findings indicate that several different precursors are highly significant in the development of drug difficulties and that each provides for a somewhat different pattern of drug-seeking behavior. Results from the Berkeley and Oakland longitudinal studies, for example, suggest that both antisocial and passive-dependent personality features are at work in elevating a person's risk of alcohol- and drug-related difficulties (Block, 1971). In these studies, persons displaying passive-dependent traits during childhood encountered few behavioral management problems as teenagers but began misusing alcohol and tobacco during middle adulthood. Persons exhibiting early antisocial behavior were also at risk for substance abuse difficulties, but followed a pattern in which thrill-seeking behavior and substance misuse surfaced during adolescence and continued into adulthood.

Investigating the personality correlates of substance abuse in a large sample of young adult respondents, Stacy, Newcomb, and Bentler (1991) determined that the six personality constructs they selected for study exerted a direct, mediating, and interactive effect on alcohol use and abuse, with sensation seeking and cognitive expectancies showing a stronger and more consistent relationship with alcohol use and problematic drinking behavior than the other four personality constructs (i.e., hostility, social conformity, parental alcohol abuse, and depressive tendencies). Other studies have also found sensation seeking to be important in defining a person's risk for drug involvement, although the sensation-seeking interests and activities displayed by persons at risk for drug-seeking behavior differ qualitatively from the sensation-seeking interests and activities of adventure-some (e.g., rock climbers) and pro-social (e.g., police, firefighters) risk takers (Levenson, 1990). Sensation seeking, in fact, is one of the developmental precursors thought to be important in the formation of a drug lifestyle (see Chapter 6).

Objective Personality Assessment: The MMPI

The Minnesota Multiphasic Personality Inventory (MMPI) is a 566-item personality measure comprising 3 validity scales, L, F, and K; 10 clinical scales, 1 (Hs: Hypochondrias), 2 (D: Depression), 3 (Hy: Hysteria), 4 (Pd:

Psychopathic deviant), 5 (Mf: Masculinity-femininity), 6 (Pa: Paranoia), 7 (Pt: Psychasthenia), 8 (Sc: Schizophrenia), 9 (Ma: Hypomania), and 0 (Si: Social introversion); and a surfeit of special scales and indexes. Modifications of item content and normative standards were recently incorporated into the MMPI and published as the MMPI-2 (Butcher, Dahlstrom, Graham, Tellegen, & Kaemmer, 1989). It stands to reason that these changes will only serve to augment the MMPI's already impressive array of research and clinical applications; a frequent criticism of the original MMPI was the outdated nature of many of its items. However, whether the retooled MMPI is any more useful than the original test or can claim the same level of predictive validity awaits further empirical analysis. The reader is referred to a recent text for more detailed information on the MMPI and MMPI-2 and on the individual strengths and weaknesses of each instrument (Greene, 1991).

Objective personality assessment research on substance abuse can be traced back to a series of studies carried out in the early 1960s on patients incarcerated at the U.S. Public Health Service Hospital in Lexington, Kentucky. The results of these preliminary studies divulged the presence of a relationship between the MMPI and addictive status, in that the MMPI effectively differentiated between groups of narcotics addicts and nonaddicted medical patient controls (Hill, Haertzen, & Davis, 1962). Research conducted since that time has continued to garner support for the discriminative power of the MMPI with respect to substance abuse (see Sutker & Archer, 1979), although as is common in many areas of psychological inquiry, there are several noteworthy exceptions to this trend in the literature. A study of Canadian heroin addicts administered by Gendreau and Gendreau (1970) is a case in point. In this study, the Gendreaus were unable to unearth support for the presence of an "addiction-prone" personality when the MMPI results of heroin addicts and a group of matched controls were compared. Findings such as these have led many to question the validity of the addiction-prone personality concept of drug use development and others to question the value of personality assessment in general.

A major goal of MMPI research is to identify any scales that are commonly elevated in specific client populations. Research indicates that Scale 4, Psychopathic deviance (Pd), is the MMPI scale most frequently elevated in groups of alcoholic and substance-abusing patients (Donovan, 1986; McKenna & Pickens, 1983), although it has been noted that Scale 2, Depression (D), may also exhibit prominent peaks on the MMPI protocols of substance-abusing clients (Hodo & Fowler, 1976; Overall, 1973). Persons attaining high scores on Scale 4 tend to be angry, rebellious, nonconforming, and unpredictable, whereas respondents with elevations on Scale 2 tend to be timid, withdrawn, overly sensitive, and generally dissatisfied with life (Greene, 1991). Such findings suggest that substance abuse is correlated with personality features of either a sociopathic or a neurotic nature, or perhaps a combination of these two patterns. The possibility that substance abuse may reflect both sociopathic and neurotic personality trends has been investigated using the high-point pair and cluster approaches to MMPI interpretation.

Research indicates that high-point pairs (the two most prominently elevated scales on a specific MMPI profile) may furnish a much greater wealth of interpretative information than the individual scales alone. The 2–4/4–2 pattern (combining the D and Pd scales) is, in fact, the mean high-point pair observed in groups of alcohol-abusing clients (Greene & Garvin, 1988). When individual records are inspected, however, there is typically no dominant modal high-point pair, although the 2–4/4–2, 2–7/7–2, and 4–9/9–4 patterns tend to be the three most familiar code types in substance-abusing populations (Greene & Nichols, 1987). Studies comparing the MMPI scores and high-point pairs attained by alcohol abusers and other substance-abusing groups like cocaine addicts find few significant differences in the MMPI performance of these two groups (Johnson, Tobin, & Cellucci, 1992). Polydrug abusers, on the other hand, often achieve higher overall profile elevations than alcohol-abusing clients and tend to generate profiles with prominent peaks on Scales 8 (Sc) and 9 (Ma). A group from the Veterans Administration Medical Center in Dallas discerned that black polydrug-abusing veterans recorded significantly fewer severely disturbed high-point pair patterns than white polydrug-abusing veterans (Penk, Woodward, Robinowitz, & Hess, 1978). On the strength of these findings, the authors concluded that African American polydrug abusers may be less emotionally disturbed than white polydrug abusers, although such a conclusion awaits further evaluation.

An appreciably more sophisticated approach to understanding and classifying within-group variability on the MMPI centers on the derivation of subclassification systems through the use of cluster analytic statistical procedures. The most popular subclassification of substance-abusing personalities follows a two-group scheme, one cluster suggesting the presence of an impulsive, acting-out pattern of behavior (elevations on MMPI Scales 4 and 9) and the other indicating an anxious, inhibited, and neurotic pattern (elevations on MMPI Scales 2 and 7; Morey & Blashfield, 1981; Skinner, 1982). Calsyn, Roszell, and Chaney (1989) utilized a four-group MMPI clustering scheme—normal, psychopathic, neurotic, and schizoid—and determined that the neurotic and schizoid groups displayed higher levels of emotional distress and psychological disturbance than subjects in the normal and psychopathic groups, that psychopathic and schizoid patients displayed more criminality than either normal or neurotic subjects, and that the normal group exhibited the best family and marital adjustment of the four patterns. Craig and Olson (1992) subjected the MMPIs of 104 cocaine abusers to hierarchical cluster analysis and identified two general groupings, one characterized by a solitary elevation on Scale *4* (acting-out pattern) and the other by a more highly elevated profile with peaks on Scales F, 4, 6 (Pa), 7 (Pt), and 8 (emotionally disturbed pattern).

EMOTIONAL DISORDER

The contemporary rise in popularity of dual diagnoses (substance abuse in persons with a formal psychiatric diagnosis) has reawakened interest in the self-medication hypothesis. Proponents of this hypothesis assert that drug-dependent persons consume chemical substances in an effort to alleviate feelings of guilt, frustration, depression, and anxiety (Khantzian, 1985). Evidence in support of this theorem takes several different forms. Of overriding concern, however, is the need to document the presence of a relationship between emotional disorder and substance misuse. Of substance abusers surveyed, between 65% and 77% exhibit concurrent psychiatric disorders, with antisocial personality and depression the two most commonly diagnosed maladies in drug abuse populations (Ross, Glaser, & Germanson, 1988; Rounsaville & Kleber, 1986). Weiss, Mirin, Griffin, and Michael (1988) identified a moderate degree of drug-diagnosis specificity in a sample of substance-abusing clients: Persons whose primary drugs of abuse were minor tranquilizers recorded a greater number of panic and anxiety disorder diagnoses, persons whose primary drug of abuse was cocaine recorded a higher percentage of affective disorder diagnoses, and persons whose primary drug of abuse was heroin recorded a higher proportion of conduct and antisocial personality disorder diagnoses.

An association has also been observed between substance abuse problems and psychopathology in studies exploring the drug use practices of psychiatric patients. Approximately 20% to 50% of patients diagnosed with schizophrenia (Drake & Wallach, 1989), bipolar disorder (Miller, Busch, & Tannebaum, 1989), major depression (McLellan & Druley, 1977), and antisocial personality disorder (Lewis, Rice, & Helzer, 1983) have a concurrent substance abuse diagnosis. The drug–psychological disorder alliance may extend even to persons who do not present clearly diagnosable psychological difficulties. Probing the self-medication hypothesis in a sample of 494 hospitalized drug abusers, Weiss, Griffin, and Mirin (1992) determined that major depression was a significant correlate of drug use, but noted that subclinical depression was an even more reliable concomitant in this group of patients. The ability of both clinical and subclinical psychiatric symptomatology to foster drug use behavior requires appreciably more attention before the strength of the drug–psychological disorder affiliation can be accurately gauged.

Once the existence of a relationship between drug abuse and psycho-pathology has been established, the next step is to determine the direction of this relationship. It could be argued, for instance, that emotional disorder is the consequence (secondary symptom) rather than the cause (primary disorder) of significant substance abuse. Hence, Udel (1984) contends that nearly three quarters of the sample of recovering physicians he interviewed reported emotional symptoms that were the consequence, rather than the cause, of their drug addiction. Other investigators note that emotional distress often precedes drug use, although the stress-dampening effects of drugs tend to be short-lived (Huba, Newcomb, & Bentler, 1986). The results of several longitudinal investigations implicate drug abuse as both a cause and effect of emotional issues like self-criticism, guilt, and shame: That is, emotional issues put a person at risk for initial drug use, the continued use of drugs exacerbates these issues, and the aggravated issues encourage further progression into drug use (Kandel, Kessler, & Margulies, 1978; Robins & Wish, 1977). There is also the possibility that some drugs, like alcohol and heroin, serve a self-medicating function, whereas other drugs, like cocaine and amphetamines, simply exacerbate preexisting psychological difficulties (Castaneda, Galanter, & Franco, 1989).

Where research may tend to support the argument that drug abuse and psychopathology are related and that psychopathology can put a subject at risk for substance abuse difficulties, a more adequate test of the self-medication hypothesis requires that the effect of drugs on a subject's current emotional state be assessed. To this end, Newcomb and Bentler (1988) observed that alcohol alleviated depression in a group of adolescents, whereas Woody, O'Brien, and Rickels (1975) advised that the antidepressant medication doxepin reduced both depressive symptoms and future substance use in long-term heroin addicts. Studies less congruent with the self-medication hypothesis note that psychiatric symptoms characteristically fall to a low level of occurrence once drug use is terminated (O'Connor, Berry, Morrison, & Brown, 1992). Post, Kotin, and Goodwin (1974) also observed results incompatible with the self-medication theorem in gauging the reactions of 23 depressed patients to low-moderate doses of cocaine. Whereas a third of the sample experienced mood elevation in response to cocaine, another third reported that their depressive symptoms worsened, and the final third showed no change. When eight of the patients were administered higher doses of cocaine, one showed improvement, and the remainder experienced no change or a serious exacerbation of depressive symptomatology. Exploring the specificity of the drug-psychological disorder nexus, Johanson and de Wit (1989) ascertained that anxiolytic (antianxiety) drugs were no more reinforcing for persons with high initial anxiety than for persons with low initial anxiety.

Although studies such as those carried out by Post et al. (1974) and Johanson and de Wit (1989) provide data inconsistent with major features of the self-medication hypothesis, there are several issues that must be addressed before this theorem can be dismissed. First, the Post et al. study demonstrates that higher doses of cocaine may exacerbate depressive symptomatology in some individuals. This finding does not mean, however, that cocaine cannot serve a self-medicating function for a select group of individuals, at certain dosages, at specific points in their addictive careers. It may well be that self-medication is a critical motivating factor in some cases and that this effect interacts with other variables in determining drug outcomes. The complexity of the issue is revealed in studies showing that many drug-involved persons continue ingesting drugs long after the self-medicating effect has worn off and been replaced by long-term deterioration in mood (Mirin, Meyer, & McNamee, 1976). In interpreting the results of the Johanson and de Wit (1989) study, it is important to keep in mind that recent evidence suggests that a complex interaction of specific drugs of abuse and risk factors may influence the degree to which a drug is reinforcing for a particular individual (cf. Ciraulo, Barnhill, Ciraulo, Greenblatt, & Shader, 1989, with Schuckit, 1989).

There is evidence, then, of a relationship between emotional disorder and substance abuse; it is further concluded that emotional disorder can put one at risk for substance abuse difficulties, and that some individuals, depending on a complex interaction of person, setting, and stage of drug involvement, may use drugs to self-medicate against anxiety, depression, guilt, or frustration. Factors other than self-medication that are potentially important in promoting a drug–psychological disorder relationship include the possibilities that (a) psychopathology interferes with a person's judgment and decision-making capabilities to such an extent that the individual fails to appreciate the deleterious effect of drugs on his or her behavior; (b) psychopathology increases the risk of dysphoria and severe withdrawal symptomatology in the absence of a drug effect and so impedes the process of desisting drug use; and (c) psychopathology encourages a person to seek out situations and affiliations found in the drug subculture to establish a new identity and achieve a sense of social acceptance (Weiss, 1992a). Whatever the explanation, the parameters of the drug–psychological disorder relationship and the factors that determine the subject, setting, and developmental features of the self-medicating effect must be investigated more thoroughly and defined in more precise terms.

CONCLUSION

The results of this review indicate that drug use is a highly reinforcing activity that both directs and motivates behavior. This chapter also reveals that people learn the techniques and attitudes of habitual drug use in much the same manner as they learn any other activity: that is, through operant schedules of reinforcement and punishment, conditioning of involuntary responses, and modeling of other people's behavior. Whereas individual differences, as represented in this chapter by personality factors and emotional disorders, may affect a person's risk of substance abuse involvement, these are the pebbles, in contrast to the ripples that are learning. Learning is one of the variables that give rise, not only to drug use initiation, but also to a drug lifestyle. For as Adesso (1985) so aptly points out, time spent in a particular addictive activity is directly proportional to the strength of the learned expectancies.

Although there is evidence that early antisocial behavior, low self-esteem, and sensation seeking may put an individual at risk for future drug use, the presence of an "addiction-prone" personality cannot be verified from the results of this literature review on the personality correlates of drug-seeking behavior. Hudleby (1986) found, for instance, that personality measures were largely ineffective in predicting later juvenile delinquency and drug abuse in 150 early adolescent boys in Ontario, Canada. Emotional disorder, although it may promote substance abuse in a subset of cases through activation of the self-medication motive, is not a complete answer to the problem of substance abuse, either. Even though a drug lifestyle may be mediated and influenced by a number of factors, the force that converts a drug lifestyle from a theoretical possibility to an observable reality exists in the form of various learning and reinforcement contingencies. The next chapter examines ways by which this learning might take place, through investigating the role of socialization in the formation of drug-seeking behavior.

Chapter 4

Sociological Factors

INTRODUCTION

In their pursuit of answers to questions concerning the nature of human comportment, sociologists opt for a situation-based interpretation of drug-seeking behavior and, accordingly, tend to see the social milieu as of vital significance in the development of deviant and nondeviant forms of behavior. This view contrasts sharply with the person-oriented inclinations of biology- and psychology-minded investigators. Thus the sociological model furnishes investigators with yet another avenue through which drug abuse may be defined and measured. However, because social structure assumes many forms and has many facets, it is necessary to restrict the scope of the present discussion to three principal areas of sociological significance: societywide effects, primary-group effects, and reference-group effects.

Studies of societywide effects consider the role of sociocultural values and normative practices in defining an individual's attitudes toward and eventual risk of alcohol and other drug abuse outcomes. Primary-group effect research, on the other hand, considers a person's relationships with family members and the impact these relationships have on the proclivity for substance abuse. The final section in this chapter, on the social environmental correlates of drug-seeking behavior, involves a consideration of reference-group effects. Here, the role of peer relations in promoting or deterring future alcohol and other drug use is scrutinized. These three categories are reviewed in an effort to form a comprehensive appreciation of sociological influences on substance use and abuse.

SOCIETYWIDE EFFECTS: SOCIOCULTURAL MILIEU

Alcoholism and drug abuse are not uniformly distributed across societies and cultures, and may vary widely even for persons living in the same general location. In New York City, for instance, where 10% of the population is Irish-American, 15% Italian-American, and 25% Jewish, the ethnic composition of one sample of alcoholics was 40% Irish, 1% Italian, and 0% Jewish (Lolli, Schesler, & Golder, 1960). Similar results were obtained in a survey of alcoholics in California (Terry, Lolli, & Golder, 1957). Cross-national differences in alcohol consumption and alcohol abuse have also been observed and documented (see Table 4-1). The issue that merits more immediate attention, however, is to explain precisely how these cross-cultural and cross-national variations originate. Cultural values

Table 4-1   Comparisons of Alcohol Consumption in 10 Countries

Nation	Alcohol use for 1985[a] (Liters of absolute ethanol per 100,000 population)				Alcohol abuse rate for 1970[b]
	All alcoholic beverages	Beer	Wine	Distilled spirits	
Canada	8.0	82.7	9.7	2.7	2,460
Fed. Rep. of Germany	10.8	145.5	25.6	2.4	4,820
France	13.3	40.1	80.0	2.3	9,050
Great Britain	7.1	108.9	10.0	1.7	2,130
Ireland	6.2	100.0	3.5	1.8	1,830
Italy	11.6	21.6	84.8	1.2	7,390
Japan	5.7	38.0	0.7	2.4	—
Sweden	5.2	46.8	11.7	2.0	1,990
Switzerland	11.2	69.2	49.6	2.2	4,420
United States	8.0	90.3	9.2	2.7	2,690

[a]Produktschap voor Gestilleerde Dranken. (1986). *How much alcoholic beverage is drunk worldwide*. Schiedam, Netherlands: Author.

[b]Per capita rate of alcohol use in excess of a daily average of 15 cl of absolute ethanol. Alcohol abuse data are from de Lint, J. (1976). The epidemiology of alcoholism with specific reference to sociocultural factors. In M. W. Everett, J. O. Waddell, & D. B. Heath (Eds.), *Cross-cultural approaches to the study of alcohol: An introductory perspective*. Paris, France: Mouton.

concerning the use of specific chemical compounds appear to be one possible explanation for cross-cultural and cross-national differences in alcohol consumption and dependence.

Investigators have traditionally assumed that the consistency and clarity of cultural norms, values, and customs relative to the use of alcohol and other substances are of key etiological significance in deciphering cross-national variations in drug use and abuse. Ullman (1958) writes that when customs and values concerning drug use are clear, consistent, and integrated, the incidence of alcohol consumption may be moderate to high, but the rate of alcohol abuse is nearly always low. This theory appears to hold, whether for the alcohol use patterns of the Jewish population of New York City or the ingestion of peyote by a Native American tribe in southern Arizona. Conversely, when rules guiding the proper use of alcohol and other drugs are lacking or incomplete, the rate of alcoholism and other drug abuse tends to be high (Larsen & Abu-Laban, 1968). Appraising theoretical conceptualizations of the drug-culture connection is the next step to understanding the effect of cultural beliefs, practices, and expectancies on a person's propensity to use and misuse chemical substances.

An early pioneer in cultural research on drug abuse, Robert Freed Bales (1946) proposed a preliminary etiological model of cross-national differences in the use and abuse of alcohol that relies principally on three categories of cultural influence. The first category involves the degree to which a culture arouses inner tension and adjustment problems in its members. The second centers on a culture's ability to provide viable tension-reducing and recreation-enhancing alternatives to alcohol and other drugs. Bales's third category of influence concerns a culture's attitude toward the use of ethanol to reduce tension and promote self-interest. Its treatment of cultural prescriptions outlining the proper use of alcohol as either a tension reducer or promoter of self-interest is the aspect of Bales's theory that has received the greatest attention from investigators in the field.

Bales subdivided cultural attitudes toward drug use into four categories, with abstinence at one end of the continuum and utilitarianism at the other. Religious groups like the Moslems and Mormons hold to an abstinent attitude that strictly prohibits alcohol and other drug use. Cultures adhering to a ritualistic attitude, the second of Bales's four categories, provide clear prescriptions for when and where drug use is appropriate. One example of the ritualistic approach to alcohol consumption is practiced in the United States by persons of the Jewish faith. Cultures with a convivial attitude, Bales's third category, view drug use as a social lubricant, whereas cultures following a utilitarian approach, the fourth category, condone the use of alcohol or drugs as a means of feeling good and relieving tension. Subsequent research has shown that cultures holding to convivial and utilitarian attitudes experience much higher rates of both alcohol use and alcoholism than cultures espousing an abstinent or ritualistic attitude (Ull-mann & Krasner, 1975).

The relationship between cultural attitudes toward alcohol and other drugs and a person's use of drugs is actually quite complex. It is generally agreed that strong prohibitions against the use of intoxicants normally lead to decreased levels of consumption in the general citizenry but encourage the development of serious psychopathology in those who do drink (Po-pham, 1959). Examining this issue empirically, Christiansen and Teahan (1987) determined that strong prohibitions against adolescent drinking in Ireland correlate with less frequent social drinking, less recurrent problem drinking, and fewer positive expectancies concerning the effects of alcohol. However, a larger proportion of the alcohol-using Irish youth population displayed drinking-related problems in the form of adverse physiological reactions, family problems, and conflict with school and legal authorities than was the case for their alcohol-using American counterparts. This outcome suggests that strong cultural prohibitions against drinking may contribute to a polarization of attitudes, in which alcohol is viewed as either all good or all bad, resulting in a low overall rate of alcohol con-sumption but a much higher rate of interpersonal conflict and other alcohol-related problems in persons who choose to drink despite the prescriptions.

The complex interplay of cultural and personal attitudes in the devel-opment of drinking behavior is illustrated in a study by Kitano, Chi, Rhee, Law, and Lubben (1992). Surveying the drinking practices of subjects of Japanese heritage living in Japan, Hawaii, and Santa Clara County, Cal-ifornia, these authors uncovered results that signified a relationship be-tween cultural norms and alcohol use behavior. Specifically, Japanese sub-jects residing in Japan displayed a more permissive attitude toward male alcohol use and a greater volume of actual alcohol consumption than Jap-anese subjects living in Hawaii or California. The researchers found that 56.5% of the Japanese-American males living in Hawaii and 53.3% of the Japanese-American males living in California could be classified as light/moderate or heavy consumers of alcohol, whereas 76.5% of the Japanese men residing in Japan could be so classified. All three groups were sig-nificantly less tolerant of alcohol consumption in women: Japanese-Americans expressed more tolerant views toward female drinking than native Japanese and, correspondingly, more Japanese women residing in Hawaii and Cal-ifornia could be classified as light/moderate or heavy drinkers than Japa-nese women living in Japan.

In a related vein, Caetano and Medina-Mora (1988) examined the association between cultural attitudes, acculturation, and patterns of al-cohol use in persons of Mexican descent residing in the United States and in Michoacan, Mexico. Concordant with the greater tolerance for alcohol use in the United States, Mexican-Americans drank more frequently and more heavily than the group that resided in Mexico. Upon Mexican subjects' relocating to the United States, an acculturation effect normally occurred in men within 5 years of arrival, whereas for females the effect was only observed in U.S.-born subjects. Caetano and Medina-Mora speculate that the traditional female roles of homemaker and daughter preclude Mexican-born women from taking advantage of the climb in discretionary funds that normally accompanies immigration to the United States, and with which alcoholic beverages are purchased. Mexican immigrant women in the U.S. must therefore wait for changes to take place in regulatory cultural norms before they can adopt the alcohol-using practices of their new country.

Culture appears to have a major effect not only on alcohol and drug use patterns, but also on an individual's behavior while intoxicated. Cinquemani (1975) compared two Central Mexican Indian tribes that routinely consume large amounts of liquor but engage in very different behavioral patterns while drinking. One of these tribes, the Los Pastores, hold to the fatalistic belief that alcohol consumption is inevitable in men and that drinking alcohol invariably provokes violence. Consequently, when men of the Los Pastores tribe drink, they are characteristically loud, boisterous, and violent. A second tribe, the Mixtecans, also drink to excess but do not associate alcohol with aggression or loss of control, and so when they drink they do so without violence. It is noteworthy that the Los Pastores have cultural proscriptions against violence during rituals and religious ceremonies and that, even though men of the Los Pastores often drink to the point of inebriation during these ceremonies, there is little if any violence. MacAndrew and Edgerton (1969) supply additional examples of how social conventions help shape cultural beliefs about personal responsibility following consumption of large amounts of an intoxicating beverage. The cultural prescriptions that delineate the range of tolerance for intoxicant use and drunken comportment provide the parameters of the socialization experience with respect to drug-seeking behavior.

The results of this review suggest that cultural values, prescriptions, and expectations are important in the development of a person's attitude toward and actual use of alcoholic beverages and other mind-altering substances. Conditions other than cultural values, however, also appear to affect cross-cultural and cross-national differences in substance use and abuse. Take, for instance, the fact that a country like Italy, which holds to a social ritualistic attitude toward alcohol imbibition in adults, suffers a much higher rate of alcohol abuse than Ireland, a country known for its utilitarian view of adult alcohol use (see Table 4-1). This finding implies that factors other than cultural attitude should be included in any explanation of the sociocultural features and correlates of drug-seeking behavior.

de Lint (1976) argues this very point in his own exegesis of cross-national differences in alcohol abuse; he incorporates both accessibility of alcohol and urbanization into his explanation of cross-national differences in problem drinking. The authority of access to help explain cross-national differences in alcohol abuse is plainly evident in the following statistical example. Assuming that the amount of alcohol consumed in a particular geographic region reflects the availability of alcohol in that jurisdiction, alcohol availability and abuse correlate .92 for the nine nations listed in Table 4-1 for which both accessibility and abuse data are available. Urbanization has also been shown to be important in explaining cross-national differences in the rates of alcohol use and problem drinking (de Lint, 1976).

Although both accessibility and urbanization should be taken into account in constructing a comprehensive model of cross-national variations in alcohol use, cultural values remain a viable explanatory concept. Therefore, attention now turns to two groups heavily involved in transmitting cultural values to children: namely, family members and peers.

PRIMARY-GROUP EFFECTS: THE NUCLEAR FAMILY

The family is frequently the first social unit with which a child interacts. Early lessons in life are ordinarily learned in interactions with parents and siblings, the results of which set the stage for future attitudinal and behavioral development. Problems arise, however, when early training is faulty, erroneous, or incomplete, or when the full protective capacity of the family is compromised by neglect, abuse, or conflict. As was mentioned in Chapter 2, drug abuse follows along family lines. One conceivable explanation for this finding is that drug-seeking behavior is influenced by heredity and that a genetic predisposition to alcohol and/or drug use is passed down from one generation to the next. It is also possible that cross-generational transmission of values and ideas capable of affecting a person's risk for substance abuse involvement takes place within the family. Family environment factors potentially linked to subsequent drug abuse behavior can be classified into three general categories: (a) parental deviance (criminality as well as drug abuse), (b) lack of an affectionate and supportive parent–child relationship, and (c) weak parental supervision.

Parental Deviance

In one of the first studies to address familial precursors of substance misuse, Teuber and Powers (1953) discovered that subjects who later developed alcohol abuse problems were raised in homes where the mother had a propensity to escape from crises through physical withdrawal, sexual promiscuity, and alcohol misuse. The modeling function of parental drug use is further illustrated in a study by Smart and Fejer (1972), where a positive relationship was recorded between parental consumption of tobacco, alcohol, and tranquilizers and a child's own use of mind-altering substances.

Needle, Lavec, Su, Brown, & Doherty (1988) reported that significantly more mothers of substance-using teenagers ingested drugs themselves than mothers of non-drug-using adolescents. Regular consumption of beer and hard liquor by parents was found to predict offspring's use of hard liquor and illicit drugs other than marijuana in one study (Kandel, Kessler, & Margulies, 1978), and use of heroin in a second (Cannon, 1976). Modeling of parental behavior in the initiation of cigarette smoking is also well documented (Shute, Pierce, & Lubell, 1981).

Ahmed, Bush, Davidson, and Ionnotti (1984) advised that alcohol and marijuana use by family members increases a child's propensity for future drug use and abuse through imitation and modeling. They noted that only 4% of children living in households where no one else smoked marijuana used cannabis themselves, compared with 23% of children residing in homes where one other family member smoked marijuana and 39% of children living in homes where two or more family members consumed cannabis on a regular or semiregular basis. Modeling exerts a clear effect on the behavior of children whose parents ingest drugs, but it is not the only means through which parental drug use may affect their offspring's risk of future drug dependency. A correlation of .35 was obtained between a composite measure of parental drug use and child drug use in a study by Dishion, Patterson, and Reid (1988), leading them to conclude that parental drug use raises a child's risk of drug involvement by increasing the availability of drugs in the home and interfering with the parent's ability to manage the child's behavior, as well as serving a modeling function. Harbin and Maziar (1975) uncovered a high incidence of drug ingestion in the family backgrounds of drug abusers and added that family separations for reasons other than death were also common in this group.

Lack of Affection

Family "breakdown" events such as death, divorce, family conflict, and parental alcohol or drug abuse are known to correlate with adolescent drug use (Friedman, Pomerance, Sanders, Santo, & Utada, 1980). Drug-abusing subjects themselves view their families of origin as less cohesive and adaptable than do subjects with no history of substance misuse (Friedman, Utada, & Morrissey, 1987). The families of substance abusers are often characterized as high in conflict and low in mutual support. Along similar lines, a group of investigators under the direction of Ronald Simons recorded a reasonably strong correlation between parental rejection and adolescent substance abuse (Simons, Conger, & Whitbeck, 1988; Simons & Robertson, 1989). Simons and his colleagues speculate that parental rejection exerts both a direct effect and an indirect effect (by damaging the child's self-esteem and encouraging him or her to affiliate with deviant peers) on

future aggression and drug use (Simons et al., 1988). Studies comparing relational family factors (e.g., cohesion, discipline, and communication) and structural family factors (parental absence, family size, and birth order) in research on adolescent drug use suggest that relational factors may be more important than structural factors in understanding the formation of a drug lifestyle (Coombs & Paulson, 1988; Piercy, Volk, Trepper, Sprenkle, & Lewis, 1991). The quality of the parent-child relationship, in fact, appears to have a bearing on whether normative experimental drug use leads to more serious patterns of drug involvement (Kandel, 1982).

According to the results of a frequently cited investigation on the familial correlates of substance abuse, serious neglect and poor interpersonal relations characterize the early family experiences of heavy drug users (Chein, Gerard, Lee, & Rosenfeld, 1964). From interviews conducted with 30 compulsive drug users, 29 normal controls, and the parents of as many of the subjects as could be located, these investigators observed that paternal absence during childhood (48% drug users vs. 17% control), weak father–son attachment (80% drug users vs. 45% control), and severely disturbed marital relations (97% drug users vs. 41% control) preceded the onset of drug problems for subjects in the compulsive drug use group. Hirschi (1969) has proposed that a weak parent–child bond makes it difficult for a child to learn rule-abiding behavior, therefore elevating his or her vulnerability to future delinquent and drug-abusing outcomes. Olson, Portner, and Bell (1982) assert that parental overinvolvement may be just as important as parental rejection in placing a child or adolescent at increased risk for involvement with alcohol or other drugs. Hence, there is preliminary support for the supposition that a weak affective bond between parent and child may increase the child's proclivity to abuse drugs by interfering with the parent's ability to influence the behavior of the child both directly and indirectly. Parental overinvolvement, on the other hand, may encourage drug-seeking behavior by stimulating an attitude of entitlement and ardent rebellion in a child who feels both spoiled and smothered by doting parents.

Weak Parental Supervision

Although the contributions of attachment and social bonding to the study of deviance development are legion, Rankin and Wells (1990) call attention to the fact that direct parental control (discipline) may be an even more potent source of influence over future delinquent outcomes, including alcohol and other drug use. Ineffective discipline, lack of consistency and structure, and a tendency to vacillate between overpermissiveness and physical or verbal violence have been observed clinically in the parents of alcoholics and drug abusers (Wurmser, 1978). There is also reason to

believe that, compared with the parents of control subjects, the mothers and fathers of heavy drug-using adolescents rely predominately on social isolation and deprivation in disciplining their children (Zucker & Barron, 1973). Research conducted at the Oregon Learning Center in Eugene demonstrates that training sessions designed to teach basic child management and disciplinary skills to the parents of high-risk and acting-out juveniles are effective in reducing subsequent drug use and delinquency on the part of these juveniles (Patterson, 1980).

Although there are no hard and fast rules when it comes to the familial correlates of alcoholism and drug abuse, research results suggest that the mothers of adolescent drug abusers are more domineering and overprotective (Zucker & Barron, 1973) and the fathers more punitive and rejecting (Prendergast, 1974) than the parents of nondrug-abusing adolescents. Many of these reports, however, are based on unsystematic clinical impressions or studies that lack sufficient methodological rigor. Employing a psychometrically sophisticated measure of parental attitude and a retrospective design, Emmelkamp and Herres (1988) surmised that drug abusers enrolled in treatment rated their fathers and mothers as more overprotective and rejecting than did controls, with the effect strongest for paternal rejection and lack of warmth. Although the problems associated with the use of retrospective accounts of family relations limit the interpretability of these findings, the outcomes obtained in this and other investigations nonetheless imply that a relationship may, in fact, exist between family climate and subsequent problems with alcohol or other drugs.

Exactly how familial overprotection and rejection support serious drug use in affected siblings remains a mystery, although a recent study by Feigelman, Hyman, Amann, and Feigelman (1990) suggests several possibilities. Upon conducting follow-up interviews with 48 young adult white male subjects 6 years after their release from an adolescent substance abuse treatment program, these authors ascertained that subjects who lived at home with their parents were more likely to have an ongoing problem with drugs than those living on their own. These results may be a function of low self-esteem or the enabling behavior of parents, but Feigelman et al. opt for an interactional-conflict interpretation, in which the young adult is reinforced for being irresponsible but is continually castigated by parents embarrassed by their offspring's behavior and lack of autonomy. A complex interplay of factors within the home was also observed in a group of 235 heroin addicts interviewed by Maddux and Desmond (1989). Familial alcoholism placed these addicts at increased risk for future substance abuse problems, but availability and other family-environmental considerations (e.g., drug use behavior of siblings) determined the actual drug of abuse.

It stands to reason that poor family relations, inadequate parental discipline, and modeling of escapist coping strategies put a person at risk for substance abuse difficulties. However, the transmission of cultural values from parent to child may also be important in defining a subject's liability for drug abuse. It is known, for instance, that clear and consistent cultural prescriptions concerning the proper use of alcohol are associated with a low rate of alcoholism, as represented by the fact that heavy alcohol consumption is most prevalent in persons raised in nonprescriptive environments (with neither approval nor disapproval of alcohol), followed by persons reared in prescriptive (approve of alcohol) and proscriptive (disapprove of alcohol) homes (Larsen & Abu-Laban, 1968). Concerning the proposed link between the familial transmission of cultural values, drinking and delinquency, and family and peer influences, Pearce and Garrett (1970) noted that 69% of delinquents in their study, as compared with 25% of a group of nondelinquent controls, initially used alcohol without parental permission. During adulthood, Pearce and Garrett's delinquents drank primarily with peers, whereas the nondelinquents did most of their drinking at home. These findings suggest that peers also serve an important socializing function with respect to the future use and abuse of alcohol and other drugs.

REFERENCE-GROUP EFFECTS: PEERS

A peer group is composed of persons with whom one associates and perceives a sense of kinship or mutual identity. Peer influence is believed to exert control over drug use in adolescents on the strength of research demonstrating that peers serve a vital reference and modeling function for children and teenagers. Studying self-reported drug use in a sample of 4859 junior and senior high school students, Napier, Goe, and Bachtel (1984) determined that peer associations and the role models these students selected for emulation exercised a formidable effect on their use of illicit substances. Akers (1984) speculated that delinquency and drug use are linked through their affiliation with a common set of social factors that include weak parental supervision, poor school performance, lack of religious training, and, most importantly, behavior of close friends. Perusing answers supplied by a group of 1381 adolescents to a survey of drug use contexts, White, Johnson, and Garrison (1985) ascertained that the behavior of friends was clearly prognostic of both delinquency and drug use. However, they found little evidence of crossover between drugs and crime and so failed to generate support for a deviant subculture interpretation of the drug–crime connection.

Utilizing concepts and postulates borrowed from Sutherland's (1939) differential association theory of delinquency and Becker's (1953) model of marijuana indoctrination, Orcutt (1987) examined self-reported marijuana use by college students as a function of attitudes toward marijuana and of the drug-involved behavior of each subject's four closest friends. Analysis of these data revealed that students who expressed positive attitudes toward marijuana were more apt to smoke marijuana themselves, whereas students who professed a negative view of marijuana personally avoided the use of this substance, except when all four of their closest friends were semiregular cannabis users. The differential association effect of peers on marijuana use was most conspicuous in subjects holding a neutral view of cannabis ingestion. When none of a subject's four closest friends were semiregular users, only 9% of neutral-view subjects reportedly used marijuana themselves. However, this figure climbed to 24% when one of a subject's four closest friends was a semiregular user of marijuana and to 50% when two or more of the subject's four closest friends were semiregular users.

It is commonly believed that the single best predictor of adolescent drug use is the degree to which an individual associates with other adolescents who consume drugs (Elliott, Huizinga, & Ageton, 1985). The results of a nationally representative survey of high school students revealed that the drinking behavior of friends accounted for 39% of the variance in drinking behavior among males and 44% of the variance among females (Harford & Grant, 1987). However, the causal order of the variables that constitute the drug-peer alliance is doubtful, and questions concerning the relative contributions of social learning versus differential association have been raised. Contrasting the social learning (modeling of peer behavior) and differential association (holding attitudes favorable to the use of drugs) interpretations of adolescent drug use, Johnson, Marcos, and Bahr (1987) accrued greater support for the social learning alternative. Further analysis of these data disclosed that social learning and social control (attachment) variables considered in combination produced results superior to those obtained from any other individual variable or combination of variables.

Oetting and Beauvais (1987) found peer influence, as defined by gang membership, having best friends, or belonging to couples, to have a direct effect on drug use in adolescents. Further analysis of these data revealed that peer influence acted as an intermediary between a set of potent social variables (community solidarity, neighborhood cohesiveness, family atmosphere, deviant role models, and religious upbringing) and drug use outcomes. Several personal variables—self-esteem, depression, anxiety, and introversion—also correlated with drug-peer associations, but at a level significantly below that attained by the social variables. In a follow-up to this study, Swaim, Oetting, Edwards, and Beauvais (1989) explored the relationship between emotional distress, peer associations, and drug use in a group of 563 11th- and 12-grade students and discovered that, whereas emotional distress accounted for 4.8% of the variance in self-reported drug use, this figure climbed to 43.4% when a measure of peer drug associations was added to the equation. These findings corroborate earlier studies in which peer association theory was shown to be substantially more predictive of drug use in adolescents than strain or emotional distress theory (Ginsberg & Greenely, 1978; White, Johnson, & Horowitz, 1986). Swaim et al. speculate that the effect of emotional distress on drug use patterns, at least among adolescents, is mediated largely by peer associations.

This positive review of peer influence as a factor in the initiation, and perhaps maintenance, of drug-seeking behavior should not be taken as prima facie evidence that adolescents are passive recipients of peer influence. Adolescents, in fact, play an active role in the peer selection process, choosing to be with certain groups while avoiding others. With this factor in mind, Fisher and Bauman (1988) have proposed an interactive model of peer influence whereby adolescents align themselves with those who share similar views. Glassner and Laughlin (1987) discovered evidence from interviews conducted among adolescents concerning their use of substances that tended to support Fisher and Bauman's hypotheses on the nature of peer influence. Of vital importance is the realization that it is not the actual use of substances by peers that most influences a child's decision to use drugs, but rather the child's perception of peer substance use (Jessor & Jessor, 1977). Accordingly, peer influence is mediated by a person's perception of others' behavior—a perception that does not need to be pro-drug to have an effect. As a case in point, several studies indicate that peers can serve a protective function in situations where they support a drug-free lifestyle and exhort others to avoid or discontinue their involvement with substances (Meier, Burkett, & Hickman, 1984; Weinstein, 1978).

Recent comparisons of the relative abilities of familial and peer factors to affect adolescent drug use outcomes imply that peer associations may wield greater authority over future drug-seeking behavior than early family relations (Marcos, Bahr, & Johnson, 1986). Swadi (1988) notes that when substance use is found in both a family member and the adolescent subject's closest friend, the probability of self-reported substance use on the part of the subject is 79%. In cases where there is no drug use in a family member or the subject's best friend, the probability of self-reported drug use falls to 13%. Comparing the relative influence of parents and peers on drug-using behavior in his sample, Swadi determined that when a family member imbibed drugs but the child's best friend did not, only 35% of the subjects used drugs themselves, compared with a rate of 60% when the subject's best friend used drugs but no family member did.

Rather than laboring to determine whether family or peer influences dominate future drug use outcomes, a more productive approach may involve a comprehensive examination of how these two forces interact. Coombs, Paulson, and Richardson (1991) remark that drug-using and abstaining juveniles both report greater affiliation with parents than with peers, but that compared with abstainers, substance-using teenagers are more likely to report being influenced by their peer group. This factor, in combination with the results of studies highlighting the role of the family in early socialization (i.e., Emmelkamp & Herres, 1988; Loeber, 1990), suggests that youths who enjoy more positive relationships with their parents are less influenced by drug-using peers and consequently less involved in drug-oriented activities.

Research studies show that adolescents look to their parents for guidance in identifying long-term career-oriented goals and values but rely on peers in defining short-term immediate goals and values (Sebald, 1986; Wilks, 1986). Adolescents who possess few future-oriented values and goals may therefore be more vulnerable to deviant peer influence because of its accent on immediacy, excitement, and irresponsibility (Simons et al., 1988), all of which may move the individual into a second stage of sociological development wherein he or she learns the techniques and attitudes conducive to continued drug involvement by modeling the behavior of drug-using peers.

CONCLUSION

This chapter has examined the sociological correlates of substance abuse as represented by the cultural, familial, and peer factors that influence a person's proclivity for involvement in drug-seeking and drug-using behavior. Culture appears to affect the probability of future substance abuse by establishing the conditions under which drug use is deemed appropriate. As was discussed previously, certain religious and cultural groups (e.g., Mormons and Muslims) strictly prohibit the use of chemicals, whereas groups like the Jewish community prescribe clear guidelines for the proper use of alcohol. Both attitudes have been shown to correlate with low levels of substance abuse. Cultural values, therefore, appear to provide general prescriptions outlining the social acceptability of individual behaviors— the degree of substance abuse adjusting itself according to the levels of approval and prohibition, and to the clarity and consistency of the prescriptions themselves.

If it can be agreed that cultural factors are capable of influencing a person's inclination toward drug use behavior, then the next step is to determine precisely how these values are conveyed to the individual. First and foremost, cultural values and attitudes are transmitted through association with family members and friends. In my own clinical work with clients, I have come to respect the power of the family to effect both positive and negative outcomes in the behavior of its members. It has been my experience that rarely are the parents of drug-abusing and acting-out children and adolescents "bad" people; it is more likely that they feel overwhelmed by the responsibilities of raising a family without solid family management skills. Often, the parents of acting-out children have never been properly parented themselves, and there is evidence that family management skills are normally passed down from one generation to the next (Patterson, 1986). Parenting is made even more arduous in situations where the society or culture lacks a clear and consistent set of guidelines for appropriate behavior. The professional community, rather than blaming parents for the negative actions of their offspring, could help prevent a certain percentage of drug abuse problems by teaching parents the skills they need to manage their children's behavior.

The third component of sociological influence in defining the risk of drug-seeking outcomes concerns peer relations. Human beings are social animals, and as such have a high need for social acceptance and affiliation. Without the guidance of parents who follow effective family management practices, children and adolescents are left defenseless against negative forces that run rampant in a society where drug and criminal opportunities abound. Inept family management practices lead to negative consequences, the list of which includes weak self-control (Gottfredson & Hirschi, 1990), low self-esteem (Patterson, 1986), and poor school performance (Loeber & Dishion, 1983). Because people are drawn to those who think and act as they do, it is little wonder that children exposed to ineffective parenting and inconsistent discipline tend to drift into relationships with similarly predisposed children. Furthermore, because parents who lack effective family management skills also have difficulty supervising the activities of their children outside the home, they are often less well equipped to protect their offspring from negative peer influence than parents with strong family management skills (Wilson, 1980).

This discussion reveals the prominence of sociological variables in affecting future drug abuse outcomes. First of all, it demonstrates that sociological variables, in this case cultural attitude, familial relations, and peer associations, are important correlates of drug-seeking behavior. Second, it suggests that sociological factors may exert their influence in an orderly, rather than chaotic, fashion. In other words, cultural prescriptions set the general tone of sociological influence; families follow suit by communicating, interpreting, and shaping this influence; and peers complete the process by reinforcing or modifying these and other social patterns. A third implication of this review is that, in order to derive a consummate appreciation of the etiological roots of a drug lifestyle, sociological variables must be worked into existing biological and psychological models. For example, the vulnerability of a child with a biological predisposition to drug-seeking behavior may be exacerbated by the presence of certain sociological conditions, which in turn may encourage the formation of psychological characteristics that impede the child's ability to relate to pro-social peers or benefit from the ameliorative efforts of school- or community-based programs.

Considering all of the conditions or pebbles reviewed in this section, it appears that sociological variables associated with future drug use fall into two general categories (see Figure 4-1). The first is organized around a theme of socialization that encompasses sociocultural teachings, family relations, and peer associations. There is every indication, à la Sutherland (1939), that the attitudes and behaviors that define a drug lifestyle are learned through intimate contact with those who are actively and regularly involved in this deviant behavior. However, there is also evidence that failure to socialize to conventional definitions of behavior—the second category—may likewise elevate the risk of future drug involvement. Secondary parameters, such as early antisocial behavior and low self-esteem, contribute to these two categories of risk directly, as well as through interaction with the primary parameters of sociocultural influence, family, and peers.

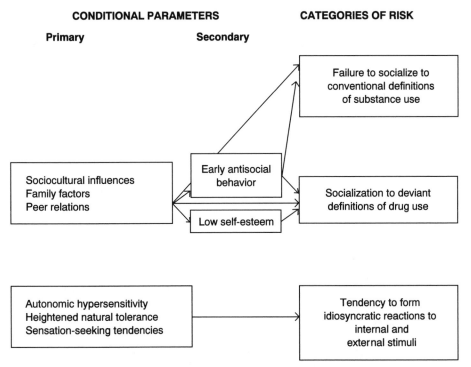

Figure 4-1 Conditional parameters and categories of risk: variables associated with future drug use. Effect of learning is represented by arrows.

A third major category of risk, which originates primarily from an interactive web of individual biological and psychological conditions (high sensation-seeking tendencies, autonomic hyperactivity, or reduced sensitivity to the inebriating effects of alcohol), concerns the disposition to react to stimuli in such a manner that drug use seems a more natural course of action than it does for most individuals. The relationships presumed to exist between key primary and secondary conditions and the three categories of risk for drug-seeking behavior are outlined in Figure 4-1. The next section explores the developmental roots of a drug lifestyle by examining how these factors form the primary domains of Person × Situation interaction.

Part 2

Development

Chapter 5

Motivational Roots of a Drug Lifestyle

INTRODUCTION

Motivation is an internal condition that activates and directs behavior. Physiological drives, such as the need for food, water, and shelter, were the first categories of motivation studied. Since that time, motivational research has expanded to include social and psychological drives as well. The work of Harlow (1959) stands as an example of this shift in emphasis. In studies originally conducted on rhesus monkeys, Harlow established the presence of an innate drive for contact comfort with important implications for future interpersonal and emotional development. Harlow's work encouraged other investigators to examine social-psychological motives and the salience of factors other than the drive to reduce tension in directing the behavior of the human organism. Maslow (1969) advanced the field of motivation further by proposing a hierarchy of needs (Figure 5-1) in which basic needs (physiological drives, safety needs) were said to require attention before higher motives (cognitive understanding, self-esteem) could be appreciated and actualized. In this chapter, three primary topics will be con-

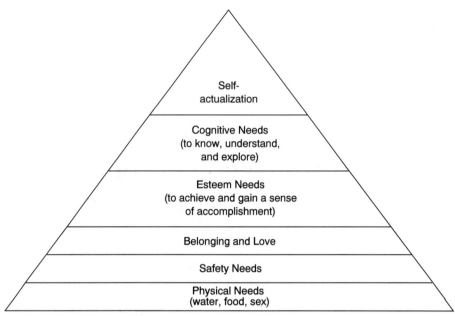

Figure 5-1 Maslow's hierarchy of needs, in which the lower (physical) needs require attention before the higher needs can be considered.

sidered in a discussion of the motivational roots of drug lifestyle behavior: (a) existential fear as the primary motivating force behind behavior development, (b) management of existential fear through adaptation and lifestyle activity, and (c) secondary organizing motives and drug use behavior.

THE ROLE OF FEAR IN LIFESTYLE DEVELOPMENT

Alfred Adler (1927), an early associate of Sigmund Freud, eventually broke away from mainstream psychoanalytic thought because his theories on the social foundations of human behavior presented too great a challenge to Freud's views on unconscious motivation and psychic determinism. Adler proposed that there is an existential sense of inferiority that confronts all people upon first entering a world populated by others who are stronger and more knowledgeable than they, and upon whom they must depend for the satisfaction of their basic needs. Another former colleague of Freud, Otto Rank (1929), believed that the trauma or shock of birth served as a catalyst for future behavioral development. The early contributions of these two psychoanalysts, in conjunction with the offerings of contemporary existential thinkers like Rollo May (1967), provide the theoretical under-pinnings for a motivation-based theory of lifestyle development. It should be kept in mind, however, that the motivational component of lifestyle theory starts off as existential fear, but soon branches off into several subordinate fears, the patterns of which are unique to each specific lifestyle.

Many persons learn to compensate for existential fear with increased adaptability, developing and exercising self-discipline, commitment, and a sense of social obligation. For a variety of reasons, not the least of which is poor negotiation of the early and later life tasks (see Chapter 6), persons predisposed to substance abuse difficulties lack a strong sense of social commitment and obligation. Therefore, instead of compensating for feel-ings of inadequacy by becoming more adaptive, learning to modify their behavior in response to environmental information, and working to balance long- and short-term considerations, persons who engage in problematic drug use behavior seek to deny, suppress, or escape from existential fear by retreating into a drug lifestyle. Individuals who form a commitment to a drug lifestyle allay existential fear and doubt by ingesting intoxicating chemicals and by distracting themselves with drug-based rituals.

According to lifestyle theory, existential fear is inevitable because change is inevitable. Existential fear is construed by the neonate as a primitive fear of nonexistence. Upon delivery into a world of constantly changing sights, sounds, and sensations, the newborn's instinct to survive clashes with the continually changing environment, which seems to threaten his or her very survival. Change brings with it the possibility of nonexistence; the fear of nonexistence, therefore, becomes a fear of change and of things unknown. The birth experience consequently gives rise to a transformation of existential fear from a physically based fear of nonexistence to a psy-chologically based fear of change. This early fear soon inspires the devel-opment of anxiety in other areas, including fear of abandonment, fear of failure, fear of commitment, and fear of responsibility, to name just a few. If not properly managed, these fears eventually infiltrate every corridor of a person's life.

For the drug abuser who has grown accustomed to a life of ineffective coping and ritualization, the demands of a lifestyle based on trust, sharing, and responsibility and the prospect of learning to cope without the use of drugs can be truly frightening. Moreover, the longer one remains locked in drug lifestyle activities, the greater the fear becomes. Early existential anxieties often metastasize into other concerns, such as the fear of being unable to succeed in a conventional lifestyle despite one's best efforts, or the consternation associated with negotiating a successful transition to a nondrug way of life and the anticipated loss of "status" or immediate gratification such a conversion entails.

RESPONDING TO EXISTENTIAL FEAR

The two primary responses to existential fear are adaptation and lifestyle recitation. These modes of fear management provide contrasting pictures of behavior. Adaptation is defined by lifestyle theory as modification of behavior in the service of knowledge acquisition and development. To accomplish the sometimes elusive objective of successful adaptation, one must consider both the long- and short-term consequences of one's behavior and seek to respond to situations in a socially responsible manner. The history of adaptation, whether for individuals, nations, or species of organisms, suggests that adaptation and its ultimate goal—survival—are guided by three primary considerations: respect for oneself, respect for others, and respect for nature. Consequently, persons who operate in an adaptation mode consider both the long- and short-term implications of their conduct, for themselves and for their wider social and physical environments.

Physiologists have found that the human body reacts to fear by activating the sympathetic branch of the autonomic nervous system to create the so-called "fight or flight" response. Adaptation is symbolized by the "fight" option, in that it represents a person's willingness to confront fear head-on. A drug lifestyle, on the other hand, is symbolized by the "flight" response, in the sense that it represents escape from existential fear. In actuality, neither fight nor flight is unique to either mode of fear management. A general who retreats in the face of overwhelming odds is actually using the adaptive mode, by modifying his original decision and increasing the chances of surviving to fight another day. By the same token, someone committed to a drug or criminal lifestyle may implement a fight response if, for instance, it is called for by the lifestyle (e.g., in situations where the person has been "disrespected"). The difference between an adaptive and a lifestyle reaction to fear is not found in the decision to make either a fight or flight response, but in the data on which the decision is based. An adaptive response relies on information provided by the environment and is balanced according to its anticipated long- and short-term consequences, whereas a lifestyle response follows from the rules, roles, and relationships provided by a particular lifestyle.

In stark contrast to the adaptive mode of fear management, which is innovative, the lifestyle mode is unimaginative, stagnant, and regressive. Instead of working to adapt their behavior in response to a constantly changing environment and to master their reactions, persons committed to a drug lifestyle seek to manipulate their environment with behaviors learned from others already familiar with this lifestyle. A lifestyle response does provide a temporary respite from existential fear in the sense that it supplies predetermined rules, roles, relationships, and criteria for success and failure. Hence, once the lifestyle is learned, the individual believes that he or she is relieved of the responsibility of thinking innovatively and begins reacting on the basis of previously learned—and often faulty—information. Rather than moving the individual forward, the lifestyle mode takes the person in circles, its object being to protect the lifestyle rather than make the individual more adaptive in the face of environmental contingencies. A major flaw, then, of lifestyle recitation in response to existential fear is that it does not allow for the long-range management of a person's fears and concerns. By hiding from fear, rather than working to master it, the person sets into motion events that allow the fear to metastasize and infiltrate all aspects of life until it is blocked by the ameliorative effects of treatment or the natural consequences of age and time.

Piaget's (1963) work on assimilation and accommodation provides a useful analog for conceptualizing the adaptation and lifestyle modes of existential fear management. Piaget has argued that a child learns and develops in interaction with his or her environment. When faced with information that can be integrated into an existing mental set or schema, the child assimilates it into the schema. When confronted by information for which he or she has no current mental representation, the child accommodates the experience by modifying an existing schema, thereby creating a new mental representation. A child who has learned to grasp a cup will learn to clutch similarly shaped objects through assimilation; however, the child's grip will be modified to handle a toy truck, demonstrating the process of accommodation in action. A person who attempts to manage existential fear with adaptation engages in both accommodation and assimilation in an effort to form a more consummate understanding of his or her environment. Someone who adopts a lifestyle mode of fear management continues assimilating new information into existing schemas but typically engages in very little accommodation. In fact, information incompatible with existing schemas will frequently be distorted in order to be fit into an existing schema. This practice leads to a state in which the subject attempts to justify and rationalize his or her actions rather than learn from his or her experiences.

Adaptation and lifestyle behavior are viewed as antithetical, in the sense that one leads to mastery and growth and the other to manipulation and excuse-making. However, most people display a combination of both approaches, the degree of each determining the extent to which the person is committed to a particular mode of fear management. The goal of lifestyle intervention is to encourage the personal growth mode by reinforcing subjects' adaptive resources and capabilities, thereby shifting the balance of influence in their lives to adaptation and discouraging the lifestyle mode of fear management. This task requires the subjects to acquire a new attitude and configuration of skills to expand their repertoire of life options. Before this task can be accomplished, however, lifestyle intervention must also consider other motivational features of the drug lifestyle in detail, because existential fear branches off into ancillary or secondary motives for drug use behavior once experience in the drug lifestyle is gained.

SECONDARY ORGANIZING MOTIVES

Lifestyle theory postulates that all behavior has its origins in a person's response to existential fear, and, thus, fear is considered to be the primary organizing motive for behavior. Secondary organizing motives, in contrast, are typically more descriptive of a person's involvement in a discrete act of drug use; they are more clearly tied to specific behaviors and therefore more accessible to conscious awareness. As a consequence, secondary organizing motives serve a validating function for the individual by acting to excuse or justify certain conduct in a specific situation or context. The primary organizing motive that subserves a criminal lifestyle, for instance, is said to branch out into four secondary organizing motives: anger/rebellion, excitement/pleasure, power/control, and greed/laziness (Walters, 1990). It is hypothesized that nearly all antisocial acts committed by persons engaged in a lifestyle pattern of criminal involvement can be traced to one or more of these four secondary organizing motives.

Surveys suggest that the secondary organizing motives for alcoholism and drug abuse fall into three primary categories: enhancement, coping, and social motives (Critchlow, 1986; Leigh, 1989). The enhancement motive entails use of intoxicants for the purpose of achieving positive affect; the coping motive entails drug use as a means of eliminating or suppressing negative affect; and the social motive entails the use of drugs, primarily alcohol, for ceremonial, religious, or social reasons. Cooper, Russell, Skinner, and Windle (1992) developed a three-factor measure of drinking incentives and discerned that enhancement motives were associated with a pattern of frequent, heavy alcohol consumption and ingestion of emotion-enhancing drugs (i.e., marijuana, cocaine, and other stimulants). Coping motives, on the other hand, were characterized by frequent, but not necessarily heavy, use of alcohol, symptoms of abusive drinking (including social and occupational dysfunction, tolerance, and withdrawal), and ingestion of emotion-dampening drugs like barbiturates and tranquilizers. Social motives predicted moderate levels of alcohol consumption, typically in social settings, but were not associated with either abusive drinking or use of other mind-altering substances independent of the coping and enhancement motives (Cooper et al., 1992).

Highlighting two of the three motives discussed in the literature, enhancement and coping, and dividing each by source (personal vs. social), lifestyle theory constructs a system of four secondary organizing motives to explain the validation of drug-seeking behavior. These four secondary organizing motives—personal enhancement, social enhancement, personal coping, and social coping—allegedly perpetuate and advance the influence of the primary organizing motive in the evolution of a drug lifestyle. The personal enhancement motive fosters the use of mind-altering substances to achieve immediate gratification and a pleasurable emotional state. The social enhancement motive, on the other hand, encourages the use of drugs for the purpose of achieving camaraderie with other drug users, as part of the superficial social network that grows up around habitual drug use and serves as a substitute for more meaningful interpersonal relationships. The personal coping motive validates drug use on the basis of a subject's stated desire to eliminate negative and uncomfortable affect, and the social coping motive promotes drug use to escape painful social relations, interpersonal isolation, or both.

CONCLUSION

As noted earlier, fear transmutes into several secondary forms in response to environmental and developmental exigencies. An individual's adaptive responsibilities also change over time, due to the evolutionary nature of existential fear and the fact that this fear conforms to certain situational parameters. Hence, the secondary organizing motives become more or less important during different stages of drug lifestyle involvement. As a way of understanding this process and its ability to induce divergent behavioral outcomes, lifestyle theory divides the drug lifestyle into developmental properties and stages. The progressive nature of drug involvement need not be viewed as unequivocal verification of the disease status of substance abuse, but it does imply that developmental factors serve as turning points in the evolution of a drug lifestyle.

Now that fear has been shown to have a major influence on human development, the next step is to examine the network of personal and situational variables, both risk and protective factors, that set the stage for later drug involvement through their complex interaction.

Chapter 6

Life Tasks

INTRODUCTION

Before a behavioral definition of a drug lifestyle can be set forth, two additional developmental issues must first be addressed. First is the question of why some people escape from fear primarily through retreating into a lifestyle while others handle it primarily through adaptation. Existential fear drives all manner of human conduct, but individual differences exist with respect to how this fear is managed. The second issue to be addressed is the lifestyle selection process; there is a plethora of potential lifestyles from which to choose. In this regard, the question is why a person selects a drug lifestyle over, for example, its criminal, gambling, or sexual counterparts. Proponents of lifestyle theory maintain that decisional factors are clearly important in defining a person's manner of contending with existential fear, as well as in determining his or her choice of lifestyle. However, conditional factors may also influence a person's risk of lifestyle involvement and choice of lifestyle, and these factors are the primary focus of this chapter.

Although individual biological, psychological, and sociological conditions have profound implications for future behavior, the manner in which these individual conditions fit into the wider network of human experience and development must also be appreciated. This developmental framework is defined by lifestyle theory as the interaction of personal (characteristics of the individual) and situational (characteristics of the environment) factors along an evolutionary continuum of early and later life tasks. These interactions occur in three primary domains of human experience—social, physical, and psychological—considered over two major life periods: ages 0 to 5 years (early life tasks), and ages 5 years and older (later life tasks). The risk and protective functions of historical-developmental conditions, and the way these conditions affect behavioral outcomes, must be examined before a detailed analysis of the interactive domains and the life tasks to which they give birth can be conducted.

RISK AND PROTECTIVE FACTORS

When considering the fact that few people can lay claim to total abstinence from mind-altering substances, one might well wonder why only a small segment of the population of the United States has ever encountered a problem with drugs. Evidently, most people's involvement with drugs is transitory, circumscribed, and nonproblematic. Why some people succumb to a lifestyle pattern of drug-seeking behavior when most people are able to limit their involvement to an occasional drink or nonabusive use of another psychoactive substance is a question that merits further study. One possible explanation is found in recent developments in research on risk and protective factors. For purposes of the present discussion, risk factors are defined as characteristics and experiences that elevate the probability of a person's future involvement in drug abuse, and protective factors as characteristics and experiences that reduce the likelihood of future drug involvement. Discerning the complex interaction of risk and protective factors is the prime concern in constructing a comprehensive understanding of drug lifestyle development.

Before continuing, the roles of biological, psychological, sociological, and developmental conditions in the evolution of a drug lifestyle must be considered. Although these conditions shape alternatives and modify options, they do not directly or solely determine behavior, deviant or otherwise, because it is choice that is awarded the prominent place in the kaleidoscope of variables that define lifestyle development. In other words, individuals choose to engage in or refrain from drug-seeking behavior, even though the information and knowledge upon which their decisions are based are regularly influenced by conditions. Hence, although risk and protective factors can increase or decrease a person's odds of engaging in drug-seeking behavior, the presence of several risk factors does not inevitably lead to a negative outcome, nor does an abundance of protective factors necessarily shield a person from all forms of negative influence.

Surveying the contributions of interacting risk factors to the evolution of a drinking problem, McCord (1988) discovered that shy-aggressive male children (person risk factor) were at increased risk for alcohol abuse if they were exposed to one of two family conditions (situation risk factor). Shy-aggressive boys living with alcoholic fathers were placed at increased risk for subsequent alcohol abuse if the mothers expressed high esteem for the fathers, and shy-aggressive boys living with nonalcoholic fathers were placed at increased risk if their home environments were characterized by interpersonal conflict and a lack of maternal control. McCord concludes that in the first instance alcoholism was engendered by the child's apparent imitation of the behavior of a respected, but nonetheless alcoholic, father, whereas in the second instance alcoholism was predicted by family problems that may have influenced him to associate alcohol use with uninhibited, and possibly even criminal, conduct. This example illustrates the complexity of the risk–behavior association, in that different conditions may account for similar behavioral outcomes through the action of two separate pathways of influence.

After conducting an extensive review of risk factors and juvenile delinquency, Loeber (1990) unearthed support for the notion that causal relationships are influenced by age and developmental factors. Loeber discerned that biological factors are of prime etiological significance in defining early risk for future antisocial involvement, whereas family factors come into play after age 2 as a consequence of the child's evolving ability to internalize select features of his or her environment. Additional developmental changes occur after age 5 in response to an expanding sphere of experience outside the confines of home; school and peer influences characteristically replace biological and family influences as the principal risk factors for antisocial involvement after this age. Loeber also contends that risk factors not only differ as a function of the developmental stage but also form interactive relationships that leave the child more or less vulnerable to later influences and the future surfacing of drug and criminal problems.

Searching for an explanation of controlled drug use in a small network of cocaine users, Murphy, Reinarman, and Waldorf (1989) conducted an 11-year follow-up of these subjects. Data obtained from this investigation demonstrated that the majority of network members encountered very few physical, interpersonal, or legal problems as a consequence of their use of cocaine, despite long-term sustained use in some instances. Factors that apparently protected many of the subjects in this network from progressing to compulsive use included avoiding routes of administration they knew from experience had a high probability of leading to addiction or compulsive use (e.g., freebasing, intravenous use), refusing to associate with compulsive drug users, and developing a positive view of themselves and their ability to refrain from abusing cocaine and other substances. Research on drug use in adolescents implies that peer influence may serve either a risk or protective function depending on the degree to which they support (White, Johnson, & Garrison, 1985) or actively discourage the subject's involvement with drugs (Meier, Burkett, & Hickman, 1984).

Studying high-risk (one or more alcoholic parents, adverse early life events) children living on the Hawaiian island of Kauai, E. E. Werner (1986) found that personal factors that served to shield these children from future alcohol and coping problems included temperaments that elicited positive attention from primary caregivers, average or above-average intelligence, good verbal skills, achievement orientation, and positive self-image. Situational factors that protected this group of high-risk children included: receiving ample attention from the primary caregiver, having freedom from any major family or domestic problems prior to age 2, and enjoying youngest-child status for at least 2 years prior to the birth of the next sibling.

Using subjects from the same cohort of children born on the island of Kauai, Werner and Smith (1977) determined that a strong mother–child bond protected children at risk for antisocial behavior (raised in poverty, parental conflict, early loss of father) from entering into various criminal pursuits. The interaction of risk and protective factors in this example helps illustrate why only a fraction of the total population of individuals exposed to drugs and crime enter into a lifestyle pattern of involvement with these activities.

EARLY DEVELOPMENTAL TASKS

Lifestyle theory maintains that conditions affect behavior through a combination of person and situation variables. Arising out of the chaos sometimes created by these bidirectional forces are specific risk and protective factors that increase or decrease a child's propensity to engage in drug-related activities. Risk and protective factors are organized by lifestyle theory into three major classes of Person × Situation interaction—social, physical, and psychological (see Table 6–1). Within the social domain of human experience, Person × Situation interactions are manifest in the early life task of attachment, while in the physical domain these interactions appear in the early life task of stimulus modulation. Interactions taking place in the psychological domain, on the other hand, give rise to the self-image life task. These interactions have been termed the "early life tasks" principally because they are universal issues confronting all persons, the

Table 6-1   The Early and Later Life Tasks by Domain

Domain of experience	Early life tasks	Later life tasks
Social	Attachment	Social bonding/empathy
Physical	Stimulus modulation	Internal/external orientation
Psychological	Self-image	Role identity

modes of resolution of which place an individual at either increased or decreased risk for future drug involvement.

Attachment

Psychologists and psychiatrists hold that early family relationships set the tone for later interpersonal associations and behavior. No two theorists are more responsible for stimulating interest in the research and clinical implications of early parent–infant attachment than John Bowlby (1982) and Mary Salter Ainsworth (1979, 1989). Ainsworth (1979), in fact, is responsible for constructing a popular system of attachment classification. Dividing attachment into three primary categories—secure, avoidant, and anxious/ambivalent—Ainsworth has argued that this system ably predicts future behavior. Research generally bears this theory out, in that avoidant children tend to be more depressed, withdrawn, somatically preoccupied (Lewis, Feiring, McGuffog, & Jaskir, 1984), and aggressive (Sroufe, 1983) than their securely attached peers, and anxious/ambivalent children tend to be more fearful, helpless, and impulsive than securely attached children (Sroufe, 1983). Ainsworth hypothesizes that a critical period exists for the formation of attachment feelings somewhere between the ages of 18 months and 36 months, although the research on this aspect of Ainsworth's theory is less confirmatory (see Herbert, Sluckin, & Sluckin, 1984). There is sufficient evidence, nonetheless, to conclude that a positive mother-infant bond encourages creativity, emotional security, and constructive exploratory behavior in a developing child, whereas a negative mother-infant bond invites entrenchment, insecurity, and fear (Main, Kaplan, & Cassidy, 1985).

The person (child) variables that are likely to contribute to future attachment problems include difficult temperament (Goldsmith & Campos, 1982), early constitutional anomalies (Connell, 1976), infant fearfulness (Goldsmith, Bradshaw, & Rieser-Danner, 1986), low birth weight (Bell, 1979), and persistent crying (Thompson, 1986). Infant responsiveness, on the other hand, may serve a protective function; it has been shown to promote secure attachment (E. E. Werner, 1986). Maternal warmth (Bates, Maslin, & Frankel, 1985), acceptance (Main, Tomasini, & Tolan, 1979), and responsiveness (Blehar, Lieberman, & Ainsworth, 1977) are among the situational (caregiver) variables commonly observed in the backgrounds of securely attached children. However, Goldsmith and Alansky (1987) concluded on the basis of a meta-analysis of the attachment literature that maternal characteristics may be less important and infant characteristics (temperament, responsiveness) more important to attachment than has traditionally been assumed. In exploring the nature of this early life task, Hazan and Shaver (1987) advise that attachment be viewed as an outcome of a complex and unique interaction of person and environment factors rather than as a specific behavioral trait.

Although there is a paucity of empirical data on the early parent–child attachments of substance-abusing adults, a fair amount of research has been conducted on the relationship between adolescent drug use and features of Hirschi's (1969) social control/bonding model of deviance development. Hirschi contends that adolescents lacking strong social attachment to their parents and other representatives of the conventional social order are at increased risk for drug involvement and criminal outcomes. The consensus of research examining Hirschi's predictions on social bonding and substance use is that, although social bonding theory does a fairly good job of explaining adolescent use of drugs like alcohol, tobacco, and marijuana, it is not particularly helpful in explicating the use of amphetamines, hallucinogens, and opiates (Marcos, Bahr, & Johnson, 1986; Taub & Skinner, 1990). Bonding to specific family members, as measured by juvenile respondents' perceived closeness to their mothers and fathers, was found to correlate inversely with initial marijuana use and early progression from alcohol to marijuana use in an ongoing series of studies directed by Kandel and Davies (1992). These findings also imply that although social bonding and, perhaps, attachment have a noticeable effect on drug use during the early stages of a drug lifestyle, other factors may play a more important role as use begins to escalate.

Although poor bonding or attachment in general may place an individual at increased risk for entering the early stages of a drug lifestyle, Ainsworth's (1979) model suggests two different styles of weak bonding to consider: avoidant and anxious/ambivalent. Avoidant styles of interpersonal adjustment are thought to be associated with future criminality (Walters, 1990) but may have relevance to drug abuse as well. However, lifestyle theory maintains that persons who have resolved the early life task of attachment by becoming anxious or ambivalent about intimate or other interpersonal relationships are at increased risk for future drug abuse. Having been exposed to early life experiences that encourage dependency and discourage self-sufficiency, the anxious/ambivalent subject is drawn to others as a source of protection and guidance. In fact, the use of mind-altering substances can be viewed as a further extension of this individual's dependency-seeking inclinations. As was demonstrated previously, paternal rejection and maternal overprotection are frequently observed in the early family relations of future alcoholics and chronic drug abusers. The dependency, fear, and confusion that arise as a consequence of growing up in a chaotic home environment form the nucleus of an attachment style characterized by anxiety and ambivalence—a mode of attachment that, according to lifestyle theory, puts a person at increased risk for drug involvement. The presence of mutual attachment between a child and parent, on the other hand, may act to protect a young child against substance misuse (Brook, Brook, Gordon, Whiteman, & Cohen, 1990).

Stimulus Modulation

Stimulus modulation is a measure of how a person perceives, interprets, and organizes sensory information to achieve an optimal level of physiological arousal. Research has found that some individuals are born with lower than normal resting levels of physiological reactivity and that such persons seek out higher levels of environmental stimulation in an effort to maximize sensory experience (Farley, 1986). One way by which such stimulation may be realized is through involvement in intellectually and physically challenging activities and tasks. Alternately, persons born with higher than normal resting levels of physiological arousal are motivated to avoid intellectually or physically invigorating activities because they view lower levels of sensory stimulation as optimal. These findings seem to imply that the stimulus modulation life task contains features of both internal and external adjustment (Farley, 1986): Internal or mental stimulation becomes expressed as ideas, thoughts, and feelings; and external or physical stimulation becomes expressed in the form of environmental manipulation and the realization of assorted physical accomplishments.

Genetics, neurological factors, and gender appear to be the person variables that contribute most to the evolution of stimulation-seeking tendencies. A genetic effect, possibly expressing itself through early temperament, appears to have a major impact on the early life task of stimulus modulation. Neurological factors, for example arousal level (Borkovec, 1970) and autonomic reactivity (Venables, 1987), not only are potentially viable markers for stimulation-seeking interests, but also provide an additional avenue through which heredity might affect stimulus modulation. Gender also appears to influence thrill-seeking and sensation-augmenting behavior: males tend to display stronger thrill-seeking interests than females (Farley, 1986), perhaps with an assist from testosterone, the male sex hormone, which studies show is linked to high levels of sensation-seeking behavior (Daitzman & Zuckerman, 1980).

Parental discipline and environmental stimulation appear to be the two situational variables of greatest significance in determining how a person manages the stimulus modulation life task. As was pointed out in the chapter on sociological correlates of drug-seeking behavior (Chapter 4), a lack of parental guidance and structure can elevate a child's risk for drug-related behaviors. It may well be that a lack of consistent parental guidance creates confusion in the young child's mind, which then interferes with the child's ability to profit from important early socialization experiences that under normal circumstances take place in the home. The volume of environmental stimulation a child is exposed to may also play a pivotal role in the formation of sensation-seeking tendencies, in that high levels of stimulation are potentially of etiological significance in the development of a drug lifestyle, and because environmental factors may interact with specific individual characteristics to increase a person's risk of drug involvement.

High sensation seeking has been shown to correlate with both drug use (Andrucci, Archer, Pancoast, & Gordon, 1989) and delinquency (Simo & Perez, 1991). One study found scores on a sensation seeking measure to be superior to personality indexes of depression and anxiety in discriminating between adolescent abstainers, novice users, and regular users of a wide array of chemical substances (Teichman, Barnea, & Ravav, 1989). The results of a second study suggest that the relationship between behavioral disinhibition and drinking behavior in undergraduate men can be attributed to the intervening effect of sensation seeking (Earlyewine & Finn, 1991). A third study witnessed an interactive relationship between sensation seeking and certain set and setting effects that correlated with the alcohol consumption practices of a large group of college undergraduates (Schall, Kemeny, & Maltzman, 1992).

Pedersen, Clausen, and Lavik (1989) calculated a canonical correlation between sensation seeking and drug use and ascertained that the disinhibition subscale of the Sensation Seeking Scale (SSS; Zuckerman, 1979) correlated with increased use of legal drugs and inhalants, whereas the experience seeking subscale correlated most strongly with the use of marijuana and tranquilizers. Zuckerman (1979) had previously explored the SSS subscale performance of young adult and middle-aged alcohol-abusing males and discerned that the younger group preferred activities incorporating uncontrolled, and perhaps even illegal, forms of behavioral expression, whereas the older group was attracted to exciting events in an effort to achieve unpredictability and relieve boredom. Although it is tempting to attribute this difference to developmental factors, it could just as easily be interpreted as reflecting a cohort or generational effect, because Zuckerman employed a cross-sectional, rather than longitudinal, design.

Newcomb and McGee (1989) compared alcohol abuse, delinquency, and thrill seeking in high school students and found some support for thrill seeking as an underlying basis for alcohol abuse and delinquency in females, but not in males. This gender effect may be due to differences in biology or temperament; such factors not only discriminate between males and females but also have been found to correlate with future drug and criminal outcomes (Tarter, Alterman, & Edwards, 1985). Lifestyle theory speculates that, in contrast to the exclusively physically oriented stimulation-seeking tendencies associated with the criminal lifestyle (Walters, 1990), persons at risk for future drug-seeking behavior exhibit a combination of both physical and mental stimulation-seeking interests.

Sensation seeking is not necessarily a bad thing; many pro-social physical feats and innovative ideas are the result of a desire to achieve maximal physical or mental stimulation. Instead, it is high sensation seeking in conjunction with deleterious environmental conditions that encourages the destructive thrill-seeking pursuits known to elevate a person's risk for drug-seeking behavior.

The risk established through the stimulus modulation life task is perhaps the most complex feature of the developmental scheme presented by lifestyle theory to explain future drug abuse behavior, because other research shows that high autonomic arousal, with a corresponding desire for less sensation, has also been observed in persons at risk for abuse difficulties (Finn & Pihl, 1978). Consequently, both exceptionally high and exceptionally low sensation-seeking tendencies may serve as risk factors for future substance abuse outcomes, depending on a complex network of moderating influences, with abuse of depressant drugs like alcohol preferred by people with low sensation-seeking tendencies and polydrug abuse preferred by people with high sensation-seeking tendencies.

Self-Image

Developmental psychologists assert that newborn infants are incapable of discriminating between themselves and their external environments (H. Werner, 1957). With time, however, a child learns to make a clear distinction between self and environment, and it is this process of differentiation that leads to self-identity. Lewis and Brooks (1978) studied this issue in two groups of children, one group aged 9 to 12 months and the other 12 to 24 months. Only children in the older group responded to a change in their own physical appearance brought on by the surreptitious placement of rouge on their noses as they gazed into a mirror, leading Lewis and Brooks to conclude that a rudimentary conception of self does not occur until the individual is at least 1 or 2 years old. Lifestyle theory contends that along with the interaction of person and situation variables comes an evolving sense of self designed to guide a child's ensuing psychosocial development along specific psychological lines.

Body type (Shelden, 1954) and minor physical anomalies like wide-set eyes or low-seated ears (Mednick & Kandel, 1988) are some of the person variables capable of influencing a person's sense of self. The hemispheric organization of the brain may also influence the self-image life task through the expression of various interests and abilities. It has been noted, for instance, that left hemisphere-dominant persons prefer verbal-comprehensive (arithmetic, vocabulary) tasks to visual-motor (spatial relations, artistic expression) tasks and normally perform better on the verbal tasks, whereas right hemisphere-dominant persons demonstrate a converse pattern of interests and abilities (Hare & McPherson, 1984).

Situational variables that potentially affect the resolution of the self-image life task include parental communication (Dishion, Stouthamer-Loeber, & Patterson, 1984) and peer relations (Panella, Cooper, & Henggeler, 1982). A child who suffers physical and/or verbal abuse at the hands of his or her parents or who feels alienated from pro-social peers will develop a self-image very different from that of a child who routinely garners the praise and support of parents and the acceptance of pro-social peers.

There is little question that drug abuse is linked to low self-esteem and other problematic psychologically based behaviors. The question is rather one of cause and effect. Findings from several studies suggest that drug use in teenage populations is the product of dysfunctional attitudes and personal characteristics that include low-self esteem, depression, and rebelliousness (Kandel, 1978). Other investigators argue that any psychological problems encountered by drug abusers, whether the drug of choice is alcohol (Udel, 1984), cocaine (Windle & Miller-Tutzauer, 1991), or heroin (Woody & Blaine, 1979) are secondary to the physical effects of the drug or the behavioral consequences of a drug lifestyle. Many early stage drug and alcohol abusers, for instance, fail to report or display low self-esteem (Cooper, 1983). One study, in fact, showed evidence of increased self-esteem in adolescents who continued using marijuana (Kaplan, 1980). The protective function of self-esteem has nonetheless been demonstrated in studies such as the one conducted by Miller and Jang (1977) in which concurrent measures of self-esteem and psychological well-being correlated inversely with alcohol abuse difficulties in a group of subjects at risk for alcohol-related problems by virtue of a family history of alcoholism.

Fenley and Williams (1991) had 41 male drug abusers, 37 male non-abusing psychiatric patients, and 44 male nonabusing technical school students complete an adjective check list in an effort to explore the self-image correlates of substance abuse. Nine scales successfully discriminated between substance abuse clients and technical school students without distinguishing between technical school students and psychiatric patients (thereby ruling out the alternative hypothesis that the substance abuse-technical school differences could be accounted for solely on the basis of psychological maladjustment). These results were interpreted by Fenley and Williams as signaling less favorability, inner strength, achievement, order, and endurance, and more self-criticism and fear on the part of substance-abusing clients. In line with these findings, the lifestyle model of drug-seeking behavior holds that persons suffering fearfulness, low self-esteem, and minimal levels of self-confidence are at enhanced risk for drug involvement.

LATER LIFE TASKS

The early life tasks are normally resolved, for better or worse, by the time a child enters school (i.e., around age 5). Development does not stop, however, simply because the child is spending more time at school and less time at home, although the primary developmental issues do shift as variables other than innate biological structure and family environment assume preeminence in motivating and directing the child's behavior. These are referred to by lifestyle theory as the later life tasks, of which there are three. Person × Situation interactions occurring in the social domain evolve out of the early life task of attachment into the later life task of social bonding and empathy. Here, a subject's willingness to consider the effect of his or her behavior on others, to cooperate in the realization of social goals, and to put off his or her own desires for the good of the group is revealed. In the physical domain, the early life task of stimulus modulation gives way to the later life task of internal/external orientation, the outcome of which confirms the direction, internal (self) or external (other), of the subject's future control efforts. Finally, in the psychological domain, the early life task of self-image is transformed into the later life task of role identity, wherein the subject decides how he or she fits into the wider world.

According to lifestyle theory, a person at risk for drug involvement may be sensitive to others' feelings and may even possess the capacity for empathy, although these characteristics do not necessarily harbor sufficient vigor to override conditions that encourage the use of drugs. Lifestyle theory maintains that such persons handle the social bonding/empathy task by adopting an ambivalent or equivocating stance in their dealings with others. With the internal/external orientation task, on the other hand, persons at increased risk for drug-seeking behavior reveal a consistent pattern of external orientation (Wright & Obitz, 1984); such individuals are said to be searching for an external solution (drug-related activity) to an internal problem (existential fear). Finally, the later life task of finding a role identity has important implications for future drug-seeking outcomes in that it affects both social alienation and role integration. Jessor, Jessor, and Finney (1973) note that heavy marijuana use is associated with alienation in women and social criticism and rejection in men. Likewise, Yamaguchi and Kandel (1984) state that failure to integrate into adult roles such as employment and marriage is prognostic of heavy substance abuse in persons who use marijuana in adolescence.

Unlike the early life tasks, the later life tasks are never fully resolved. Consequently, they not only guide behavioral development from age 5 until death, but are also amenable to intervention. Although it may not be possible to promote a secure sense of attachment in a 9-year-old child who is ambivalent or avoidant, intervention is still feasible through development and fortification of a client's social bonding and empathy skills. Furthermore, because resolution of the early life tasks normally precedes a person's initial use of drugs, these substances play no direct role in the pattern or outcome of the early life tasks. The same cannot be said of the later life tasks, however. In fact, drug use often has a profound effect on the drug abuser's negotiation of the later life tasks. It is fairly well established, for instance, that early onset of drug use is strongly prognostic of future drug abuse and other life problems (Kaplan, Martin, & Robbins, 1984). This finding indicates that early drug use can have a deleterious effect on a person's initial approach and eventual handling of later life tasks, while other research suggests that drug use and abuse may interfere with subsequent social development (Newcomb & Bentler, 1988).

CONCLUSION

This chapter on the early and later life tasks and their implications for future drug abuse liability illustrates how an interactive model of drug-seeking behavior can be assembled without resorting to the aphorism, "Everything causes drug abuse." Although it may be true that many variables enter into the equation used by lifestyle theory to explain a person's risk of drug abuse, the fact that these variables can be grouped into three primary domains of Person × Situation interaction is of both scientific and practical significance. Scientifically, this approach supplies researchers with a finite number of areas for investigation that can be organized into a manageable number of testable hypotheses. It should be noted that the three early life tasks—attachment, stimulus modulation, and self-image— correspond to the three categories of risk identified in the conclusion of Chapter 4: failure to socialize to conventional definitions of drug use, idiosyncratic responses to internal and external stimuli, and socialization to deviant definitions of drug use, respectively. The practical significance of an interactive model of lifestyle development is that it allows clinicians an opportunity to identify salient risk and protective factors, toward an eventual goal of constructing effective programs of prevention and intervention—in lieu of hunches, fads, and approaches that are no longer relevant to the vast majority of substance-abusing clients.

Philosophers have long pondered the question of whether the universe is ordered and predictable or random and unpredictable. Lifestyle theory adopts a compromise position, arguing that the universe is qualifiably ordered but never fully predictable. By concentrating on the three primary domains of Person × Situation interaction, lifestyle theory strives to instill order in the complex web of variables that contribute to the formation of a drug lifestyle. However, the theory also recognizes that these interactions do not follow a fatalistic blueprint drawn up by deterministic-minded philosophers. The lifestyle view consequently necessitates a shift in perspective reminiscent of the one that took place in the field of physics earlier in this century. Physicists have seen the Newtonian view of an ordered universe replaced by Einstein's theory of relativity, Heisenberg's uncertainty principle, and recent developments in the area of chaotic processes. If the science of human behavior is to progress likewise, then the uncertainty of human behavior must be studied rather than denied. Choice and cognition must be effectively integrated into mainstream behavioral science. The final chapter of this section (Chapter 8), in fact, considers the contributions of choice and cognition to drug lifestyle development. First, however, the developmental transitions that take place as individuals become increasingly preoccupied with drugs must be explored.

Chapter 7

Developmental Transitions

INTRODUCTION

Thus far, it has been learned that existential fear provides the impetus for behavioral development (Chapter 5), and that a person's response to this fear, shaped by an interactive network of conditions, forms the nucleus of reactions to various early and later life tasks. Because individuals' stated motivations for using mind-altering substances may change with their commitment to a drug lifestyle, it is essential that the progressive nature of drug abuse be explored and verified. Because drug abuse is an evolving process, it must be examined in a dynamic, rather than static, way. In an effort to depict the progressive nature of a drug lifestyle, this chapter identifies three key behavioral transition points: initiation, escalation, and cessation. Once described, these transition points are used to construct a four-stage model of drug lifestyle progression.

BEHAVIORAL TRANSITION POINTS

Why some people use drugs occasionally, socially, or not at all while others exhibit a pattern of problem drug use is a question for which there is as yet no simple answer. What is known is that the reasons people give for their initial use of drugs often diverge from those they give to support their continued use of an abusable substance. The progression from use to abuse, to dependence, to abstinence, regression, or relapse has been discussed by Donovan, Jessor, and Jessor (1983), Kandel (1984), and Clayton (1992). It is important to note, however, that this progression is not inexorable, and that most people exit a drug lifestyle, with or without assistance, before it becomes terminal. Occasionally, a subject may even drift from a later stage of lifestyle development to an earlier one, although it is more typical for an individual to demonstrate forward progression. The present discussion considers three behavioral transition points—initiation (onset of drug use), escalation (significant increase in the severity and/or intensity of drug use), and cessation (termination of drug use)—toward a goal of constructing a workable lifestyle developmental model.

Initiation

In light of the fact that 81% of the high school graduating class of 1990 reported prior use of alcohol, 27% acknowledged prior use of marijuana, and 5% confessed to having tried cocaine at least once (Johnston, O'Malley, & Bachman, 1991), it is evident that drug use initiation applies to a major cross-section of the general public. Of the conditional factors potentially important in understanding drug initiation, perhaps none are more powerful than exposure to drug-using peers (Brook, Cohen, Whiteman, & Gordon, 1992; Newcomb & Bentler, 1988). The effect of peer associations and school experience may, in fact, supersede family factors in explaining drug use initiation (Johnson Marcos, & Bahr, 1987). It is more plausible, however, that family and peer factors interact and influence each other in elevating or lowering a person's risk of drug involvement. Hence, family conflict may encourage a child to turn to a drug-using peer group for support (Panella, Cooper, & Henggeler, 1982); inadequate parent-child attachment may produce a child more concerned with earning the respect of a drug-using peer group than currying favor with his or her parents (Brook et al., 1992); and lack of effective parental supervision may leave a child vulnerable to the influence of a drug-using peer group (Wilson, 1980).

Peers are not the only important influence in the initiation of drug-seeking behavior. Walters (1994a) asked 120 inmates enrolled in a comprehensive residential drug treatment program to list the factor or factors they perceived as responsible for their inaugural use of drugs. Although 63% indicated some form of peer influence, another 18% mentioned curiosity and excitement. Other investigators, although acknowledging the strength of peers to prompt drug experimentation, have found curiosity and the desire to be part of the "drug culture" to be equally important in prompting subjects to use drugs for the first time (Hser, Anglin, & McGlothlin, 1987). To complicate matters even further, Kandel and Davies (1992) note that both association with a delinquent peer group and high educational aspirations predict incipient marijuana use. On the basis of these data, Kandel and Davies conclude that there are two general types of individuals who experiment with marijuana: those who use marijuana out of curiosity and normative adolescent rebelliousness, and those who use marijuana because they are alienated from conventional society and prone to engage in delinquent behavior. Whereas persons in the first group normally terminate their involvement with marijuana after a relatively brief period of experimental use, juveniles in the second group are more liable to engage in a distinct pattern of escalating marijuana and other drug use.

It is worth noting that aggression, rebelliousness, general deviance, and rejection of dominant social values tend to correlate with initial drug use (Penning & Barnes, 1982). This finding not only suggests substantial overlap between drug use and delinquency initiation, but also lends support to Jessor and Jessor's (1977) general deviance explanation of problem behavior, in which adult antisociality is viewed as emerging from a self-reinforcing cycle of adolescent-stage activities that includes rejection of conventional social norms, family conflict, legal problems, and drug use. Several recent studies provide support for the general deviance theory through identification of a single underlying common factor for adolescent behavioral problems (Farrell, Danish, & Howard, 1992), the composition of which tends to vary as a function of the developmental stage into which a subject falls (McGee & Newcomb, 1992).

Prompted by data identifying a sequential pattern of drug use in substance-abusing adolescents, Kandel argues that juvenile drug use follows a specific progression, from legal drugs (alcohol or cigarettes) to marijuana, to illicit drugs other than marijuana, and finally to medically prescribed psychoactive substances (Kandel, Yamaguchi, & Chen, 1992). Although research has tended to contradict the fixed sequence of stages proposed in Kandel's "gateway" theory of deviance development, there is confirmation of a developmental progression of increasing severity and deviance for substance abuse in adolescent subjects (Ellickson, Hays, & Bell, 1992; Newcomb & Bentler, 1990). It seems likely, then, that both the general deviance and gateway hypotheses are valid to some degree and that a meaningful integration of these two perspectives holds promise, although it must be kept in mind that sociocultural factors (e.g., cultural attitudes as reflected in movies, television shows, and commercials) probably interface with both perspectives in promoting or inhibiting the initiation and subsequent escalation of drug-seeking interests.

Escalation

Escalation is more difficult to pinpoint than initiation because it encompasses a wider range and more gradual progression of behavior rather than a discrete event. For the sake of the present discussion, escalation is defined as a significant and sustained (6 months or longer) increase in the frequency and/or intensity of drug use. There are, in fact, two schools of thought on the proposed relationship between drug use and drug abuse: the continuity or pharmacological model and the disengagement or two-phase model. The pharmacological model postulates that drug use is a necessary and sufficient condition for drug abuse: that is, that drug abuse is simply increased drug use. Newcomb (1992) has investigated this hypothesis and discovered that whereas alcohol and marijuana use are necessary for subsequent alcohol and marijuana abuse, neither is sufficient to explain the abuse of these substances. The lack of continuity from use to abuse noted in the Newcomb study substantiates the disengagement model, suggesting that progression from drug use to abuse should be conceptualized as a two-stage process in which initiation is a necessary prerequisite for escalation but in which other factors are also influential.

Of the factors that are foreseeably linked to drug use escalation, age of onset, peers, social bonding, and negative affect have received the greatest amount of empirical attention and support to date. Research on age of onset indicates that the earlier an individual commences the use of marijuana, the greater his or her chances of progressing to daily or near-daily use of this substance (Kandel & Davies, 1992; Kandel et al., 1992;). A relationship has also been noted between early age of first drug use and later abuse of a variety of different chemical substances (Robins & Przybeck, 1985). One possible explanation for the relationship between age of onset and escalation of drug use is that significant deviance during the formative years interferes with the negotiation of important developmental tasks and the actualization of basic skills; the lack of these skills then impedes the individual's efforts to integrate into conventional society. This hypothesis is supported by a longitudinal investigation of adolescent drug use by Newcomb and Bentler (1988).

Peers may be as closely tied to drug use escalation as they are to initiation. In a bid to address this issue, Simons, Conger, and Whitbeck (1988) determined that the children of parents who used drugs and exercised minimal control over the activities of their offspring were more inclined to seek immediate gratification than children whose parents did not use drugs and did exercise firm control. This tendency, in turn, placed the first group of children at increased risk for drug experimentation. The introduction of a drug-using peer group into this scenario greatly enhanced the probability of drug use escalation. Other investigators have also unearthed evidence in support of the etiological role of peers in drug use initiation and escalation (Swaim, Oetting, Edwards, & Beauvais, 1989).

A third factor relevant to drug use escalation is lack of bonding to the conventional social order. It was noted in Chapter 4 that poor mutual attachment to one's parents, coupled with exposure to a deviant peer group, places a child at increased risk for drug initiation. It also appears that lack of commitment to conventional goals and social institutions, which may have its roots in weak parent–child attachment, elevates the risk of drug progression. Yamaguchi and Kandel (1984) maintain that young adults who smoke marijuana on a regular basis participate less often in conventional social activities like marriage and employment than young adults who do not. Whether this lack of commitment to the conventional social order has its foundation in a weak parent–child relationship or in negative labeling experiences during the initial stages of drug involvement (Kaplan & Johnson, 1992), it appears to play a facilitative role in the development and intensification of deviant behavior.

Positive affect frequently encourages initial use of drugs. Although positive affect may also inspire drug escalation, negative affect appears to supplant it in significance as a drug lifestyle evolves. Research probing the relationship between negative affect and drug use escalation show that high levels of arousal and negative affect (anxiety, depression) greatly increase a person's chances of escalation (Pandina, Johnson, & Labouvie, 1992). Furthermore, initial drug use as a means of alleviating negative affect portends a greater likelihood of escalation than initial drug usage designed to promote a positive affective state (Kaplan & Johnson, 1992). Other studies indicate that whereas drug initiation is mediated largely by social factors and positive outcome expectancies, drug escalation and heavy drug involvement are more often driven by self-medication motives (McKay, Murphy, McGuire, Rivinus, & Maisto, 1992).

Cessation

Cessation of drug use, like escalation, presents several noteworthy definitional problems. Should the definition of cessation be restricted to total abstinence, or should occasions where intake has been "significantly" reduced also be included? Another question concerns chronological age, which may or may not be an important correlate of cessation depending on the definition of cessation. Research shows that people tend to reduce their intake as they get older (Waldorf, 1976) although a substantial number fail to achieve continued abstinence even as they age, dabbling in drug use from time to time, slipping back into a brief period of abuse, or relapsing into a drug lifestyle after a period of abstinence or decreased involvement. For the purposes of this discussion, cessation is defined as voluntary abstinence from drug use for a period of 1 year or longer in someone who has progressed beyond the initiation and escalation stages for that specific drug. Whether the relationships observed when this definition of abstinence is employed hold in situations when an individual achieves a significant reduction in drug-related activities but falls short of abstinence is an issue that requires further study.

Vaillant and Milofsky (1982) studied 110 men with prior histories of alcohol abuse, 49 of whom had achieved voluntary abstinence for a period of 1 year or longer, in an attempt to identify predictors of alcohol use cessation. The severity of prior alcohol abuse was the single most powerful predictor of continuous abstinence, although four other factors were also important in promoting desistance in these 49 subjects. One such factor was a substitute dependency, whether a replacement drug like tobacco, marijuana, or Valium; compulsive eating, gambling, or work habits; or regular attendance at Alcoholics Anonymous (AA) meetings. The development of a new intimate relationship uncontaminated by prior resentments was a second. A third abstinence-promoting influence uncovered by these authors was the formation of a stable source of social support, hope, and self-esteem. Finally, the majority of subjects who abstained from alcohol for 1 year or longer benefitted from a naturalistic behavior modification experience where the negative consequences of their continued involvement with alcohol were brought to the fore, with the aid of disulfiram treatment, aggravation of a serious medical condition, or compulsory supervision by an employer or the courts.

Tuchfeld (1981) reviewed the life histories of a group of chronic alcoholics and determined that financial problems, legal entanglements, and educational programming were much less effective than health considerations and concern for loved ones in encouraging abandonment of an alcohol-based lifestyle. A process of identity transformation also took place in many of these subjects, whereby newfound values, priorities, and feelings of self-confidence replaced negative attitudes, beliefs, and expectancies. Like Tuchfeld, Ludwig (1985) ascertained that stable economic and social conditions assisted individuals in making the transition from a drug lifestyle to a regular pattern of responsible living. Perceiving themselves as having "hit bottom" also apparently motivated many of the subjects in Ludwig's sample to abandon their abusive relationship with drugs. Hitting bottom (82%) and growing tired of "the hustle" (83%) were factors cited by a group of long-term heroin addicts to explain their rationale for eventually rejecting a heroin-based drug lifestyle, often without benefit of formal treatment (Simpson & Marsh, 1986).

With cessation comes the possibility of relapse. Factors with known value in predicting drug relapse include major depression and antisocial personality (Rounsaville, Dolinsky, Babor, & Meyer, 1987), external locus of control (Shelton, Parsons, Leber, & Yohman, 1982), failure to assume responsibility for negative outcomes or viewing negative outcomes as uncontrollable (Bradley, Gossop, Brewin, Phillips, & Green, 1992), and poor ability to identify and manage high-risk situations and drug-related cues, thoughts, and feelings (Marlatt & Gordon, 1985). The maintenance of a vow of absolute and total abstinence may also promote relapse in some individuals through what Marlatt and Gordon (1985) refer to as the Abstinence Violation Effect (AVE). This issue clearly warrants further examination; empirical data addressing the validity of the AVE concept are mixed and inconclusive (Collins & Lapp, 1991; Birke, Edelmann, & Davis, 1990). Relapse and relapse prevention figure prominently in the final part of this book, which discusses intervention and change.

DEVELOPMENTAL STAGES OF DRUG LIFESTYLE INVOLVEMENT

To provide a conceptually functional and clinically practical approach to drug use progression, lifestyle theory organizes the behavioral transition points, discussed in the previous section, into four stages of drug lifestyle involvement. Perhaps the most famous synopsis on the progressive nature of drug use and abuse is the one offered by Jellinek (1960) in his now-classic stage-based theory of alcoholism. Jellinek contends that the alcoholic advances through four stages of a disease process that is progressive, inexorable, and fatal if not treated. The first stage, labeled "prealcoholic" by Jellinek, is characterized by the abuse of alcohol for the express purpose of alleviating anxiety and stress. The second or "prodromal" stage of alcohol abuse gives rise to the putative first- and second-rank symptoms of alcoholism (blackouts, surreptitious drinking, and abnormal tolerance) and the formation of a denial or alibi system. The third or "crucial" stage of alcoholism, according to Jellinek, is distinguished by a complete lack of control over drinking behavior and the appearance of physical addiction. In Jellinek's fourth or "chronic" stage of alcohol involvement, reverse tolerance, physical deterioration, memory problems, and moral/ethical degeneration assume diagnostic preeminence.

The developmental stages of drug involvement proposed by lifestyle theory differ from Jellinek's model in several key respects. First, contrary to Jellinek's formulations, peer influence, not stress, is seen as the primary motivating force behind initial drug use (Swaim, Oetting, Edwards, & Beauvais, 1989; White, Johnson, & Horowitz, 1986). Second, the lifestyle model takes exception to Jellinek's position on abstinence and treatment as the only avenues through which one may exit a drug lifestyle, on the strength of research suggesting that controlled drinking is possible (Marlatt, 1983) and that many persons who have had problems with alcohol or drugs mature out of these problems without benefit of treatment (Anglin, Brecht, Woodward, & Bonett, 1986; Vaillant & Milofsky, 1982). The disease and lifestyle models of stage development also differ widely on the variables they use to define drug abuse. Whereas the former emphasizes the physical symptoms of alcoholism and drug abuse, which research suggests are mutable and indistinct (Schuckit, 1987), the latter accentuates the role of lifestyle factors in initiating and sustaining drug-oriented activities.

Age is an important correlate of drug involvement, and the results of several studies indicate that alcohol use responds to age-related factors (Fillmore, 1988; Grant, Harford, & Grigson, 1988). Self-reported alcohol, marijuana, and polydrug use, for instance, tends to peak around age 20 and then fall off (Menard & Huizinga, 1989)—a finding that has been documented both cross-sectionally (Temple & Ladouceur, 1986) and longitudinally (Roizen, Cahalan, & Shanks, 1978). Although there may be a meaningful connection between age and substance abuse, this relationship appears to be complex and mutable. Hence, despite the fact that problem drinking tends to be more serious and common in young adult males, younger men are also more likely to desist from problem drinking than older men (Roizen et al., 1978). There is also evidence to suggest that the age-substance abuse relationship shifts as the definition of substance abuse changes (Cahalan & Room, 1974). Therefore, although age shows some concordance with stage of drug involvement, there are many exceptions to this rule that make age an unreliable marker of developmental progression. As a result, behavioral and motivational factors should be considered in combination with age to derive an accurate representation of developmental stage demarcation, which in the present model consists of the pre-drug, early drug, advanced drug, and burnout/maturity stages of drug involvement.

Pre-Drug Lifestyle Stage

The pre-drug lifestyle stage spans the adolescent and early adult years, normally commencing at around age 12 and culminating at around age 21 or 22. The point made earlier concerning the obstacles inherent in using age as the primary differentiator of stage must be reiterated; the age ranges used to delineate the four stages of drug lifestyle involvement vary from case to case. Consequently, an individual's age must be considered in conjunction with information on his or her behavioral and motivational state in determining his or her current level of development. It is not uncommon, for instance, to find a 20-, 30-, or even 40-year-old individual functioning at a pre-drug stage of lifestyle development, or, conversely, a 16- or 17-year-old who has already progressed beyond the pre-drug stage and is operating in an early or advanced stage of drug lifestyle involvement. It is equally important to note that the age ranges provided in this section have been calibrated using research on persons whose primary drug of abuse was alcohol or heroin. Investigators may therefore find it necessary to lower, compress, or otherwise modify the age ranges when investigating a drug lifestyle founded on cocaine or another stimulant drug, given the likelihood of accelerated progression and burnout with such drugs.

Primary motives for drug use during the pre-drug lifestyle stage include desire for peer acceptance, search for excitement, and pursuit of pleasure (Walters, 1992). Interviews conducted with high volume drug abusers enrolled in a comprehensive drug treatment program revealed that peers (61%) and curiosity and excitement (20%) were the primary reasons given for initiation of drug-related activities (Walters, 1994a). To satisfy curiosity and pursue excitement, individuals immersed in a pre-drug lifestyle stage of lifestyle development experiment with a wide assortment of chemical compounds. Because they are unfamiliar with the physiological action of many of these substances, individuals in the pre-drug lifestyle pattern of behavior are at greater risk for overdose than more experienced users. However, the ultimate goal of the pre-drug lifestyle stage substance abuser is self-enhancement rather than self-destruction, and the primary motivation for drug use during this stage is to feel good and be part of a wider group of individuals who also use drugs and feel good.

A comparatively large number of persons enter the pre-drug stage of lifestyle development, but many drop out before advancing to the next stage. Surveys suggest that drug use is common (82%, 28%, and 12% of a group of 18- to 25-year-old respondents reported using alcohol, marijuana, and cocaine, respectively, during a 12-month period; U.S. Department of Health & Human Services, 1990) and problems relating to the use of drugs, although less conspicuous, occur on a fairly regular basis (of the 18- to 25-year-old respondents who used alcohol within a 12-month period, 24% experienced at least one blackout, 25% reported drinking fast in order to get an effect, and 26% reported getting angry or cross with another person while drinking; U.S. Department of Health & Human Services, 1990). However, compulsive or progressive use of drugs in adolescents and young adults continues to be the exception rather than the rule, and the vast majority of persons who have used drugs at a pre-drug lifestyle level do not progress to a more advanced stage of drug lifestyle preoccupation (Johnston, O'Malley, & Bachman, 1991). Persons who desist from drug abuse during the pre-drug lifestyle stage frequently report doing so out of fear that continued involvement will damage their health, disrupt their long-term plans, or ruin their reputations (Stuck, Ksander, Berg, Loughin, & Johnson, 1982). The experimentation of youth soon gives way to the realization that there are consequences to drug abuse that most people view as incompatible with their life goals. Those who do not take heed of the warning signs progress to the early stage of drug involvement.

Early Drug Stage

The early drug stage normally extends from young adulthood (ages 21-22) to around age 32. It is during the early stage of drug lifestyle involvement that a commitment to a drug-oriented way of life first materializes. This stage also gives rise to a corresponding shift in motivation in which drugs are used for the purpose of eliminating stress, pressure, and frustration rather than simply for excitement, curiosity's sake, and peer acceptance. It is at this stage that the early warning signs of physical and psychological dependence make their appearance, along with an increased tolerance to the primary drug of abuse and the emergence of craving when the drug is no longer available (Hughes, Power, & Francis, 1992). Perhaps the cardinal diagnostic feature of this stage, however, is a noticeable increase in subjects' preoccupation with drug use; their thoughts and actions are dominated by drugs even when they are not actively engaged in using them.

Even though many persons who commit to a lifestyle pattern of drug abuse do not have a clearly defined drug of choice (see Walters, 1994b), a drug abuser normally becomes more selective in his or her use of chemical substances when moving from a pre-drug to an early drug stage of lifestyle involvement. There is also a corresponding shift in behavior in which non-drug interests, relationships, and commitments are replaced by a growing preoccupation with drug-related activities and pursuits. Research, in fact, suggests that young adults who reject conventional social roles like marriage and stable employment are at increased risk for drug use escalation and for early stage drug lifestyle commitments that replace investment in conventional social roles (Kandel, Simcha-Fagan, & Davies, 1986). It is not that a spouse or steady job necessarily insulates an individual from the ravages of a drug lifestyle, but the early stage drug abuser's avoidance of such responsibilities signals an unwillingness to abandon the self-centered pursuit of pleasure in favor of a lifestyle in which the concerns and interests of other people are sometimes placed ahead of the individual's own immediate goals and desires. Beyond the hindrances encountered during the early stages of drug lifestyle involvement, even more serious hurdles await someone who moves into an advanced stage of drug-based activity.

Advanced Drug Stage

The general time frame for the advanced drug stage extends from age 32 or 33 to somewhere during the fifth decade of life (ages 40-49). Again, there are many exceptions to the general age guidelines, but the single factor that most clearly defines the advanced stage is the presence of maximal commitment to drug lifestyle activities. Voluntary attrition reaches its lowest point during this stage. Chief motives for drug use during the advanced stage converge around subjects' efforts to silence the fear and anxiety that stem from their belief that they have lost control over their lives. These individuals may also engage in compensatory displays of anger and retaliation designed to exert control over their surroundings. Overdose and suicide display rising rates during this stage, in part because these actions offer advanced stage drug abusers an opportunity to assert control over their physical being, and in part because these individuals begin to place less value on human life, including their own lives. Job and family pressures, although they may have been present during the early stage of drug involvement, become clear sources of stress and frustration during the advanced stage and provide further grist for the drug lifestyle mill (Cahalan & Room, 1974).

The advanced stage of drug lifestyle involvement is characterized by the subject's unconditional commitment to a drug-oriented way of life, and it is during this stage that the individual is most dangerous to him- or herself directly and to others indirectly. Direct danger to the user is represented by increased rates of overdose deaths, suicide attempts, and self-destructive behavior as the user becomes increasingly preoccupied with drug lifestyle activities. The indirect danger to others is a function of drug-influenced behavior that, despite an absence of malicious intent, ends up causing significant harm to others. Such behavior might include the commission of sundry criminal acts or operating an automobile under the influence of alcohol or another intoxicant. The subject's growing dependence on drug-oriented thinking, much of which has become automatic by the time he or she reaches an advanced stage of drug lifestyle involvement, is clearly evident in the subject's thoughts, actions, and demeanor. It is for this reason that there are minimal levels of voluntary attrition from this stage and many advanced-stage individuals wind up dead, hospitalized, or in trouble with the law.

Stage of Burnout and Maturity

The final stage in the drug developmental sequence is composed of two interrelated but distinct processes. "Burnout" refers to reductions in physical strength, stamina, and pleasure that accompany entry into the fifth decade of a drug user's life. Some may take issue with the term, but this is an expression that many drug abusers themselves use to identify the physical fatigue and malaise they suffer after many years of drug-based activity (Speckart & Anglin, 1986). The second process, maturity, unfolds as the individual begins to reevaluate his or her life goals. This process is similar in many ways to the midlife crisis described in the writings of Levinson, Darrow, Klein, Levinson, and McKee (1978), where middle-aged males are said to experience a sense of loss and panic in response to the dawning awareness that many of their life goals and objectives will never be realized. A reevaluation of life's priorities also takes place during the maturity phase of this stage, in which the individual demonstrates increased investment in meaningful long-term relationships and decreased interest in the pursuit of immediate pleasure.

Drug use that occurs during the burnout/maturity stage tends to be sporadic, although it may persist if psychological maturity does not accompany physical burnout. Winick (1962) was one of the first to propose that chronic drug addicts frequently mature out of their addiction with age, and Waldorf (1976) discerned that the two best predictors of voluntary abstinence were age and the number of years addicted. Although studies have failed to provide universal verification of the maturing out process, abstinence rates of 10% to 57% have been reported in samples of untreated opiate addicts (Maddux & Desmond, 1980), alcoholics (Hermos, Locastro, Glynn, Bouchard, & DeLabry, 1988), and cocaine abusers (Murphy, Reinarman, & Waldorf, 1989) in follow-ups spanning 4 to 12 years. Vaillant and Milofsky (1982) obtained complete drinking histories on 400 men and observed that 49 of the 110 individuals who experienced a problem with alcohol between the ages of 20 and 47 subsequently achieved continuous abstinence for 1 or more years, most without benefit of formal treatment. Likewise, only 20% of a cohort of recovered male alcoholics interviewed two decades after their initial admission to an inpatient substance abuse treatment facility attributed their recovery to the effects of program intervention (Nordstrom & Berglund, 1987).

Anglin, Brecht, Woodward, and Bonett (1986) observed a relatively high rate of voluntary abstinence in a large sample of heroin addicts, most of whom were able to desist from further opiate use without benefit of treatment. However, regular participation in criminal activity, including drug dealing, acted to suppress the maturing out process in this group of individuals. The most noteworthy feature of this study is that it highlights a potential area of overlap between the drug and criminal lifestyles, with implications for the treatment and management of drug-involved individuals. Anglin et al. speculate that participation in an ongoing series of drug-related crimes, perhaps because it makes chemical substances more available to the individual or possibly because it reinforces a related set of cognitive-behavioral thinking styles, serves to interfere with the maturing out process, in turn decreasing an individual's chances of remaining drug-free in the community.

The progression of developmental stages in a drug lifestyle is neither as distinct nor as deliberate as this discussion might make it seem; it is variable and indeterminant rather than fixed and methodical. It is not uncommon to observe movement both forward and backward in the developmental stage sequence; it has even been observed that a person previously functioning at the burnout/maturity stage can revert to an early or advanced stage of drug involvement, often with a new primary drug of abuse (see Lehman, Barrett, & Simpson, 1990).

Equally important is the fact that when people enter an inpatient drug treatment facility, certain facets of their drug lifestyle go into remission while other facets remain active. The structure provided by most inpatient drug programs may permit a higher level of adjustment than is typical of an individual's daily routine in the community. If a subject does not lay a foundation for change or take pains to modify his or her thinking, then he or she will likely reenter society with the same cognitive and behavioral patterns that necessitated treatment in the first place.

CONCLUSION

The behavioral transition points and developmental stages discussed in this chapter are clearly related. In fact, the developmental stages are designed to provide a clinically useful integration of transition point data with the conditions, behaviors, and motives that define drug use behavior. Comparing the behavioral transition system and the developmental stage system across time reveals that initiation precedes the pre-drug lifestyle stage; initiation is a necessary but not sufficient condition for enrollment in the pre-drug stage, which requires both drug initiation and a regular and potentially problematic pattern of drug-based activity. The escalation transition point, on the other hand, may be part of either the pre-drug or early drug stage, although it normally signals the occurrence of issues that originally make their appearance in the early drug stage. Finally, cessation may occur during any of the four stages of a drug lifestyle but is most commonly observed during the burnout/maturity stage. The putative relationships between the behavioral transition points discussed in the first section of this chapter and the developmental stages presented in the second section are set out in Table 7-1.

As mentioned earlier in this chapter, lifestyle theory is in agreement with features of both the general deviance and gateway theories of drug use development. Aspects of the general deviance model in line with lifestyle theory include a focus on the interactive nature of human development (including the view that drugs and crime are interdependent). Interactionalism (defined as the study of the interactive relationship between an or-

Table 7-1   Temporal Relationship Between the Behavioral Transition Points and Developmental Stages

Behavioral transition points	Developmental stages
Initiation	
	Pre-drug-lifestyle stage
Escalation	
	Early drug stage
	Advanced drug stage
	Stage of burnout/maturity
Cessation	

ganism and its environment) consequently plays a fundamental role in both the general deviance and lifestyle models of human behavior. The drug–crime relationship is viewed by both these models as stemming from an extensive overlap of related conditions, choices, cognitions, and behaviors. Lifestyle theory also finds itself in agreement with certain features of the gateway theory of drug-seeking behavior, through the latter's emphasis on development. It is not that using alcohol or marijuana inexorably leads to the use of "harder" drugs, but the use of these substances acquaints a person with a lifestyle in which the use of drugs is encouraged and experimentation with a wide assortment of substances is commonplace. Thus, lifestyle theory aligns itself with both the general deviance and gateway theorems by holding to an interactive-developmental view of drug-seeking behavior.

Chapter 8

Behavioral Patterns

INTRODUCTION

Thus far, the focus has been on the conditional aspects of the structural model of lifestyle theory. However, historical-developmental conditions, such as those surveyed in previous chapters, are only one factor in the equation used by lifestyle theory to delineate a drug lifestyle. Of equal significance in ascertaining the nature of a drug lifestyle are the current-contextual conditions, choices, and cognitions that research suggests are correlated with drug-seeking behavior. This chapter examines the effect these three factors have on the development of a drug lifestyle and how their interaction gives rise to behavioral patterns that help define drug lifestyle involvement. Commencing with a brief dialogue on the differences between historical-developmental and current-contextual conditions, this chapter then touches on the choice and cognition aspects of the structural model of lifestyle theory as well as the interaction of conditions, choices, and cognitions in the formulation of a behavioral definition of the drug lifestyle.

CONDITIONS

Lifestyle theory considers two general categories of conditional influences: those provided by historical-developmental conditions and those provided by current-contextual conditions. Historical-developmental conditions are features of the individual, environment, or Person × Situation interaction that place a subject at increased or decreased risk for drug use. Research on the historical-developmental correlates of drug-seeking behavior was covered in Chapters 2, 3, 4, and 6; the current-contextual conditions, on the other hand, require additional explanation.

Conditions of the current-contextual variety exist as features of a person, situation, or Person × Situation interaction that enhance or minimize the odds of a concurrent drug use episode. As the expression implies, these conditions are more immediate, and therefore more amenable to direct control and intervention, than historical-developmental conditions. Current-contextual variables are said to exert either an exacerbatory (increasing the probability of a concurrent drug use outcome) or mitigatory (decreasing the probability of a concurrent drug use outcome) effect on the behavior of individuals, who may or may not be at high risk for future drug use. As a case in point, having a bad day at work may serve an exacerbatory function in a high-risk individual or someone with a history of substance abuse, whereas it may have no bearing on the actions of someone who is at low risk for future drug use behavior.

Faupel (1985) has studied the influence of current-contextual conditions on drug abuse outcomes by cross-tabulating dichotomized measures of drug availability and life structure (regularly occurring patterns of occupational, domestic, recreational, and criminal activity). High availability of or access to drugs combined with high life structure falls within the purview of the stabilized addict role, whereas low drug availability coupled with high life structure is characteristic of the occasional user role. High availability and low life structure demarcate the freewheeling addict role, and low availability and low life structure define the street junkie role. Research has shown that heroin addicts may be more vulnerable to arrest during the street junkie phase than when other current-contextual conditions prevail, because they are more apt to engage in impulsive or high-risk crimes in this role than when either drug availability or life structure is high (Faupel, 1987). The nature of the drug-crime connection may also vary as a function of these roles, with little drug-crime crossover for persons adopting the occasional user role, a directional relationship with crime serving as the putative causal agent in the stabilized addict and freewheeling roles, and a directional relationship with drug addiction serving as the putative causal agent in the street junkie role (Faupel & Klockars, 1987).

Lifestyle theory maintains that the same condition may provoke either a historical-developmental or current-contextual effect. Peer influence, for example, could place an individual at higher or lower risk for future drug seeking (historical-developmental function) or increase the probability that this individual will engage in a specific drug use episode (current-contextual function). Current-contextual conditions are therefore of prime etiological and practical significance in understanding drug use behavior. However, current-contextual conditions offer more than simple clarification of the evolution of specific drug use events and the connection between past and present conditional effects. There is evidence, for instance, that current-contextual conditions may influence the treatment process and the propensity for relapse, because, unlike historical-developmental conditions, current-contextual conditions are oriented to the present and so are more amenable to intervention and modification. Limiting access to drugs, learning to deal more effectively with stress, and avoiding drug-related cues can all be conceptualized as current-contextual conditional management strategies with implications for the treatment of drug-involved persons. In fact, these strategies form the conditional arm of structural lifestyle intervention, a topic discussed in Chapter 9.

CHOICE

The decisions a person makes comprise the second major category of influence delineated by the structural model. It is proposed that conditions affect behavior by narrowing or restricting a subject's options in life, constraining the subject's choice. The decision-making process is construed by theoreticians operating out of the rational choice perspective as an optimizing enterprise marked by an exhaustive review and evaluation of the relative costs and benefits of alternative courses of action (G. S. Becker, 1968). The trouble is, research indicates that the human decision-making enterprise is neither as methodical nor as analytic as these theorists have traditionally assumed. Evidence of perseverative choice selection (Einhorn & Hogarth, 1978), shortcut decision making (Corbin, 1980), and impulsive evaluation of alternatives (Fattah, 1982) all argue against a simple economic or rational choice interpretation of the choice process. Furthermore, research delving into the decision-making processes that support drug abuse (Bennett, 1986) and crime (Weaver & Carroll, 1985) implies that these decisions are frequently biased in favor of one or two alternative avenues of action with which the individual is most familiar or feels most comfortable.

Lifestyle theory posits that the choices individuals make rarely conform to the underlying tenets of rational choice theory. Specifically, the human decision-making process is viewed by lifestyle theory as influenced extensively by nonrational forces, prior experience, and developmental contingencies. Paternoster (1989) reports that extralegal factors like moral values, opportunity, and informal sources of social control were significantly more prognostic of future marijuana use in a group of adolescent respondents than the perceived certainty of getting caught and punished for such behavior. Even when individuals do consider the legal ramifications of their actions, their ability to analyze, store, and utilize this information is limited by the flawed nature of the human decision-making process. Reitman (1974), for instance, observed a substantial loss of information when subjects attempted to organize, integrate, and combine information from widely divergent sources, which in turn interfered with their ability to generate an optimal solution to a particular problem. This factor is something that should be taken into account in constructing a program of treatment intervention.

People characteristically engage in those actions for which they are most consistently reinforced while avoiding behaviors they find unrewarding or punishing. Regular drug use helps create a situation in which the subject anticipates increasing rewards from continued involvement in a drug lifestyle and decreasing rewards from participation in non-drug-related activities. In fact, a drug-involved individual may attempt to discredit, discount, or belittle the benefits of a nondrug lifestyle. For this reason, not all options for or alternative solutions to a particular situation are given equal weight in a person's evaluation of the alternatives. Take, for instance, the fact that positive outcome expectancies for alcohol have been found to be effective in predicting problematic drinking behavior (Christensen & Goldman, 1983). Because the short-term effects of drug use tend to be positive and the long-term effects negative, it can be anticipated that persons committed to a drug lifestyle have problems balancing long- and short-term expectancies: They are inclined to accentuate the positive short-term effects of drug use at the expense of a thorough examination of the negative long-term effects. A subject's reinforcement history, drug-related expectancies, and evaluation of short- and long-term consequences of substance use must therefore all be taken into consideration in drafting an effective program of treatment intervention.

The decision-making process, in addition to being technically flawed and influenced by past patterns of reinforcement, clearly responds to developmental contingencies and influences. Piaget (1963) advised that a child's cognitive capabilities grow as he or she gains environmental experience. The interaction between a child and the environment results in early learning experiences and increased awareness of the consequences of actions taken. As a direct consequence, informed decision making becomes progressively more available to the child. Neurocognitive development also has an effect on preparedness for learning (Piaget, 1963). Thus, the evolution of informed decision making is a function of both neurocognitive development and of interaction with an environment replete with new learning opportunities.

COGNITION

Cognitive patterns are the third key element in the structural model of lifestyle theory. It is proposed that once the conditions have been established and the initial choices made, an individual seeks to justify his or her actions and decisions by modifying or distorting the thinking behind them. Because this facet of lifestyle development is geared more toward self-defense than self-education, the self-talk (rationale) of someone committed to a drug lifestyle is not always consonant with traditional standards of rational thinking and effective problem solving. Furthermore, because the thoughts involved in rationalizing a drug lifestyle are often repetitive, they become automatic over time. What has been referred to in traditional substance abuse treatment circles as "denial" is, in fact, a reflection of this rationalizing pattern of thought. This cognitive pattern is expressed in eight separate thinking styles—mollification, cutoff, entitlement, power orientation, sentimentality, superoptimism, cognitive indolence, and discontinuity—each of which is discussed briefly in this section.

Mollification

Denying responsibility for drug use and the consequences of such use by projecting blame onto external situations, other people, or the capriciousness of fate is a prime example of mollification, the intent of which is to avoid change. If a person is unwilling to accept responsibility for his or her actions, then he or she has, in effect, shut off all avenues of change. Someone operating on the basis of mollification views his or her problems as stemming from external conditions and reasons that if only these condition changed so would the situation. What such people need to realize is that their lives will not change until they stop offering excuses for their behavior, start taking responsibility for their actions, and begin learning to make better decisions.

Cutoff

Deterrents to drug use can be either internal (moral values) or external (legal sanctions). Lifestyle theory argues that all people are capable of being influenced by deterrents, but persons committed to a drug lifestyle have trouble guiding their life on the basis of internal and external deterrents, partly because they are able to cut off, or "implode," these deterrents at a moment's notice. The most commonly employed cutoff with respect to drug use is a two-word phrase ("fuck it"), although there are many forms of cutoffs available to someone interested in eliminating the fears, concerns, and rational considerations that prevent most people from engaging in drug abuse behavior. In fact, drug use may serve a cutoff function for itself in persons previously or currently committed to a drug lifestyle. Take as a case in point someone who plans to limit himself to two drinks, or to a few drags off a marijuana cigarette, but who then ends up consuming substantially more alcohol or marijuana than was originally intended. This situation can be attributed to the implosive nature of those first few drinks or puffs of marijuana in eliminating commonsense deterrents to further drug use.

Entitlement

Before a person can participate in drug use, he or she must first grant him- or herself permission to engage in such behavior. Permission to use drugs often derives from an attitude of entitlement, in which the subject reasons that because he or she grew up in a disadvantaged home, had a difficult week at work, or spent 5 years in prison, he or she is entitled to indulge. The attitudes of ownership, privilege, and uniqueness that characterize the thinking style of entitlement not only supply the individual with permission to use drugs, but also endorse whatever actions are "necessary" to obtain access to drugs. Many substance abuse programs unwittingly reinforce the entitlement aspect of a drug lifestyle by overemphasizing the physical roots of drug-seeking behavior. The concept of addiction, in fact, supports both entitlement and mollification by exonerating drug use on the basis of lack of choice, and by attributing activities secondary or preparatory to drug use to the overpowering effects of addiction. In light of this finding, lifestyle theory asserts that the concept of addiction must be reevaluated.

Power Orientation

Drug-inclined individuals are clearly interested in achieving a sense of control over the external environment. When such persons find their control efforts thwarted, they experience a sense of powerlessness, known as the "zero state" (Yochelson & Samenow, 1976). Power-oriented individuals attempt to extricate themselves from a zero state by engaging in a "power thrust," whereby they attempt to exert control of their situations by drawing attention to themselves or by putting another person down. The power thrust can be physical, verbal, or mental. Drug abuse itself can be seen as a form of power thrust, in that individuals are able to achieve a sense of control by manipulating their own moods through the use of chemical substances. This motive may explain why some people continue ingesting drugs even when these substances no longer produce the subjective effects that first made them attractive.

Sentimentality

Persons who have committed themselves to a drug lifestyle usually have engaged in many activities that have been harmful to themselves and others. As a means of denying injury to others, such individuals may perform "good deeds" designed to make a good impression. These might include buying an expensive gift for a spouse, taking a group of neighborhood children to an amusement park, or trying to talk a friend or relative out of using drugs despite the subjects' own commitment to such activities. Such sentimentality protects the drug lifestyle by deluding individuals into believing that their few "good deeds" counterbalance the harm and pain they have caused themselves and others, so that there is no need for them to change their behavior. The characteristic that separates sentimentality from true caring is that the primary goal of sentimentality is self-centered rather than other-centered; the subject is either trying to make him- or herself feel good about the lifestyle or expects something tangible in return for "altruistic" behavior.

Superoptimism

By the time individuals have progressed into the middle and later stages of a drug lifestyle, they have observed and known people who have lost their jobs, families, or lives over drugs; and although many of the same types of problems may be present in their own lives, such individuals superoptimistically convince themselves that there is no way any of these things could ever happen to them. If such things did happen, they reason, it would be because of some external situation and not their own behavior. In contrast to sentimentality, which exists as a denial of injury to others, superoptimism is a denial of injury to self. In fact, superoptimism grows as a direct consequence of a person's use of drugs and ability to withstand the negative consequences of a drug lifestyle. In other words, many categories of drugs, but most prominently stimulant drugs like cocaine and amphetamines, augment and reinforce a person's sense of grandiosity and invulnerability—and the belief that the person can continue avoiding the negative consequences of a drug lifestyle indefinitely. The resilience of the human body also contributes to the formation of superoptimism; an individual normally must consume relatively large amounts of a chemical substance over a relatively long period of time before encountering any long-range physical problems.

Cognitive Indolence

Most successful people recognize the necessity of proceeding in an orderly fashion toward an objective by pursuing and integrating compatible short-range, intermediate, and long-range goals. Persons committed to a drug lifestyle, on the other hand, frequently attempt to dodge essential steps in the goal attainment process by seizing on opportunities for shortcut solutions. The inclination to opt for a short-term answer to a long-term problem is a hallmark of cognitive indolence, or lazy thinking, which leads the individual in the direction of short-term benefit at the expense of long-term success and happiness. Until such time as the individual possesses increased critical thought and greater resolve in the face of frustration, and forms an ability to balance long- and short-term expectancies, this situation will likely remain in effect.

Discontinuity

The drug lifestyle engenders weak continuity of thought and action. Persons committed to a drug lifestyle may initiate many projects but end up completing very few. They have trouble following through on initially good intentions because they often lose sight of long-term goals in favor of short-term pleasures like drug use and drug-related activity. Another manifestation of discontinuity occurs when subjects selectively symbolize certain behaviors and attributes into awareness, while discounting or denying personal qualities they prefer to forget. This thinking eventually leads to a situation in which individuals compartmentalize experiences and fail to recognize the contradictions of thought and action that shield them from the truth about their behavior.

As was implied in the opening paragraph of this section, the eight thinking patterns can be considered different facets of what has commonly been referred to as denial. Lifestyle theory labors to make the denial process more specific by breaking it down into its component forms. Besides allowing individuals to disavow the severity or scope of their drug use, these thinking styles also provide an avenue through which they may trivialize or discount certain basic features of normal human experience in a manner that takes them away from adaptive goals and encourages adoption of drug-oriented goals. Mollification, for example, trivializes the fundamental human trait of personal accountability and furthers drug lifestyle goals by furnishing substance abusers with rationalizations for disclaiming personal responsibility for the consequences of their involvement in drug-related rituals and relationships. Table 8-1 lists the discount and denial coordinates of drug-oriented thinking, from mollification to discontinuity.

CONDITION-CHOICE-COGNITION INTERACTIONS

It has been argued that textbooks often fail to capture the complexity of the subject they are attempting to explain, whether it is psychiatric diagnosis, zoological nomenclature, or lifestyle theory. As presented, the condition-choice-cognition sequence seems ordered, logical, and coherent. However, what at first seems methodical and crystal-clear may soon become disordered and enigmatic in light of the interconnectedness of conditions, choices, and cognitions. Although conditions define the limits of a person's choices, they are also, to a certain extent, a product of these choices. Likewise, cognitions not only surface in support of the choices a person makes in life but also affect the decision-making process from whence these choices originate. The bottom line, then, is that conditions, choice, and cognitions are connected in ways that are multidirectional and complex, rather than unidirectional and simple—all of which makes for potential confusion.

One way to address the crossover between conditions, choices, and cognitions is by examining the behavioral patterns that arise from their interaction. Lifestyle theory maintains that the behavioral patterns or styles that ensue from the interactive blueprint of conditions, choices, and cognitions thought to be responsible for the evolution of a drug lifestyle also define this lifestyle. It can be argued that the distinct patterns of drug lifestyle development, involvement, and commitment owe their existence to discrete patterns of conditions-choice-cognition interaction in persons whose principal preoccupation is with drugs. The four behavioral patterns

Table 8-1 The Eight Thinking Styles: Discounting of Basic Human Attributes and Denials Associated With Problematic Drug Use

Thinking style	Discounts	Denials
Mollification	Personal accountability	Responsibility
Cutoff (implosion)	Rational thought	Weak emotional control
Entitlement	Social responsibility	Impertinence
Power orientation	Self-control	Impotence
Sentimentality	Charity	Injury to others
Superoptimism	Self-confidence	Injury to self
Cognitive indolence	Ambition	Negative consequences
Discontinuity	Indivisibility	Negative behaviors

that define a drug lifestyle—irresponsibility/pseudoresponsibility, stress-coping imbalance, interpersonal triviality, and social rule breaking/bending—are discussed next.

Irresponsibility/Pseudoresponsibility

The drug lifestyle engenders a repetitive pattern of irresponsible behavior in which the individual is generally unresponsive to personal and social obligations, is readily sidetracked by environmental distractions, and has trouble following through on initially good intentions. On a day-to-day basis, the subject fails to fulfill his or her obligations to family, friends, and others to whom he or she is personally accountable. There are some drug-involved persons who project a persona of responsibility by maintaining steady employment, managing their finances, and avoiding serious legal trouble. Beneath this veneer, however, lies a pattern of pseudoresponsiblity; such subjects frequently neglect the personal and psychological needs of loved ones because their primary commitment is to a drug lifestyle. Hence, although these subjects may keep food on the table and a roof over the heads of their families, they are often unavailable for important social engagements and obligations and, consequently, often fail to respond to the psychological needs of family members, due largely to a preoccupation with drugs and drug-related activities.

Stress-Coping Imbalance

Initial drug use is characteristically driven by social and enhancement motives. In other words, initial motives for drug use arise from curiosity, excitement, and peer relations; those who continue using drugs generally do so because they like the effect drugs have on their mood and behavior. However, as drug use evolves into a lifestyle, social and enhancement motives decrease in importance, whereas coping motives designed to eliminate negative affect increase in importance. Thus, drug use for the purpose of managing stress, reducing frustration, and resolving the problems of everyday life gradually takes on added significance, and drug use for the purpose of achieving pleasure begins to fade in prominence. Persons engaged in a drug lifestyle find themselves locked into an escalating pattern of social and environmental pressure, which they attempt to alleviate through the use of drugs. The problems created by a stress-coping imbalance are twofold: (a) the individual's habitual manner of coping (drug use) reduces short-term pressure but, because of its social, physical, and legal ramifications actually contributes to a long-term buildup of stress; and (b) because drug use provides short-term relief from the problems of everyday living, the individual has little motivation to learn alternative avenues of stress management and consequently limits opportunities to develop more effective coping strategies.

Interpersonal Triviality

Persons ensconced in a lifestyle pattern of drug abuse tend to avoid meaningful human interaction; they opt instead for the superficial bantering of drug associates and the ritualistic use of drugs and drug paraphernalia. As an individual becomes increasingly preoccupied with drugs, he or she develops certain drug-based rituals around the procurement, preparation, and use of these substances. These rituals serve to extend the duration of the drug experience and soon become as important as the pharmacological effects of the chemical substance in directing future drug-seeking activities. The subject typically also engages in frivolous conversations with other drug users as part of the interpersonal triviality behavioral style. This not only becomes a way of passing time, but also serves the interests of sentimentality by allowing individuals to feel good about themselves and their lifestyle. Whether the topic is politics, the economy, sports, or the individual's plans for the future, the drug-inclined individual spends an inordinate amount of time engaging in frivolous exchanges with other drug users. Consequently, although some drug abusers continue to engage in intimate relationships with persons they knew prior to entering a drug lifestyle, these relationships assume diminished significance and superficial drug-centered associations become more important as they move into the advanced stages of a drug lifestyle.

Social Rule Breaking/Bending

Persons who have committed themselves to a drug lifestyle routinely violate the rules and norms of society to obtain access to drugs. Some drug-dependent individuals, however, are able to avoid serious legal trouble even though they may be preoccupied with drugs, because such individuals are well practiced in the art of social rule bending. Instead of blatantly violating the rules and laws of society, a person with allegiance to a drug lifestyle often bends the rules through misrepresentation, manipulation, and subterfuge because these methods are less apt to lead to serious legal repercussions. In other words, many drug-inclined persons will lie, cheat, and manipulate before they will steal or violate the personal rights of others because they realize that social rule-bending behavior is less likely to land them in a place (i.e., jail or prison) where they will, at least theoretically, have less access to drugs. Most drug abusers resort to social rule-breaking conduct in situations where they view this to be their only recourse; social rule-bending alternatives are clearly preferred.

The Drug Lifestyle Screening Interview (DLSI) is a structured interview procedure that provides scores for each of the four primary behavioral characteristics that are components of a drug lifestyle: irresponsibility/pseudoresponsibility, stress-coping imbalance, interpersonal triviality, and social rule breaking/bending (see Figure 8-1). Scores on each of the four component scales of the DLSI range between 0 and 5 and summed together yield a total cumulative index that varies between 0 and 20. A total cumulative index of 10 or higher is postulated to reflect a significant pattern of commitment to drug lifestyle activities. Research has shown that the DLSI possesses moderate internal consistency ($\alpha = .66$) and a moderately high degree of interrater reliability ($r = .83$). The initial validation of the DLSI demonstrated that each of the scales, as well as the cumulative index, successfully discriminate between individuals categorized as exhibiting a high versus a low volume of past substance misuse (Walters, 1994a). Although these preliminary results are encouraging, a great deal more work needs to be done with the DLSI before it can be considered appropriate for general clinical use.

SPECIFIC COGNITIVE-BEHAVIORAL CLUSTERS

Whereas all eight thinking patterns correlate with each of the behavioral styles that define a drug lifestyle, certain cognitive-behavioral clusters are thought to be more prominent than others. Hence, although mollification and cutoff correlate with all four of the behavioral styles that define a drug lifestyle, it is believed that they correlate most forcefully with stress-coping imbalance. Likewise, entitlement and power orientation are connected to all four behavioral styles but are most vigorously associated with the social rule breaking/bending behavioral style. Cognitive indolence and discontinuity are most strongly associated with the irresponsibility/pseudoresponsibility behavioral style, and sentimentality and superoptimism align themselves best with the interpersonal triviality style, according to this formulation. The cognitive-behavioral connections proposed by lifestyle theory remain largely a matter of conjecture at this point, requiring a great deal more study before they can be considered anything other than speculative.

Lifestyle theory submits that behavior is a function of an integrated network of conditions, choices, and cognitions. Specificity may exist, however, in the relationships hypothesized between specific cognitive and behavioral styles. The glue that holds these cognitive-behavioral clusters together is thought to be derived from the goals that motivate drug use. Research in the area of substance abuse suggests that drug use is inspired by one of three primary motives, commonly referred to as the enhancement, coping, and social motives. Taking two of these motives, enhancement and coping, and dividing each into sources (personal vs. social),

DRUG LIFESTYLE SCREENING INTERVIEW
Glenn D. Walters, Ph.D.

I. Personal Data

Name _____ Reg. No. _____ Sex _____

Age _____ Race _____ Education _____ Marital _____

II. Irresponsibility/Pseudoresponsibility

a. Did you drop out of high school before completing the 12th grade?   _____

b. Have you ever been fired from a job or quit a job without warning?   _____

c. Have you ever gotten into trouble for not paying your bills?   _____

d. Have you ever been cited for failure to pay child support?   _____

e. Did you regularly neglect the psychological needs of loved ones?   _____

Note: Responding Yes receives a score of 1 and responding No a score of 0.

Irresponsibility/Pseudoresponsibility Score _____

III. Stress-Coping Imbalance

a. On a scale from 1 to 3, 1 representing a low level of stress and 3 a high degree of stress, rate your level of stress:

    1. Right before you began using drugs _____

    2. After you had been using drugs for six months _____

b. How did you handle stress during the period you were using drugs?

_____

Note: Score 2 points if subject responds by using drugs, 1 point if they report some other form of escapism, and 0 points if they appeared to use more effective coping strategies.

Stress-Coping Imbalance Score _____

IV. Interpersonal Triviality

a. Did you spend more time with drug users or non-drug users?

    1. Before you started using drugs yourself _____

    2. During the early stages of your drug usage _____

    3. During the advanced stages of drug involvement _____

b. A ritual is a routinized pattern of behavior which accompanies use of a particular drug. Indicate the degree to which rituals were part of your use of drugs (check one of the options listed below):

Not at all _____ (0)

To a moderate degree _____ (1)

To a high degree _____ (2)

c. List the specific rituals individual engaged in while using drugs.

_____

_____

_____

_____

d. Did you find yourself engaging in empty and meaningless conversations ("bullshit") with other drug users once you became involved in regular drug usage?

_____ Yes (1) _____ No (0)

Interpersonal Triviality Score _____

Figure 8-1 The Drug Lifestyle Screening Interview, Copyright 1992 by Glenn D. Walters.

V. Social Rule Breaking/Bending
a. Have you ever engaged in the following behaviors (one point each):
1. panhandling _____ (SRBe)
2. burglary _____ (SRBr)
3. lying to family members in order to get money for drugs _____ (SRBe)
4. selling drugs _____ (SRBr)
5. suspension from school for misbehavior _____ (SRBr)
6. acting as a go-between in a drug deal _____ (SRBe)
7. writing bad checks you intended to cover the check later _____ (SRBe)
8. stealing money mother's purse/father's wallet < age 14 _____ (SRBr)
b. Age of onset: Rule Breaking _____   Rule Bending _____

Social Rule Breaking/Bending Score _____ - _____

TOTAL DLSI SCORE _____

Figure 8-1 The Drug Lifestyle Screening Interview (*Continued*).

lifestyle theory proposes a system of four primary motives: personal enhancement, social enhancement, personal coping, and social coping.

Assemblages of behavioral styles, motives, and cognitive patterns eminent in drug lifestyle development are portrayed in Figure 8-2. As this figure illustrates, irresponsibility and pseudoresponsibility arise out of the interactions between sundry conditions, choices, and cognitions coordinated around lazy and discontinuous thinking and motivated by a desire for personal enhancement and self-gratification. The stress-coping imbalance behavioral style is also motivated by personal issues, but here the emphasis is on eliminating negative affect (coping) rather than generating positive feelings (enhancement) by attributing the blame for personal problems to external factors (mollification) or imploding frustration (cutoff). The third behavioral style, interpersonal triviality, derives principally from sentimentality and superoptimism, with assistance from social enhancement motives (feeling good through superficial interactions with others); and the fourth, social rule breaking/bending, evolves out of interactions in which the thinking patterns of entitlement and power orientation and social coping motives (avoiding bad feelings by exerting control over the external environment) assume center stage.

Several factors must be taken into account in any evaluation of the interrelationships between behavioral styles, cognitive patterns, and motives for drug use behavior. First, the relationships are seen as relative rather than absolute in the sense that, whereas the sentimentality and superoptimism of the drug lifestyle correlate most reliably with the behavioral style of interpersonal triviality and social enhancement motives, these two thinking patterns also correspond with the irresponsibility/pseudoresponsibility, stress-coping imbalance, and social rule breaking/bending styles and the personal coping, social coping, and personal enhancement motives, at a slightly lower level. It is critical to keep in mind, also, that

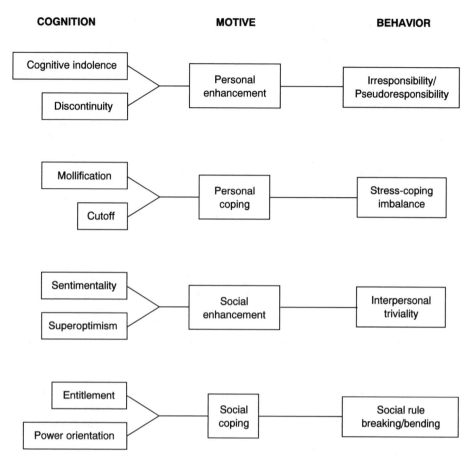

Figure 8-2 The relationship between specific behaviors, motives, and cognitions that define the drug lifestyle.

lifestyle theory maintains that as a drug lifestyle progresses the behavior styles become less clearly tied to one or two specific thinking patterns and more generally aligned with all eight. As a lifestyle evolves, the thinking and behavioral patterns become increasingly intertwined and mutually dependent.

CONCLUSION

The purpose of this chapter was to clarify and explore the interactive components of lifestyle theory with respect to conditions, choice, and cognitions. However, lifestyle theory is concerned with more than just condition-based Person × Situation interactions and the affiliation of individual conditions, choices, and cognitions. This model is most interested in how the individual self-interacts. Magnusson (1988) has argued that people develop in interaction with their environments—an argument that finds support in the drug abuse research literature (Brook et al., 1992). Lifestyle theory accepts this proposition and adds to it the conviction that the human organism is also in reciprocal interaction with itself. The conditions, choices, cognitions, motives, and behaviors that define both the individual and his or her lifestyle interact to such an extent that the individual is in a constant state of flux. Every thought, action, and experience brings with it unmistakeable change, although in many cases the alterations are subtle and barely perceptible. Lifestyle theory is highly interested in how a subject confronts these changes, because a subject's reactions provide clues to his or her habitual style of fear management: adaptive living versus lifestyle recitation.

Invariability, or the appearance of invariability, is largely a consequence of a person's attempts to fit his or her thoughts and perceptions into preconceived categories derived from old learning experiences, many of which may no longer be applicable to the person's present circumstances. The cognitive rigidity and distortion that give rise to invariability are particularly characteristic of a drug lifestyle. As research has shown (Miller, 1991), the drug lifestyle—as is true of any deviant lifestyle, whether the focus is crime, gambling, or drug abuse—promotes stereotypic thinking and behavior, such that the individual's ability to adapt to a changing social environment is severely compromised. This, then, is the problem created by a person's decision to manage existential fear through lifestyle recitation rather than through adaptive living. As a consequence, one of the principal goals of lifestyle intervention is to enhance the subject's problem-solving capabilities and fortify his or her adaptive resources by challenging stereotypic thinking and providing the skills necessary to function as a responsible member of society. Many of these skills, in fact, are intended to reinforce the individual's adaptive resources as well as his or her ability to implement innovative solutions to everyday problems.

It is clear that lifestyle theory conceives of human experience much as Heisenberg conceived of matter: that the act of observing a phenomenon, whether it is human behavior or a molecule of water, irrevocably alters the subject of observation. The observer could be a social scientist, probation officer, parent, or next-door neighbor; in each case, human behavior is a function of the relationship between the individual and his or her environment, which includes the observer. Lifestyle theory maintains that drug use moves in the direction of becoming a lifestyle as the behavior becomes more patterned. Patterning appears to be largely a function of the interaction between life conditions, choices, and cognitive styles. Conditions exert their influence by affecting schedules of reinforcement and establishing certain conditioned responses. Choices subsequently enhance and perpetuate these responses. Cognitions are then drafted to protect and justify the choices made. Some of the limitations of a drug lifestyle are that the conditional reinforcement strategies are oriented almost exclusively toward short-term gain, the decision-making processes are flawed and narrow, and the thinking patterns are irrational, automatic, and self-justifying.

In the final section of this book, attention is drawn to the issues of intervention and change. Lifestyle theory contends that psychological efficiency and well-being are largely a matter of how one manages existential fear—that is, to what extent an individual's behavior is directed by adaptive versus lifestyle motives. Interventions designed to reinforce the adaptive mode of fear management focus on ways individuals can be taught to balance short- and long-term contingencies, make reasoned decisions, and think in a manner that is appreciably more rational, controlled, and self-educating than the manner to which they are accustomed.

Although adaptability is relatively easy to appreciate, it can be exceedingly difficult to accomplish, because internal and external environments change regularly, and individuals regularly undergo alterations in development and experience. The psychologically mature individual manages these changes by learning from the environment and adjusting his or her behavior; the psychologically immature person, on the other hand, resorts to cognitive distortion and behavioral repetition. In the chapters that follow, the discussion converges on change strategies designed to enhance adaptability as a means of realizing long-term success and personal contentment.

Part 3

Treatment

Chapter 9

Structural Model of Lifestyle Intervention

INTRODUCTION

The structural model of lifestyle intervention is directed by three primary goals: (a) management of current-contextual conditions, (b) formation of better choice and decision-making strategies, and (c) modification of cognitive patterns. This model, like all facets of the structural branch of lifestyle theory, is organized around conditions, choice, and cognition, each of which is addressed in an effort to construct a meaningful program of lifestyle intervention. The conditions section of this chapter focuses exclusively on current-contextual conditions; the specific historical-developmental conditions that contributed to a client's behavior no longer exist and so are not amenable to direct intervention. (However, historical-developmental conditions may nonetheless provide clues to early prevention; these variables will be examined in Chapter 11, where drug abuse prevention is discussed.) This review of the structural model of lifestyle intervention commences with a critique of management strategies directed at current-

contextual conditions and is followed by an in-depth analysis of choice-
and cognition-based intervention strategies.

CONDITION-BASED INTERVENTIONS

It can be inferred from research on relapse in substance-abusing populations that social pressure, unpleasant mood states, interpersonal conflict,
cognitive factors, external events, urges and temptations, drug-related cues,
drug availability, and withdrawal symptomatology are important aggra-
vating conditions when it comes to drug relapse (Bradley, Green Phillips,
& Gossop, 1989; Marlatt, 1978). Studies suggest that precipitants to relapse
can be grouped into three primary categories of influence: cognitive factors,
negative affect, and external events (Bradley et al., 1989). The cognitive
precipitants of relapse will be examined in a later section. Negative affect
and external events (cues, availability, and interpersonal relations) are
discussed here. Substitution works its way into the present discussion because of its indisputable relevance to relapse prevention and its potential
utility in organizing research on the management of current-contextual
conditions.

Affect Regulation

Stressful life events, chronic stress, and the negative affect to which they
give rise are known to correlate with abusive drinking in adult samples
(Brennan & Moos, 1990) and seem to bode poorly for future treatment
outcomes (Brown et al., 1990). Yet it is difficult to determine the direction
of this relationship with any degree of certainty from retrospective accounts
of subjects. As a case in point, Hall, Havassy, and Wasserman (1990)
conducted weekly follow-up interviews with 225 subjects (85 alcoholics,
72 opiate abusers, and 68 cigarette smokers) who had just completed
abstinence-oriented treatment programs. They failed to uncover a connection between stress (negative affect) and relapse when considered on
a week-by-week basis. However, subjects frequently mentioned stress and
negative affect in their retrospective (after 12 weeks) accounts of relapse
situations. These authors speculated that the subjects' retrospective accounts may have been colored by their efforts to rationalize their recent
relapses. The researchers concluded their discussion by admonishing ex-
perimenters to exercise caution in interpreting retrospective reports of
substance-abusing subjects in research on the conditional determinants of
relapse behavior.

Hall et al.'s caveats notwithstanding, there may still be a meaningful
connection between stress-related negative affect and drug-seeking behavior, although this relationship is probably mediated by a number of other

variables. Marlatt, Kosturn, and Lang (1975), for instance, observed that heavy drinkers consumed considerably more ethanol when frustrated or provoked by an annoying confederate than heavy drinkers spared such an encounter. Marlatt et al. noted further that frustration and anger plummeted when subjects were given the opportunity to retaliate against the confederate through administration of a bogus electrical shock in a standard "teacher-learner" research paradigm. Hence, subjects faced with stressful life circumstances may be in a better position to regulate negative affect and prevent relapse if they have been instructed in alternative coping strategies to replace their previous reliance on alcohol and/or other drugs.

Because negative affect appears to be largely a matter of an inability to manage stress, it makes sense that stress management training should figure prominently in the treatment of clients reporting problems with negative affect. The power of stress management techniques like relaxation training (Davidson & Schwartz, 1976), meditation (Shapiro & Walsh, 1984), and biofeedback (Khatami, Mintz, & O'Brien, 1978) to achieve a calm, positive physical and mental state is well documented, although the direct applicability of these procedures to drug abuse is less thoroughly understood. Strickler, Bigelow, Wells, and Liebson (1977) utilized biofeedback training with a group of alcohol-abusing clients and found it to be an effective adjunct to other forms of alcohol abuse treatment; and Denney, Baugh, and Hardt (1991) found increased levels of abstinence in alcohol rehabilitation patients exposed to at least six biofeedback training sessions. Marlatt and Marques (1977) carried out a study in which heavy drinkers were randomly assigned to a progressive muscular relaxation, meditation, bibliotherapy, or no-treatment control group and discovered that shortly after treatment all three relaxation groups showed signs of improvement, but that these gains failed to persist through the follow-up evaluation conducted some 6 to 7 weeks later.

Therapists may also want to take advantage of the stress-reducing properties of aerobic exercise. Folkins and Sime (1981) have reviewed the literature on physical fitness and mental health and discovered that regular exercise may contribute to the formation of a lifestyle in which the individual exudes a general sense of well-being and enjoys improved sleeping habits, decreased negative affect, and an enhanced ability to handle stressful life events. Murphy, Pagano, and Marlatt (1986) reported that heavy drinkers are less likely to express a desire to drink if they have completed a jog at the end of the day. In this study, Murphy et al. compared subjects randomly assigned to a meditation group, an aerobic exercise group (30 min of running or a combination of running and walking), or a no-treatment control group. After 8 weeks of treatment, both the meditation and aerobic exercise groups displayed significant reductions in their alcohol intake, although only the exercise group registered outcomes superior to those recorded by the control group. Six weeks later, a follow-up indicated that 57% of the meditation group and 62% of the aerobic exercise group were still practicing their techniques. However, where the aerobic exercise group was using alcohol significantly less often than the control group, the meditation group had relapsed to a baseline (pretreatment) level of consumption.

Social skills training, where assertiveness, anger management, and communication skills are taught, is yet another way by which stress and negative affect may be mastered. One study found assertiveness skill deficits on the part of alcohol abusers (Miller & Eisler, 1977), and a second showed that alcoholics are no less skilled than social drinkers in general social situations but are significantly less skilled in alcohol-related social situations (Monti, Abrams, Binkoff, & Zwick, 1986). Be this as it may, assertiveness training has been found to be effective in the treatment of persons with substance abuse difficulties, particularly when refusal skills (i.e., resisting the pressure to drink: Chaney, O'Leary, & Marlatt, 1978) and behavioral rehearsal (i.e., role playing of assertive responses: Ingram & Salzberg, 1990) are included in the treatment package. Finally, studies contrasting the relative efficacy of interpersonal communication skills training with an intrapersonal coping skills program credit the former with being a better retardant of relapse than the latter (Monti et al., 1970; Rohsenow et al., 1991).

Cue Control

The opponent-process model of drug-seeking behavior attributes the subjective experience of craving to the presence of exteroceptive (external) cues that elicit a drug-opposite or homeostatic effect, which prepares the organism for drug ingestion (Siegel, 1988). In evaluating this hypothesis, McCusker and Brown (1990) discovered that subjects exposed to exteroceptive contextual cues linked to alcohol use (simulated lounge/bar) reported subjective feelings of craving for more alcohol, whether they consumed a small amount of alcohol or an alcohol-like placebo, to a significantly greater degree than subjects who consumed alcohol or an alcohol-like placebo in the absence of such cues. Binkoff et al. (1986) found that clients who reported more craving and anxiety in a role-play scenario where alcohol was present were at greater risk for alcohol consumption 6 months after treatment than clients who described lower levels of craving and anxiety in the same scenario. It has also been shown that alcohol-related cues can adversely affect an alcohol abuser's perceived ability to resist the urge to drink heavily (Sobell, Sobell, Toneatto, & Leo, 1993). The craving for opiates (Childress, McLellan, & O'Brien, 1986) and cocaine (Childress,

McLellan, Ehrman, & O'Brien, 1987) can also be explained, in part, by the action of exteroceptive contextual cues.

Interoceptive (internal) cues are also capable of eliciting urges, craving, and relapse, as represented by the reinstatement paradigm. This model holds that behaviors previously conditioned to the introduction of a chemical substance and subsequently extinguished can be reinstated through random noncontingent injections of the "training" substance. Reinstatement in animals has been shown to be pharmacologically specific, to the extent that drugs from the same general pharmacological class as the training drug elicit the conditioned response, whereas drugs with dissimilar pharmacological properties have no such effect (Young & Hurling, 1986). Reinstatement has been observed in humans trained on alcohol (Bigelow, Griffiths, & Liebson, 1977), amphetamines (Chait, Uhlenhuth, & Johanson, 1986), and morphine (Preston, Bigelow, Bickel, & Liebson, 1987). Other classes of interoceptive cues, such as drug-based rituals (behaviors leading to the procurement, preparation, and use of a substance that tend to be repeated in ritualistic fashion), positive outcome expectancies (Marlatt, 1985), and automatic and nonautomatic cognitive processes (Tiffany, 1990), are also capable of eliciting urges and precipitating relapse. Interoceptive cues are therefore defined as features of the internal physiological, subjective, or behavioral state of the individual that set the stage for future episodes of drug self-administration.

One way of reducing relapse-promoting urges is to eliminate the precipitating environmental cues, a procedure known as cue avoidance. Hinson, Poulos, Thomas, and Cappell (1986) noted that opiate-addicted rats often stopped self-administering morphine when they were placed in a new environment. The fact that only 12% of servicemen previously addicted to heroin in Vietnam became readdicted once back in the United States, even though half used heroin one or more times after their return (Robins, Davis, & Goodwin, 1974), has been attributed to cue-related factors, in that the stimulus (and interpersonal) conditions that supported heroin use in Vietnam were no longer present once the servicemen returned home (Siegel, 1988). To appreciate the significance of this finding, this 12% rate must be compared with the 90% rate of relapse traditionally obtained by treated opiate addicts who have returned to the environments in which they first acquired their heroin habit (Cushman, 1974). Studies conducted specifically on geographic change as a remedy for heroin abuse have found this procedure moderately effective in curtailing relapse in addicts living in Detroit, Michigan (Ross, 1973), San Antonio, Texas (Maddux & Desmond, 1982), and Sweden (Frykholm, 1979). Of course, environmental or geographic change as an intervention for cue-related craving is limited by the fact that cue avoidance is not always possible. As a consequence, other stimulus control procedures, such as extinction or cue exposure, must be considered.

The extinction paradigm calls for exposing individuals to urge-producing stimuli while preventing them from engaging in the behavior (drug use) that has relieved the craving in the past. Continued presentation of a craving-based stimulus in the absence of the prohibited behavior weakens the cue-behavior bond, thereby diluting the urge to use drugs. Blakey and Baker (1980) used this procedure successfully to treat a group of alcohol abusers; although alcohol-related urges and general anxiety rose in response to a series of alcohol-related cues (e.g., the sight and smell of alcohol), both fell to low levels of occurrence as treatment progressed. Cue exposure techniques have also been used to reduce craving in cocaine-dependent subjects (O'Brien, Childress, McLellan, & Ehrman, 1990). On the other hand, even though exteroceptive cues were found to stimulate craving in a group of heroin addicts, the capacity of cue exposure to lessen their urge to use drugs was limited (Powell et al., 1990). Cooney, Baker, and Pomerleau (1983) remarked that the efficacy of extinction and cue exposure strategies may be enhanced by using them in conjunction with cognitive control techniques like imagery, relabeling, and distraction.

Aversion therapy is another form of counterconditioning potentially capable of reducing or eliminating the craving brought on by alcohol- and drug-related cues. Disulfiram is a drug that, when taken regularly, causes an aversive reaction (nausea, headaches, vomiting) in the presence of alcohol. Early studies on disulfiram were quick to proclaim this substance as an effective treatment in the battle against alcoholism (see Liskow & Goodwin, 1987). More recently administered studies, however, have failed to furnish support for this procedure, because few meaningful differences have been noted between subjects randomly assigned to disulfiram and placebo therapy and followed for 1 or more years (Fuller, 1984). A major problem with disulfiram therapy is that it is an aversive technique self-administered by the client, who is free to stop taking the medication or to "drink over" the nausea produced by the disulfiram. Consequently, compliance and professional supervision are required for effective implementation. Studies show that this method of intervention is most effective with married clients who take their daily dose of disulfiram in the presence of their spouses (Azrin, Sisson, Meyers, & Godley, 1982).

Effective treatment of cue-related craving requires an appreciation of the interactive relationship between interoceptive and exteroceptive cues. It is well known that exteroceptive cues are capable of stimulating internal thoughts, feelings, and sensations that are interpreted by the subject as craving. It is also plausible, however, that interoceptive cues, whether in the form of expectancies, sensations, or drug-based rituals, may motivate the individual to seek out an environment (exteroceptive cues) in which drug use has previously taken place. Consequently, the union of extero-ceptive and interoceptive cues in both time and space is a particularly potent current-contextual exacerbating condition capable of producing re-lapse. Hence, effective treatment requires that both internal and external cues be addressed and that efforts be made to prevent the temporal and spatial intersection of these two forms of current-contextual influence, through effective management of both the person and his or her environment.

Access Reduction

It is only logical that drug abuse requires or presupposes access to abusable substances; thus, one way to reduce drug abuse is to limit the availability of drugs and restrict drug use opportunities. Crowley (1988), for instance, observed that pharmaceutical prescriptions for cocaine, benzodiazepine, methaqualone, and other abusable medications were 2 to 17 times more frequent in a Colorado ski community than in other areas of Colorado. This proportion was found to correlate with a similarly disproportionate number of adults classified as "involved and dysfunctional" drug abusers in the ski community (24.3%), compared with the state average of 6.8%. Likewise, a group of heroin addicts pointed to the accessibility of heroin as one of the primary reasons for their initial use of this substance (Simpson & Marsh, 1986). The availability of opiate drugs is also a common precip-itant of relapse after a period of treatment and/or voluntary abstinence, according to the self-reports of relapsing heroin addicts (Meyer & Mirin, 1979).

Studies supplying animals with unlimited access to cocaine show es-calated use and frequent toxicity over and above that observed in studies where access is controlled by the experimenter (Johanson, 1988). Avail-ability also appears to be an important source of influence in the abuse of substances during both the early (Gillmore et al., 1990) and advanced (Barrett, Joe, & Simpson, 1990) stages of a drug lifestyle. There are also data to suggest that a noticeable increase in the availability of drugs, as represented by a sudden rise in discretionary income, may promote ac-celerated drug use (Faupel & Klockars, 1987), although this effect does not operate independent of certain sociocultural influences and factors (see Caetano & Medina-Mora, 1988). Although availability operates at both the individual and group/community levels, individual-level access-reducing in-terventions, like throwing away cigarettes in response to a lapse on the part of someone trying to quit smoking (Brandon, Tiffany, & Baker, 1986), are probably less effective than group- or community-level interventions.

An access-limiting intervention occurring at the society or community level (strengthened intradiction policies) was primarily responsible for the 1972 East Coast heroin shortage that saw significant reductions in both drug use and drug-related crime (Research Triangle Institute, 1976). Moore (1984) notes that reducing the availability of alcohol by increasing the price has resulted in a lower rate of alcohol consumption, a decreased incidence of alcohol-related traffic fatalities, and a decline in the number of cirrhosis deaths in states and jurisdictions adhering to this policy of abated availability. In contrast, time series analyses of Iowa liquor sales subsequent to statewide privatization of bottled wine and liquor distribution show that the increased availability of alcohol created by privatization failed to exert a lasting effect on alcohol consumption in that state (Mulford, Ledolter, & Fitzgerald, 1992). These divergent outcomes may be attributed to variations in location, procedure, or focus (Moore was primarily concerned with efforts to reduce problem behavior by reducing availability, whereas Mulford et al. were interested in the effect of increased availability on alcohol consumption) between the two studies.

Modification of Interpersonal Relationships

Social pressure, in the form of verbal coercion and voluntarily establishing relationships with persons who use drugs, was the single most important determinant of relapse in a group of heroin addicts discussing their past difficulties with drugs (Marlatt & Gordon, 1980). It may be possible for a person to increase his or her prospects of remaining drug-free by avoiding areas where drug use is rampant and avoiding persons who are known to be actively involved in drug use. This hypothesis is supported by research showing that geographic change may prevent relapse in heroin addicts (Maddux & Desmond, 1982). However, there is no way to determine from the results of these studies whether the effect was a function of changed interpersonal relationships or the avoidance of drug-related cues. It does make sense that clients who avoid interpersonal situations where drugs are available have a better chance of remaining drug-free than clients who maintain regular contact with drug users. Replacing negative social affiliations with more positive associations is consequently an important feature of lifestyle change.

As noted in previous chapters, positive interpersonal relationships may serve to retard relapse by providing a constructive focus for clients interested in resisting temptation to use drugs. Booth, Russell, Soucek, and Laughlin (1992) note that support from family and friends predicted good adjustment in a group of persons released from an inpatient alcohol treatment program because of an increased sense of self-worth inspired by this interpersonal support. Of even greater significance is the fact that this effect was independent of patients' histories of prior treatment failure. Incorporating a social support segment into a televised smoking cessation intervention was shown to improve treatment outcomes over a 24-month period of follow-up (Gruder et al., 1993). Furthermore, alcohol abusers who abandoned an alcohol-based drug lifestyle reported that their actions were motivated by the formation of a new network of friends or the reestablishment of a previously supportive relationship (Vaillant & Milofsky, 1982; Tuchfeld, 1981). The development of positive interpersonal affiliations, however, requires a capacity for personal responsibility.

A procedure known as behavioral contracting, or contingency management, may be useful in stimulating and encouraging personal accountability in persons previously committed to a drug lifestyle. Bigelow, Stitzer, Griffiths, and Liebson (1981) demonstrate the applicability of contingency management principles to the treatment of substance abuse by suggesting that a therapist and client draw up a drug relapse prevention contract. According to Bigelow et al., the steps to be taken in the event of a relapse are clearly spelled out in the body of the contract, as are the consequences (such as donating money to an undesirable individual or political group) of violating any part of the agreement. In a recent clinical study on drug dependency using this and related techniques, contingency management and community reinforcement were found to be effectual in promoting initial cocaine and marijuana abstinence and sustaining cocaine, but not marijuana, abstinence 5 months subsequent to treatment termination (Budney, Higgins, Delaney, Kent, & Bickel, 1991).

Substitution

Abandoning a pleasurable or reinforcing activity like drug abuse often presupposes an ability to identify a suitable replacement. Cessation of drug lifestyle activities frequently leads to a sharp rise in discretionary or spare time. This time presents both a choice and a dilemma for a newly recovered individual, who must fill the void with constructive activities or risk returning to a self- and other-destructive pattern of behavior out of boredom. Vaillant and Milofsky (1982), for instance, found that nearly half the "successfully" recovering alcoholics they interviewed engaged in some form of substitute behavior. Their list of substitutes included candy, tobacco, marijuana, benzodiazepines, prayer or meditation, compulsive work habits, compulsive eating, compulsive gambling, and regular attendance at AA meetings. Persons who have exited alcohol-related lifestyles without benefit of treatment often cite the availability of and desire for non-alcohol-related substitute activities as vital to their continued abstinence (Ludwig, 1985; Tuchfeld, 1981). Furthermore, spontaneous recovery from alcohol, tobacco, or opiate abuse is often facilitated by identification of substitute activities, like jogging, meditation, and absorption in work, that serve to decrease the urge to use drugs and assist the client in finding purpose in life (Stall & Biernacki, 1986).

For substitution to be an effective means of conditional management, the new activities and social relationships must be more positive than the old. Joining a skydiving club, for example, might be a positive substitute for the excitement of a cocaine-centered lifestyle. Replacing alcohol with valium or tobacco would be less desirable than abstinence from all substances, although if the individual used these substances less often than alcohol, and/or these substances were less disruptive to the person's overall level of functioning, then a positive change would have taken place. Substitution, as conceived by lifestyle theory, presumes displacement of a harmful activity with a less harmful, harmless, or constructive activity. The odds of the new activity being constructive or harmless, rather than simply less harmful (and therefore presenting a strong likelihood of directing the individual back into a drug lifestyle), are enhanced if subjects address the current-contextual conditions that support their use of drugs and seek to improve their decision-making and self-evaluation skills, both of which will be discussed in subsequent sections of this chapter.

CHOICE-BASED INTERVENTIONS

The two principal pathways through which a change in choice behavior may be realized find their expression in option-augmenting strategies and competence-promoting strategies. Problem-solving training, which incorporates both the option-augmenting and competence-promoting functions into a single intervention, has been found to be particularly effective in reducing the probability of relapse in alcohol abusers (Chaney, O'Leary, & Marlatt, 1978) and heroin addicts (Platt & Metzger, 1987). Furthermore, it has been suggested that problem-solving training may be a cost-effective alternative or adjunct to traditional substance abuse treatment offered through employee assistance programs (Hermalin, Husband, & Platt, 1990). Platt, Perry, and Metzger (1980) implemented an interpersonal problem-solving approach with heroin-addicted adult male offenders and discerned significant treatment-control differences in drug use and criminal recommitments 2 years after treatment termination in favor of subjects given the problem-solving training.

Problem-solving training seems to be sufficiently effective for use with alcoholics and drug abusers. There are, however, certain conditions and parameters that may either enhance or limit the usefulness of this particular treatment approach. Modeling is critical to the success of problem-solving training and other skill-based approaches. Modeling of social and communication skills, for instance, was found to reinforce and extend the effect of social-communication skills training in a group of alcohol-dependent Veterans Administration (VA) inpatients (Monti et al., 1990). Behavioral rehearsal or role playing also contributes to the efficacy of interpersonal problem-solving training. Studies show that behavioral rehearsal effectively promotes change in persons previously dependent on alcohol (Sjoberg, Samsonowitz, & Olsson, 1978) and tobacco (Sjoberg & Johnson, 1978). Although the problem-solving model is composed of five stages—general orientation, problem definition, generation of alternatives, evaluation of alternatives, and verification (D'Zurilla & Goldfried, 1971)—this discussion will focus on the third and fourth stages, as represented by option-expansion and competence-promoting strategies.

Option-Expansion Strategies

Generating alternative solutions to a problem situation is an integral step to solving that problem; individuals can increase the odds of attaining an optimal solution by expanding their fund of knowledge and resources and exploring their options. From a program development point of view, there are a variety of ways by which a client may enlarge his or her repertoire of options—developing new interests, erecting new friendships, learning new skills. Because several of these option-expansion techniques were discussed earlier in this chapter, the present discussion concentrates on three visibly credible and situationally potent option-expansion techniques: training in lateral thinking, in social skills, and in basic life skills.

Lateral Thinking Skills   Thinking can be classified as either convergent or divergent. Whereas convergent thinking entails paring down alternatives in an effort to derive the optimal solution to a problem, divergent or lateral thinking is designed to expand a person's list of options. The fact that convergent thinking has been emphasized over lateral decisional processing in traditional educational circles has contributed to a choking off of creativity and innovation. Practical exercises were used by de Bono (1981) to illustrate the importance of suspending judgment, restructuring perception, and challenging accepted concepts in deriving solutions to various problem situations. With an eye toward facilitating recall of the critical features of the lateral thinking process, de Bono (1981) proposed several methods, two of which are discussed here. The PNI method refers to a procedure wherein the positive, negative, and interesting (PNI) aspects of an idea or concept are thoroughly explored before a decision is rendered. The acronym CAF (Consider All Factors) serves to remind the client that he or she must inhibit the natural tendency to react emotionally or impulsively to a new idea and consider how the idea or option may affect him- or herself, others, and society in general. Although de Bono's program requires empirical validation, it seems well suited to many of the goals of option-expansion forms of intervention.

Social Skills   Research indicates that the social skills of problem drinkers (Hover & Gaffney, 1991) and drug users (Linquist, Lindsay, & White, 1979) are deficient. Social skills training (SST) may therefore be of some assistance to persons with alcohol and/or other drug problems, despite evidence to suggest that, even though SST produces short-term reductions in substance use (Eriksen, Bjornstad, & Gertestam, 1986), its long-term benefits are uncertain (Hawkins, Catalano, Gillmore, & Wells, 1989). One subcategory of social skills intervention, communication skills training, shows promise for providing long-term benefit to substance abusers, particularly if family members are included in the treatment process (Sisson & Azrin, 1986). Even when family members are not included, social and communication skills training is capable of retarding relapse and facilitating recovery in persons previously committed to a drug lifestyle (Monti et al., 1990). There is also some indication that communication skills training may be applicable to a wider audience of clients than more traditional treatment strategies because it is less constrained by level of education, anxiety, substance abuse, and behavioral skill (Rohsenow et al., 1991).

Life Skills   The types of skills most people take for granted, whether they involve filling out a job application or shopping for groceries, are precisely the skills many drug-involved persons lack. Various life skill deficits, in fact, probably contribute to a significant portion of the relapses suffered by persons released from traditional drug treatment programs, where life skills training is often ignored. Basic life skills training is yet another option-expanding technique potentially capable of supporting recovery and preventing relapse in persons previously committed to a drug lifestyle. A recent review of life skills training suggests that such training may be effective in reducing alcohol consumption, cigarette smoking, and the frequency and volume of marijuana use in high-risk youths (Dusenbury & Botvin, 1992). The cultivation of occupational and educational skills may also serve a relapse-retarding function by increasing a person's opportunities for employment, participation in supportive social networks, and cognitive understanding.

Competence-Promoting Strategies

Before a client's decision-making competence can be addressed, he or she must appreciate, accept, and embrace the logic of the problem-solving process. Besides furnishing individuals with a mechanism for evaluating the relative strengths and weaknesses of various life options, competence-promoting treatment strategies call attention to the role of priorities and expectancies in the initiation, escalation, and cessation of drug lifestyle activities. Priorities are discussed next, under the heading of values-based interventions, and expectancies will be covered as part of the discussion on goal-setting interventions.

Values-Based Interventions   Students who endorse personal responsibility as a core value, particularly if this value is congruent with the opinions of parents and peers, earn higher achievement test scores and grades, meet with fewer school disciplinary problems, and are more apt to graduate from high school than students who do not view personal responsibility as important (Hanson & Ginsburg, 1988). Because values normally can be traced back to early childhood experiences, parents and peers play an integral role in molding a child's value system. Experiences during adolescence and early adulthood, however, also contribute to a person's constellation of life values. The practice of assigning social sanctions to normative experimental drug use is thought to promote subsequent drug use by branding the offending adolescent, encouraging him or her to adopt a deviant value system in an effort to cope with feelings of social alienation and rejection (Kaplan, Johnson, & Bailey, 1986). If Bush (1983) is correct in asserting that drug use is largely a matter of adopting deviant values, then effective treatment for substance abuse needs to address the issues of values clarification and reorientation.

Values clarification is a procedure in which personal values are identified, surveyed, and modified toward an ultimate goal of clarifying a person's priorities and reorienting his or her value system. Linkenbach (1990) describes a values clarification program developed at the Colorado State University Center for Alcohol Education in Fort Collins. Persons participating in this program are taught to actualize specific life options and enhance their decision-making competence by emphasizing empowerment and values reorientation over impotence and anomie in a nonthreatening environment where subjects are encouraged to explore their thoughts, feelings, and priorities. Brown and Peterson (1990) considered the assorted contributions of values reorientation training to traditional spirituality-oriented treatment, à la Alcoholics Anonymous, and report that this intervention is an effective means of addressing the elusive spirituality issue. The literature on values clarification as a treatment strategy for persons previously committed to a drug lifestyle implies that this is a potentially viable treatment approach, capable of identifying priorities, modifying the strength of values that support deviance, and reinforcing values that promote desirable behavior (Rokeach, 1983).

Logotherapy is another procedure potentially capable of stimulating the values reorientation process. Logoanalysts espouse an existential philosophy of intervention in which the client is presumed to have lost sight of basic life values and consequently to have become preoccupied with one or more features of the neurotic triad of addiction, aggression, and depression (Frankl, 1984). It has been noted that subjects completing a 10-week logotherapy experience prior to being discharged from a VA inpatient alcohol treatment program displayed greater behavioral change congruent with "quality sobriety" (follow-up questionnaire measuring alcohol consumption, AA attendance, and postrelease employment status) than program graduates who either did not participate in or did not complete the logotherapy (Hutzell, 1984). Although suggestive, these results are limited by the fact that the follow-up period was exceedingly short and varied across subjects (ranging from a few days to several weeks after discharge).

There are at least three advantages to using logotherapy to identify, clarify, and reorient personal values. First, many of the techniques can be integrated with and adapted to lifestyle theory (Walters, 1993). Second, a structured workbook of logotherapeutic exercises for the purpose of enacting systematic values-based interventions is available to clinicians (see Hutzell & Eggert, 1989). A sample exercise taken from Hutzell and Eggert's workbook is reproduced in Figure 9-1. Third, logotherapy not only considers the identification of basic values but also the development of goals (another form of intervention that can assist with the evaluation of alternative options) designed to actualize these values. A program capable of integrating values clarification with logotherapeutic principles by emphasizing the identification and modification of life priorities appears to be a particularly effective means of addressing the decision-making component of choice-based intervention.

Goal-Setting Interventions   The results of several studies indicate that impulsivity (Brook, Whiteman, Gordon, & Brook, 1983) and inadequate forethought or planning (Shedler & Block, 1990) frequently portend future drug-related problems. The goal-setting technique may therefore be a useful intervention strategy because it seems capable of addressing, and possibly ameliorating, the impulsivity and weak life direction of someone committed to a drug lifestyle. Interventions stemming from the goal-setting approach instruct the client in ways of identifying short-, intermediate-, and long-term goals by examining the anticipated short-, intermediate-, and long-term consequences of a particular action. Rohsenow, Beach, and Marlatt (1978) state that the probability of drug abuse is a complex function of the expected consequences of drinking, the subjective value assigned to each consequence, the anticipated probability that each consequence will occur, and the subjective expected immediacy of each consequence. These authors argue that negative consequences are generally not given the same measure of consideration as positive consequences because they are characteristically less immediate—a supposition that finds support in the results of a recent study by Leigh and Stacy (1993). Such clients must therefore be taught to balance long- and short-term goals and expectancies better.

RECENT EVENTS EXERCISE

In the left-hand column, list up to five recent events you attended by your own choice. In the right-hand column, list three values you would fulfill by attending

EVENT	VALUES

*   *   *

*   *   *

*   *   *

*   *   *

Figure 9-1. Logotherapy exercise (Hutzell & Eggert, 1989).

Drug expectancies have been studied using what has come to be called the balanced design. This design calls for random assignment of subjects to one of four conditions: expect drug and receive drug; expect drug and receive placebo (inert substance made to look and taste like the drug being tested); expect placebo and receive drug; expect placebo and receive placebo (Rohsenow & Marlatt, 1981). Studies employing this design note that the expectation of an effect for alcohol can produce a subjective reaction even in the absence of actual alcohol consumption. This expectancy effect is strongest for social behaviors like aggression (Lang, Goeckner, Adesso, & Marlatt, 1975) and sexual interest (Briddle et al., 1978) and weakest for physical effects like body sway and reaction time (Marlatt & Rohsenow, 1980). After consuming a beverage they were told contained alcohol (whether or not there was any ethanol present in the drink), heavy drinkers, 90% of whom held positive outcome expectancies toward alcohol, were less verbally aggressive when provoked and more liable to report feelings of pleasure than heavy drinkers who believed they were ingesting tonic water (Rohsenow & Bachorowski, 1984).

A study conducted by Mann, Chassin, and Sher (1987) demonstrated a clear relationship between expectancies and behavior. Light-drinking high school students reported expectations of altered social behavior with alcohol imbibition, whereas heavy-drinking students held alcohol-related expectancies of enhanced cognitive and motor functioning, tension reduction, and power attainment. In a study of alcoholic patients, Eastman and Norris (1982) observed that alcoholics who attributed positive outcomes to drinking and drunkenness were significantly more likely to suffer a relapse than alcoholics with negative expectancies. There is also confirmation of the observation that when the expected and actual effects of alcohol do not concur, as in someone who is experiencing a highly stressful situation or an increased tolerance to alcohol, a subject is motivated to augment alcohol intake as a means of achieving the anticipated effect (Fromme & Dunn, 1992). Along similar lines, other investigators have shown that expectancies may be more important than the amount of alcohol consumed in stimulating a desire for ethanol or initiating "loss of control" drinking in persons with a history of alcohol abuse difficulties (Berg, Laberg, Skutle, & Ohman, 1981; Marlatt, Demming, & Reid, 1973).

Of related interest in the implementation of the goal-setting technique is what is referred to by Marlatt and Gordon (1985) as Apparently Irrelevant Decisions (AIDs). These are seemingly inconsequential decisions that gradually lead the individual back into a drug lifestyle through a series of successive approximations. For example, a client may initiate the AIDs process by taking an innocent walk through his or her "old neighborhood." To take this scenario a step or two further, walking through the old neighborhood greatly increases the chances of encountering "old" drug associates. These encounters may then lead to intimate or extended contact with persons actively involved in the use of drugs, to the extent that the client eventually relapses. The point is that for persons intent on remaining drug-free, the path to relapse is marked by a series of decisions that may at first seem inconsequential, but that have the capacity to lure the individual insidiously back into a drug lifestyle. The client must therefore possess the requisite skills and knowledge to discontinue the decisional sequence while it is still in its infancy. These skills can be attained, in part, through the use of cognition-based intervention strategies.

COGNITION-BASED INTERVENTIONS

There are features unique to cognitive therapy that make it applicable in a variety of settings. These features are summarized in the following postulates (Dobson & Block, 1988):

1 Cognitive activity affects behavior;
2 Cognitive activity can be monitored; and
3 Cognitive activity can be modified to effect changes in behavior.

Thus, cognitive therapy forges a link between thought and action by asserting that thought is the principal cause of action. According to cognitive theory, a feeling or action is not principally attributable to any specific environmental event, but rather to the person's interpretation of that event. An individual who characteristically overreacts to problem situations will customarily respond to a lapse or slip by generating a string of negative or irrational self-statements that increase his or her probability of relapse. This approach contrasts sharply with that of an individual who assumes a coping posture in the face of disappointment and failure and views a lapse or slip as a cue to activate certain basic coping and self-management skills. Four models of cognitive intervention have been selected for review based on their current popularity and relevance to major features of lifestyle change. These four strategies are imagery training, self-regulation, cognitive reframing, and cognitive restructuring.

Imagery Training

Imagery training uses mental images to create a particular emotional state (e.g., disgust), physical condition (e.g., relaxation), or behavioral outcome (e.g., increased assertiveness). The principal advantage of imagery training in the treatment of alcohol and drug abuse is that it provides clients with a cognitive map for change. Its primary limitation is that not all clients possess strong visualization and mental imagery skills. More to the point with respect to cognitive change strategies for drug-involved persons, clients who have abused or continue to abuse substances may have definite problems generating the internal pictures necessary for successful implementation of the imagery technique due to the extreme external orientation adopted by many such individuals. Practical exercises for stimulating and expanding clients' visualization skills are available (see Sommer, 1978) and may well be worth the effort to employ, given the fact that Tarbox, Weigel, and Biggs (1985) found internal scanning ability to be prognostic of good treatment outcomes in a group of severe alcohol abusers.

The imagery technique has received scant attention from researchers in the drug abuse field, although imagery designed to induce a relaxed state has enjoyed some measure of success in the treatment of drug and alcohol abuse problems (Kutner & Zahourek, 1989). Marlatt and Gordon (1985) describe a procedure that makes liberal use of mental imagery in the management of drug urges. Their "urge surfing" technique entails visualizing the urge to use drugs as a wave, with peaks and valleys that a person can learn to control. With practice, clients can become quite proficient in managing urges using this technique, which in turn contributes to a growing sense of confidence and self-efficacy. Walters (1990) discusses the use of imagery in assembling a foundation for change as part of the functional model of lifestyle intervention (see Chapter 10). Although initially introduced for use with criminal populations, this technique appears to be just as useful in substance abuse treatment settings. Therapists utilizing this approach attempt to condition disgust to past lifestyle activities by directing the client to form visual images of the people they have harmed as a consequence of their involvement in a drug lifestyle and then pairing these negative images with the client's current desire to use drugs, past memories of drug use, or any drug-oriented thoughts the client may have.

Self-Regulation

There is every indication that clients who have trouble monitoring their behavior, regulating their impulses, and maintaining a goal-oriented attitude experience a higher rate of relapse than persons capable of self-regulation (Miller, 1991). Accordingly, self-regulation and self-control are two procedures of potential use in the treatment of individuals previously committed to a drug lifestyle. Research suggests that self-control and self-regulation procedures are superior to a purely educational approach (Brown, 1980) or no-treatment control (Harris & Miller, 1990) in managing the problem of excessive drinking. Rate control, limit setting, relationship enhancement, and other self-regulation strategies have been found to be effective in reducing alcohol consumption and alcohol-related problems in college students (Werch, 1990) and young adult felons (McMurran & Whitman, 1990). These procedures appear to have value in promoting abstinence in persons whose identified drug of abuse is heroin, cocaine, or alcohol (Wilkinson & LeBreton, 1986).

There is ample evidence to support the claim that self-monitoring alone may be sufficient to bring about a significant change in behavior in some situations (Emmelkamp, 1986). Clients who self-monitor their drinking behavior, for instance, have been known to reduce their alcohol intake based simply on this feedback (Skutle & Berg, 1987). The motivation or rationale for self-monitoring may also influence the efficacy of a self-regulation intervention, as shown by the results of a study by Greenfield, Guydish, and Temple (1989). These authors discerned that college students who engaged in self-regulation of alcohol use as a way of achieving increased intrinsic control over their actions were appreciably more successful in acquiring such control than students attempting to self-regulate alcohol in response to external pressure. Motivational enhancement may also be a powerful adjunct for use with self-regulation strategies, as shown by a study in which the introduction of a brief motivational component into a 6-week cognitive-behavioral self-monitoring program resulted in a 40% reduction in alcohol imbibition in moderately high-drinking young adults over that obtained by the cognitive-behavioral program alone (Baer et al., 1992).

Self-regulation in the form of cognitive-behavioral diversion may also assist in managing urges and craving. As discussed previously, there are a number of explanations for drug-related urges, several of which involve cognitive factors. Two of the more popular cognitive explanations for craving are Tiffany's (1990) automatic-nonautomatic cognitive processing model and Marlatt's (1985) positive outcome expectancy model. Even though cognitive stimuli may be managed with behavioral counterconditioning or stimulus control procedures, other forms of intervention are also possible. The simplest of these techniques, attention diversion, may be either cognitive (concentrating on a mental image or idea incompatible with the urge-provoking thought) or behavioral (engaging in an activity designed to divert attention away from the urge-provoking thought). Attention diversion strategies, like therapist-guided imagery and video game playing, have been found to be effective in reducing postsurgical pain (Pickett & Clum, 1982) and the nausea brought on by cancer treatment (Redd et al., 1987). Marlatt and Gordon (1985) discuss the use of diversion techniques in managing the urge to use drugs, although the efficacy of this approach is unknown at this time.

Cognitive Reframing

Cognitive reframing is a technique designed to modify a client's perception or interpretation of an event. Research indicates that cognitive reframing procedures facilitate the acquisition of problem-solving skills (Miller &

Osmunson, 1989). However, the primary application of cognitive reframing to the problem of substance abuse is as a method of preparing clients for the prospect of future lapses. Therapists employing this procedure encourage the client to reinterpret lapses as predictable occurrences with which they can cope. Marlatt and Gordon (1985) theorize that relapse is least likely in situations where lapses are reattributed to external, unstable, specific, and controllable factors. Although the available data have not always corroborated the validity of Marlatt and Gordon's ideas on attribution and relapse (Huselid, Self, & Gutierres, 1991), there is little question that preparing clients for lapses, and reframing these slips as learning experiences, can have an ameliorative effect on future relapse in both alcohol abusers (Rodin, 1976) and heroin addicts (McAuliffe & Ch'ien, 1986). A therapist should exercise caution, however, in utilizing this procedure with persons ambivalent about change because it could potentially provide a convenient excuse for drug use and relapse in persons less than fully committed to the treatment process.

Cognitive Restructuring

Cognitive restructuring represents a direct attack on the eight thinking styles that support a drug lifestyle. The manner of intervention that defines cognitive restructuring derives from the work of such notable theorist-clinicians as Aaron Beck (1976), Albert Ellis (1970), Donald Meichenbaum (1974), and Maxie Maultsby (1975). Interventions emanating from lifestyle theory, however, center on the eight thinking styles, rather than on Beck's cognitive distortions, Ellis' common irrational beliefs, Meichenbaum's self-talk, or Maultsby's self-defeating verbalizations. What follows is a brief review of treatment considerations with respect to each of the eight thinking patterns believed to support a drug lifestyle (see also Chapter 8).

Mollification People who attempt to evade responsibility for their behavior by shifting blame for their actions onto external circumstances, other people, or society in general tend to resist change. Attributing responsibility for drunken comportment to the inebriating effects of alcohol is one example of how mollification may encourage the display of behaviors that are normally inhibited when the individual is sober (Marlatt & Rohsenow, 1980). Rational confrontation and information-based approaches are two common forms of intervention for persons who defend their behavior on the basis of mollification. Reed and Janis (1974), for instance, presented a group of heavy smokers with common rationalizations for smoking behavior and then exposed half the group to a series of tape-recorded messages containing factual information rebutting each rationalization. Smokers who heard the tape-recorded messages subsequently displayed a less positive attitude toward smoking and a greater sense of vulnerability to the harmful effects of tobacco than smokers not exposed to the rebuttal.

Cutoff   The cutoff, also known as implosion, embodies the rapid elimination of common deterrents to drug use. This can be accomplished through a simple phrase ("fuck it") or mental image, or it may be accessed by use of a psychoactive compound (e.g., alcohol, cocaine, or heroin) that reduces inhibitions and interferes with judgment. It has been suggested that negative affect is a common cause of substance abuse relapse (Marlatt & Gordon, 1985). Lifestyle theory maintains that negative affect has the power to stimulate a cutoff response, particularly the "fuck it" mentality. It is difficult to address this response through a rationally based intervention because of the ardent spontaneity of the cutoff response; consequently, interventions directed at implosive self-talk must be preventive in nature. Whether the therapist employs stress management, emotions management (Ross & Fabiano, 1985), or anger control training (Novaco, 1975), instructing the client in ways of effectively managing negative affect can help avert the implosive flurry of emotion that frequently gives rise to a cutoff response.

Entitlement   Like each of the eight thinking patterns known to support a drug lifestyle, entitlement becomes automatic with practice. Therefore, even though the conditions that originally spawned a client's attitude of entitlement may be gone, their influence lingers, and because the connections between these formative conditions and the client's belief in entitlement have been severed by years of disuse, the client simply accepts entitlement as a "fact of life" and goes about reframing new experiences in light of this belief. As a person's preoccupation with drugs grows, so too does his or her attitude of entitlement. One feature of this progression is that the client eventually starts using his or her *addiction* to justify continued use of substances, on the basis of both mollification and entitlement. In fact, the tendency on the part of some professionals in the drug treatment community to overemphasize the physical roots of drug use and tolerance acts to reinforce entitlement in the minds of many drug-involved persons. Accordingly, the therapist must offer a vigorous challenge to a client's attitude of entitlement through a rational examination of the client's inflated sense of privilege and propensity to misidentify wants as needs.

Power Orientation   Drug abusers look to gain external power and control as a means of compensating for feelings of inadequacy and low self-esteem. Penk, Robinowitz, and Fudge (1978) noted a high degree of drug abuse in persons who felt thwarted in attaining power and achieving goals. It is speculated that when power-oriented people are impeded in their attempts to achieve external control, they look to alternative avenues of expression; but, lacking a clear sense of internalized self-discipline, they pursue an external solution (i.e., drugs) to an internal problem (i.e., existential fear). Lifestyle theory argues that mood manipulation made possible through drug use is highly reinforcing in such an individual. Therapeutic interventions directed at power orientation require the use of both cognitive and behavioral strategies. Cognitively, the belief that external control is the preeminent goal in life must be challenged; the therapist should encourage the client to explore alternative life views (e.g., self-control, interpersonal cooperation). Behaviorally, response prevention may be of some value in reducing a client's power-thrusting inclinations. To be effective, however, this procedure must be conducted in a highly controlled setting where the client is provoked to anger, prevented from engaging in a power thrust, and guided through the use of alternative forms of anger management (e.g., relaxation, negotiation, rational thinking).

Sentimentality   The "good guy" image many drug abusers cultivate to justify and excuse their drug-seeking lifestyle is considered a clear example of sentimentality and a prime target for intervention. Sentimentality may be addressed through the following sample exercise: After instructing the client to divide a sheet of paper into two columns, the therapist asks the client to list the positive actions taken over a specified period of time in the left-hand column and any negative actions performed during the same time period in the right-hand column. Once this has been accomplished, the client is queried as to whether the positive behaviors in the left-hand column compensate for the negative behaviors listed on the opposite side of the page. If the client is at all honest, he or she will find it difficult to justify right-hand column behaviors on the basis of left-hand column activities. A direct confrontation of the client's past efforts at sentimentality may therefore be the most effective avenue of intervention for this thought process. However, the therapist should avoid offering too vigorous a challenge to sentimentality until the client has started forming alternative strategies of guilt management, because sentimentality is frequently a client's chief defense against the pangs of conscience.

Superoptimism   The very act of seeking (or being coerced into seeking) treatment for a drug problem contradicts the superoptimistic attitude that one can escape the negative consequences of a drug lifestyle. Even clients who have minimal investment in the treatment process appear willing to accept the fact that superoptimism played a role in their actions. Unfortunately, this dawning realization is sometimes accompanied by a new shade of superoptimism, in which clients believe they will be able to manipulate their way out of problem situations or change their lifestyles with minimal effort. Rychtarik, Prue, Rapp, & King (1992) speculate that one of the chief reasons discharge self-efficacy ratings are so ineffective in predicting release outcome is that many program graduates have an inflated sense of self-efficacy that borders on superoptimism. The overriding intent of rational restructuring is to expose the irrational roots of this particular style of thought by illustrating how inconsistent it is with objective reality and then to provide the client with realistic alternatives. It is also important to keep in mind that reasoned self-confidence is the natural product of a therapeutic program that teaches clients basic social and coping skills and provides them with the opportunity for success and the development of a general sense of accomplishment.

Cognitive Indolence   The lazy, shortcut thinking that leads many drug abusers to sacrifice long-term satisfaction in the name of immediate gratification is referred to by lifestyle theory as cognitive indolence. The results of one study uncovered reduced vigilance, a hallmark of cognitive indolence, in the thinking of treated heroin addicts headed for relapse (Litman et al., 1983). It is well to keep in mind, then, that cognitive indolence, like superoptimism, is a major cause of initial treatment failure. Increased vigilance and critical reasoning skills are vital to the preservation of treatment gains, and cognitive indolence promotes a style of thinking that runs counter to these ideals. Absent strong vigilance and critical reasoning skills, a client is at the mercy of the automatic drug-oriented thoughts that have created problems in the past and that, if left unchecked, substantially increase the risk of relapse at some point in the future. Critical reasoning skill deficiencies must be ameliorated if the client is to have a reasonable chance of remaining drug-free upon being released from treatment.

Discontinuity   In contrast to superoptimism, which is relatively easy to spot, discontinuity is exceedingly difficult to identify and highly resistant to change. It is a function of thought process rather than thought content, whereas superoptimism is more reflective of thought content. These factors make discontinuity a particularly elusive target for intervention. Goal-setting techniques can be efficacious in establishing continuity of thought, as can regular and consistent feedback. This last point illustrates the preferability of conducting lifestyle interventions in a group setting. Yochelson and Samenow (1976) present a self-monitoring technique that is potentially applicable to interventions aimed at modifying the discontinuity of a drug lifestyle. This procedure calls for the documentation of unedited thoughts as they occur to the client over the course of a day. Self-monitoring not only provides the client with an opportunity to observe discontinuity, but may also ameliorate the problem to some extent, because self-monitoring alone can sometimes produce a reduction in the behavior (or cognition) being monitored (Emmelkamp, 1986).

CONCLUSION

Whether the purpose of an intervention is to assist clients in managing current-contextual conditions, making better choices, or controlling their thinking, the primary objective for therapists using the structural model of lifestyle intervention is to define targets for change. The implementation of such a program, however, demands that a comprehensive assessment of pertinent issues, skills, and behaviors take place, because not all program participants require the same level or type of assistance. Exposing a client with a master's degree in chemical engineering to job skills training makes about as much sense as teaching social skills to an insurance salesman or a politician, both of whom have probably spent many years developing the fine art of persuasion. However, job skills training would be invaluable to a client with no work history, and social skills training would be indispensable for a client who lacks poise in interpersonal situations or who has trouble standing up for his or her rights. Consequently, a purposeful and continuing assessment of major skill areas is imperative in effective drug abuse programming as a way of pinpointing areas of deficit and eliminating treatment goals that are superfluous to a client's assessed needs.

The structural model of lifestyle intervention does a creditable job of identifying targets for change. There is at least one area, however, that is not covered by the structural model: the affective features of a drug lifestyle. Structural lifestyle interventions are normally directed at specific cognitive and behavioral targets, because they tend to be more amenable to change than the affective responses for which they are responsible. Equally important is that fact that when a client begins mastering his or her thinking and behavior through reconditioning, skills training, cognitive restructuring, and priority reorientation, a positive affective change frequently follows (Baker, 1969). Self-worth, self-esteem, and an increasingly positive outlook on life are therefore potential side benefits of effective cognitive-behavioral intervention. To the extent that the affective features of a drug lifestyle are causally linked to a client's current difficulties, these factors should also be addressed directly. This is the topic of the next chapter.

Chapter 10

Functional Model of Lifestyle Intervention

INTRODUCTION

Conceptually, the core goal of functional lifestyle intervention is to enhance a client's adaptive resources. It is exceedingly difficult, however, to effect change in someone who is actively using drugs. Hence, the first goal of intervention is to arrest, at least momentarily, lifestyle activities. Cessation of drug use can occur in response to external pressure from others (e.g., an ultimatum from a spouse or employer), placement in a situation where the opportunity to use drugs is severely restricted (e.g., in a prison or hospital), or formation of a temporary sense of disgust with the negative consequences of a drug lifestyle (which in some circles is referred to as "hitting bottom"). Once a drug lifestyle has been temporarily arrested, the next step is to prevent relapse by arming the client with fundamental thinking and coping skills and general life management ability. The third goal of functional lifestyle intervention is to arrange effective aftercare and follow-up services.

The three goals of functional lifestyle intervention described in the preceding paragraph correspond in general to the three stages of process intervention described in Walters' (1990) work on the criminal lifestyle. From this point on in this chapter, *functional intervention*, *process intervention*, and *intervention* will be used interchangeably.

The foundation for change is the initial stage of functional (or process) intervention. Here, with the assistance of mental imagery techniques and what lifestyle theory refers to as the attribution triad, the individual acquires a sense of disgust with his or her past drug-related activities and current drug-oriented thinking as a means of arresting lifestyle development and terminating various lifestyle activities and commitments. Once this foundation has been laid and the lifestyle has been interrupted, the next step in the treatment process is to assist the client in identifying, developing, and applying vehicles for change. This stage is designed to actualize the second goal of functional lifestyle intervention by instructing the client in basic coping, social, thinking, and life management skills. The third and final stage of the treatment process is the erection of a reinforcing nondrug lifestyle through implementation of a formal system of community follow-up, which coincides with the third goal of functional lifestyle intervention.

Since lifestyle theory equates mental health and psychological efficiency with adaptation, it should come as no surprise that the overriding purpose of functional lifestyle intervention is to stimulate, promote, and enlist a client's adaptive resources. Whereas a drug lifestyle encourages entrenchment, adaptation fosters change. Due to the regressive, defensive nature of a drug or other lifestyle, persons who engage in a lifestyle follow a desultory life pattern. The drug lifestyle insulates clients from the reality of their situations, making it all but impossible for them to take full advantage of sundry learning opportunities. Supplying these individuals with a sense of direction by reinforcing their adaptive resources is consequently one of the principal goals of lifestyle intervention. Achieving this goal, however, requires considerable time and effort, as well as reliance on the three phases of functional lifestyle intervention: that is, the foundation, vehicles for change, and reinforcing the nondrug lifestyle stages of the lifestyle change process.

FOUNDATION

The first phase, the foundation for change, is defined by lifestyle theory as disgust with past drug-related activities and current drug-oriented thinking. In encouraging clients to adopt a different perspective on their past behavioral difficulties, lifestyle theory seeks to replace the excitement and rewards of a drug lifestyle with revulsion, using principles borrowed from social learning theory and the classical conditioning model of human behavior. This foundation not only provides the client with a rudimentary sense of direction, but also counteracts the drug abuser's natural inclination to be inconsistent and lazy. It may be based on images of people the subject has harmed, directly or indirectly, as a consequence of involvement in a drug lifestyle, or it may be subsumed in a growing fear of repercussions. Either way, the foundation for change has a sobering effect on the individual and may be viewed by some clients as unnecessarily negative. What such clients must realize is that, while the foundation may create an uncomfortable affective state, these feelings are essential to the formation of a healthy substructure for personal growth and change. The attribution triad can be particularly helpful in forming and supporting a foundation for change.

Attribution Triad

Attribution is the process of drawing causal inferences about another person's motives and intentions from observations of that person's behavior. Attribution considers several key behavioral elements, none more important than perceived locus of causality. This facet of human cogitation determines whether the observer views the subject's behavior as dispositional (internal) or situational (external) in nature. Kelley (1973) argues that the internal-external attribution decision is composed of three elements: behavioral consensus, consistency, and distinction. An internal attribution is made in situations where the observer believes the subject has acted in a manner different from the way most other people would have acted under similar circumstances (low consensus), but which is consistent for the subject under similar (high consistency) and dissimilar (low distinctiveness) circumstances. High consensus, low consistency, and high distinctiveness, on the other hand, are associated with external attributions.

Attribution also influences how an individual views his or her own behavior. Weiner (1974) has argued that attributions for success and failure vary along three dimensions and have direct applicability to self-perception and self-attributions. These three dimensions include locus of causality (whether the cause is perceived to be internal or external), stability (whether the causative factors are perceived to be stable or unstable), and controllability (whether the causative factors are perceived to be within or outside an individual's volitional control). Abramson, Seligman, and Teasdale (1978) identified a fourth dimension, global versus specific, in their attempts to formulate an attribution-based theory of clinical depression. This fourth dimension appears to be potentially relevant for research into the self-perceptions of drug abusers and has found its way into Marlatt and Gordon's (1985) relapse prevention model of substance abuse treatment.

Attribution errors also interest psychologists and others who study human comportment. For example, one such error, the fundamental attribution error, occurs when the subject overestimates the effect of internal dispositions on behavior and underestimates the effect of situational factors. This perception is selective, however, in that most people choose to attribute dispositional causes to others and situational causes to themselves. This is the second attribution error, known in attribution circles as the actor–observer effect. A third common form of attribution error is self-serving bias, where the subject attributes success to stable internal factors and failure to unstable external ones. This particular error serves to protect the subject's self-esteem by minimizing self-blame in situations when the subject falls short of his or her goals (Weary et al., 1982). These three errors form the nucleus of attribution theory's views on the development of self- and other-perception.

The degree to which a recovering drug abuser attributes his or her success to stable internal factors and his or her initial lapses to unstable situational factors is said to correlate with the ability to avoid relapse (Marlatt & Gordon, 1985). Coggans and Davies (1988) interviewed a group of heroin addicts, and, consistent with the theories of Marlatt and Gordon, found evidence of an actor-observer effect: Better-outcome subjects believed that their drug use was motivated by positive factors and that they possessed the requisite skills to stop using drugs once they experienced negative consequences, whereas they viewed others as using drugs for the purpose of alleviating negative affect. However, results incompatible with Marlatt and Gordon's position on the facilitative role of attribution-based errors in preventing future occurrences of substance abuse have also been recorded (see Huselid, Self, & Gutierres, 1991).

One reason for the lack of congruence in studies on attribution bias is that such bias does not lend itself to simple, unitary analysis; it comprises a complicated network of components that are only modestly correlated with one another (Iso-Abola, 1985). This factor has led to the conceptualization of a tripartite system of beliefs referred to by lifestyle theory as the attribution triad. The attribution triad is considered a prerequisite for change; it is thought that clients lacking any portion of it will retain insufficient motivation and confidence to commence, let alone complete, the change process. The attribution triad consists of: belief in the necessity of change, belief in the possibility of change, and belief in one's own ability to effect change. These three beliefs will be examined next, followed by a discussion of the other two stages of functional lifestyle intervention: vehicles for change and a reinforcing nondrug lifestyle.

Belief in the Necessity of Change Problem resolution or behavioral transition requires that one assume accountability for the problem or behavior. Although lifestyle theory is more than willing to concede that external conditions can influence the onset and evolution of a problem behavior, it also maintains that the individual must accept responsibility for his or her part in the problem and work to rectify the thoughts, actions, and feelings that support it. These issues speak directly to the attribution-of-blame component of the attribution triad—the belief in the necessity of change. Blaming one's problems on external factors (other people's actions, environmental conditions, bad luck) interferes with the change process because change must come from within. Persons committed to a drug lifestyle, however, often demand that their surroundings change in the belief that these external conditions are responsible for their problem. Drug-abusing patients interviewed by Obitz, Cooper, and Madeiros (1974), for example, were more likely to attribute life outcomes to luck, destiny, or other people than non-using controls. Lifestyle theory argues that this style of thought is conducive to entrenchment rather than adaptation; accepting responsibility is a necessary, although not sufficient, condition for change.

Identification and amelioration of a problem situation require avoidance of the natural human tendency to offer rationalizations for one's conduct in place of accepting full responsibility. There is evidence that self-blame facilitates the change process by arming the individual with an increased sense of personal control over future negative events (Janoff-Bulman, 1979). Studying this issue in a group of 80 opiate addicts, Bradley, Gossop, Brewin, Phillips, and Green (1992) discovered that opiate addicts who accepted greater personal responsibility for negative life outcomes relapsed less often than addicts expressing no or little interest in accepting personal responsibility. Baumann, Orbitz, and Reich (1982) witnessed an attributional shift in male alcohol abusers, marked by increased congruence with the attributions of non-abusing controls, over the course of treatment. An internal orientation appears to be conducive to the formation of personal responsibility in clients enrolled in drug rehabilitation programming, whereas an external orientation may encourage continued drug use by projecting blame onto others and fostering an attitude of denial. Strassberg and Robinson (1974) note that heroin addicts with a more internalized locus of control enjoy higher self-esteem, better psychological adjustment, and more encouraging treatment outcomes than addicts with an external locus of control.

On the basis of the preceding discussion, it makes sense that failure to accept responsibility for one's actions creates personal and interpersonal problems and impedes change. How, then, is it possible to effect acceptance of personal responsibility in clients who insist on seeing themselves as victims of diabolical life circumstances? There is little a therapist can do to convince individuals of their personal responsibility if they are unwilling to examine their behavior. Many people who enter into a drug abuse treatment program, however, have experienced difficulties relative to their lifestyle and therefore may be receptive, at least temporarily, to intros- pection. Even when a client has been forced into treatment and is ambi- valent toward or resists change, the events leading up to involuntary con- finement in a hospital or jail may spark a transient interest in the prospect of change, which can be exploited by the therapist for the purpose of entering into a therapeutic alliance with the client. For clients who express a passing interest in change but who do not possess a belief in the its necessity, procedures like reattributional training (Forsterling, 1985) may be of assistance, although such training has been known to exacerbate depressive symptoms in vulnerable clients. For this reason, a thorough clinical evaluation should be conducted prior to using this procedure.

Lifestyle theory views development of belief in the necessity of change as a three-step process. The first step is to educate the client about choice and personal responsibility. It is sometimes helpful to have a client draw up lists of situations in which he or she has encountered problems with alcohol or other drugs. If the client has been engaged in a drug lifestyle for any length of time, then this exercise should yield a diverse list of such situations. The second step, or follow-up, is to have the client realize that because he or she is the common denominator in all the problem situations listed, he or she must assume a rightful share of responsibility for these problems before meaningful change can occur. The third step in the de- velopment of a belief in the necessity of change is to challenge thinking patterns that minimize personal responsibility—mollification and senti- mentality in particular. It is crucial that the therapist lay bare the irrational and self-defeating roots of these thinking patterns and work toward a rapprochement of rational thinking and constructive behavior. Although none of these steps are guaranteed to inspire a belief in the necessity of change, they can be helpful in establishing the proper conditions for an evolving sense of personal responsibility.

Belief in the Possibility of Change.   Like belief in the necessity of change, belief in the *possibility* of change is a precondition for self-modi- fication. Simply believing that one is responsible for a particular problem behavior will have little bearing on future treatment outcomes if one does not also believe that change is personally attainable. Therefore, the first two components of the attribution triad are complementary. Fisher and Farina (1979), for instance, reported that patients furnished with a bio- logical or genetic interpretation of a problem behavior were much less likely to cope constructively with the problem and its consequences than patients provided with a social learning interpretation. It is also worth noting that subjects receiving treatment for insomnia were better able to avoid relapse if they were led to attribute improvement to their own actions (relaxation training and time management) rather than to an optimal dosage of sleeping medication (Davison, Tsujimoto, & Glaros, 1973). Likewise, subjects receiving intrinsic self-help training in smoking cessation made fewer external attributions for success and remained abstinent longer than subjects treated solely or principally with nicotine gum (Harackiewicz, Sansone, Blair, Epstein, & Manderlink, 1987).

With the possibility of change comes the possibility of relapse. While it is critical that successes be attributed to the actions of the individual, it is equally imperative that failures be attributed to potentially controllable events and situations. Hence, attributions that hold external circumstances responsible for an initial lapse reduce an individual's chances of continued use and eventual relapse (Kirschenbaum & Tomanken, 1982). Marlatt and Gordon (1985) add that persons who attribute lapses and slips to global, stable deficiencies (e.g., lack of will power) are at much greater risk for relapse than persons who attribute lapses to a specific, unstable cause (e.g., temporary lack of effort brought on by fatigue). Gutierres and Reich (1988) noted that whereas self-esteem rose over the course of treatment in a therapeutic community, only attributional style (dispositional for success, situational for failure) effectively predicted reduced levels of drug use and criminality 3 months after treatment termination. Program efficacy apparently depends not only on clients' taking responsibility for their own actions, but also on their attributing success to personal resolve and failure to coping skill deficits that can be remedied through learning, practice, and increased effort.

The possibility of change can be demonstrated to clients using Ellis' (1970) rational-emotive imagery technique. This procedure calls for the recollection of an event about which the client has experienced anger, depression, or fear. Upon recapturing the negative feelings associated with this event, the client is instructed to rate the emotion on a scale from 1 (a very low level of emotion) to 10 (a very high level). The therapist then guides the client down the scale to diminish the negative feelings and then asks, first, whether the client was successful in descending the scale, and, second, how he or she was able to accomplish this seemingly arduous task. Most clients are able to move down at least three or four levels, and most responses indicate that a change in thought or perception preceded the movement down the scale. This simple exercise not only illustrates the possibility of change but also provides a mechanism (cognitive modification) through which such change can be realized. Another procedure useful in illustrating the possibility of change is to expose program participants to persons who have successfully abandoned the drug lifestyle, who can provide participants with some understanding of the problems and possibilities they will encounter as they themselves attempt to exit the drug lifestyle.

The necessity, inevitability, and possibility of change must be clearly defined for clients. It is essential, therefore, that therapists discuss with clients the fact that change, although possible, can be a difficult and frustrating process. Anguish, disappointment, and emotional discomfort must be anticipated and managed effectively. Summoning the courage to confront their fears is consequently a critical step in clients' construction of a belief in the possibility of change. It may be useful to share with clients the observation that hiding from fear by seeking refuge in a lifestyle simply reinforces the fear, making them less adaptable and increasing their chances of winding up in a prison, hospital, or morgue. To prevent such an occurrence, clients must develop a belief in the possibility of personal change. With this possibility, however, comes the responsibility of pursuing whatever resources are available to expand options, enhance decision-making capabilities, and minimize irrational, self-defeating forms of mentation.

Belief in One's Ability To Effect Change   One can recognize that change is both necessary and possible, yet still not be prepared for it due to a lack of confidence in one's ability to bring it about. This particular branch of the attribution triad derives from Bandura's (1982) work on self-efficacy, a concept he defines as a person's perceived confidence in his or her ability to cope with a specific prospective situation. There are four sources of information on which self-efficacy judgments are based—performance accomplishments, vicarious observation of others' behavior, external persuasion and social influence, and emotional arousal—and three primary dimensions along which self-efficacy judgments may vary—level, strength, and generality (Bandura, 1982). Marlatt, who has extended Bandura's self-efficacy conceptualization to substance abuse treatment, argues that motivation is a necessary, but not sufficient, condition for change. He states further that clients must retain the requisite coping skills and self-efficacy for change to occur (Marlatt & Gordon, 1985). High-risk situations stimulate conflict between the motive for change and the desire to yield to the impulse to engage in lifestyle activities; self-efficacy enters into the equation on behalf of the motive for change.

Self-efficacy consists of a cognitive appraisal of one's ability to cope with a particular situation; it is known to correspond with decreased levels of alcohol consumption (Sitharthan & Kavanagh, 1990) and increased willingness to enroll in aftercare programming on the part of clients previously dependent on drugs (Heller & Krauss, 1991). Condiotte and Lichtenstein (1981) measured self-efficacy in persons participating in one of two smoking cessation programs and determined that self-efficacy rose over the course of treatment, accurately predicted relapse, and pinpointed the circumstances under which specific clients relapsed. In other words, clients who demonstrated little confidence in their ability to resist the temptation to use drugs in the presence of old drug associates normally relapsed in response to social pressure; clients reporting minimal self-efficacy in managing stress without drugs normally relapsed in response to feelings of anger, depression, and frustration.

The situational specificity of the self-efficacy concept reflects the concept's behavioral roots and provides potential avenues for remediation. Examining a group of female alcohol abusers, Rist and Watzl (1983) ascertained that subjects who reported low self-efficacy in alcohol-related situations were more apt to relapse than subjects reporting high self-efficacy in the same situations. However, relapsing and nonrelapsing subjects did not display different patterns of self-efficacy in situations not related to alcohol. Of equal significance is the fact that self-efficacy is most reliably correlated with relapse during the first several months of the postrelease period (Rychtarik, Prue, Rapp, & King, 1992). This finding suggests that low self-efficacy creates problems for newly released clients and also demonstrates a decreasing level of predictive value over time, perhaps because self-efficacy grows as a client's interval of drug-free living lengthens.

There is little doubt that self-efficacy plays a pivotal role in the success of drug abuse treatment. There is some question, however, as to when in the treatment process self-efficacy should be assessed. Solomon and Annis (1990) noted that self-efficacy measures taken during the intake phase of treatment, but not at discharge, correlated with alcohol relapse 3 months after treatment, as opposed to Baer, Holt, and Lichtenstein (1986), who recorded a relationship between discharge self-efficacy and relapse in smokers 6 months posttreatment. Burling, Reilly, Moltzen, and Ziff (1989), on the other hand, discerned that self-efficacy measures taken at intake and discharge were equally ineffective in predicting relapse, although an increase in self-efficacy from intake to discharge was a good prognostic sign. More recently, Rychtarik et al. (1992) uncovered a meaningful connection between intake, but not discharge, measures of self-efficacy and increased involvement in aftercare and decreased rates of relapse in 87 male alcohol abuse patients 6 months to 1 year after their release from a Veterans Administration inpatient alcohol treatment program. These authors speculate that discharge self-efficacy measures may be ineffective in predicting release outcome because some clients overestimate their level of self-efficacy on being discharged from a substance abuse program.

The first step in teaching self-efficacy is to obtain an accurate estimate of this particular precondition for change. Self-efficacy instruments have been constructed for the purpose of assessing a client's belief in his or her ability to master such diverse challenges as stuttering (Ornstein & Manning, 1985), infant care (Froman & Owen, 1989), and computer skills (Murphy, Coover, & Owen, 1989), as well as such traditional substance abuse concerns as drug-seeking behavior (Annis & Davis, 1988), alcohol consumption (Annis, 1982), and tobacco use (Condiotte & Lichtenstein, 1981). Once areas of low self-efficacy have been identified, the next step is to provide remediation. Goldfried and Robins (1982), in their work on the facilitation of self-efficacy, describe cognitive strategies for enhancing self-efficacy, and Marlatt and Gordon (1985) review ways by which self-efficacy may be reinforced in persons previously committed to a drug lifestyle. Hence, self-efficacy, like the other two components of the attribution triad, must be modeled, learned, and nurtured before it can exert a positive effect on behavior.

VEHICLES FOR CHANGE

Once a reasonably solid foundation has been laid, the next stage of functional lifestyle intervention involves identifying vehicles for change. These vehicles are programs, activities, and experiences employed by the individual to challenge drug-oriented thoughts and actions. Another way to conceive of vehicles is as agents designed to separate the individual from a past drug lifestyle by increasing his or her adaptive resources. Many of the strategies outlined in Chapter 9 (e.g., problem solving, goal setting, lateral thinking) serve as potential vehicles of change, because lifestyle theory is primarily concerned with skill development—enhancing a person's adaptive resources and decreasing reliance on lifestyle activities—to manage existential fear and its derivatives. This review of vehicles for change would be incomplete, however, if on fear-centered intervention strategies and the role of affect in treatment were not at least mentioned.

Fear-Centered Intervention

Although it is true that lifestyle theory takes a cognitive-behavioral approach to treatment, this approach does not mean that lifestyle theory ignores a client's feelings. Lifestyle interventions are normally directed at the cognitive and behavioral targets responsible for affective reactions because these are generally more amenable to modification than the reactions themselves. In other words, it is as clients begin to achieve a sense of mastery over their thinking and behavior, via reconditioning, skills training, cognitive restructuring, or priority reorientation, that they also begin to feel better about themselves (Baker, 1969). Self-worth, self-esteem, and an increasingly positive outlook on life are all potential benefits of the interventions aimed at specific cognitive and behavioral markers. Nonetheless, affect and emotion should be included in the treatment package and warrant attention in proportion to the extent to which they are causally linked to a client's current difficulties. This appears to be the case, in particular, when addressing the issue of existential fear.

Fear, according to lifestyle theory, is an existential condition from which there is no escape. The fear that gives rise to a drug lifestyle can be characterized as a fear of change. To counter this fear, interventions need to be directed at reinforcing clients' adaptive resources and addressing the secondary and tertiary fears that spring from it. These secondary and tertiary fears normally find their expression in the later life tasks (see Chapter 6), which continue to evolve over the course of a person's life. By way of review, the later life tasks occur in three domains of human experience: the social, physical, and psychological domains of the Person × Situation interaction. The later life task that unfolds from the early life task of attachment, and that owes its existence to interactions in the social domain, is referred to as social bonding/empathy. The early life task of stimulus modulation interacts with other variables in the physical domain to give rise to the later life task of internal-external orientation, and the early life task of self-image interacts with variables in the psychological domain to evolve into the later life task of role identity.

Whereas the primordial or existential fear, which gives birth to secondary and tertiary characterizations of fear, is often free-floating, the fears that influence resolution of the later life tasks normally congregate around specific situations, events, people, and themes. Take, for instance, the case of the later life task of social bonding/empathy. Here, the predominant concern is fear of rejection. People may cope with this fear by rejecting others before they have a chance to be rejected themselves. In so doing, they retreat into superficial interpersonal relationships that serve as their primary source of social interaction and support. Social skills training can be helpful in encouraging adaptation and relationships in which intimacy, honesty, and commitment predominate over immediacy, exploitation, and triviality. However, it is also imperative that the fear of rejection be addressed and the necessity of taking positive risks in the development of pro-social interpersonal relationships be stressed as part of a comprehensive treatment program for drug abusers, some of whom have never known intimacy or commitment in their interactions with others.

The fears that emanate from interactions in the physical domain (internal-external orientation) often concern the issue of control. Individuals who are committed to a drug lifestyle strive for interpersonal power or manipulate their mood with drugs because they fear being unable to exert self-control through self-discipline. Looking for an external solution to an internal problem, such persons erroneously conclude that their fear of losing control can be effectively managed by exerting power over others or by ingesting drugs capable of providing them with temporary respite from their feelings of powerlessness. Evidence of an external orientation in drug abusers (Wexler, 1975) has been reported in the literature, although a great deal more work needs to be done before an external orientation can be considered a strong correlate of drug abuse. For the purpose of treatment, many of the techniques for change discussed in this and the previous chapter presuppose the capacity for internalization. Self-awareness, problem solving, and self-monitoring are prerequisite skills for effective implementation of the intervention techniques reviewed in this book. Their absence would require almost exclusive reliance on behavior-oriented strategies that are concrete and highly circumscribed.

The final later life task is that of role identity, and its particular interactive domain (psychological) gives rise to a resurfacing of the fear of nonexistence that occurs at birth. Someone who struggles with the role identity life task is preoccupied with how she or he fits into the wider social world. Such an individual fears falling short of fulfilling the roles he or she has established and of being "found out" and humiliated in the process. Tertiary fears that stem from the secondary fear of nonexistence include the fear of failure, the fear of success, and the fear of fear. People who find a haven in a drug lifestyle measure themselves by the actions they engage in as part of this lifestyle. Accordingly, their identity might be that of a "dope fiend," "acid head," or "space cadet." Some persons appear to have no unifying self-identity at all, flitting back and forth between one role and another in response to environmental contingencies. Successful disengagement from a drug lifestyle presumes the formation of a new identity capable of guiding the individual toward a more productive way of living. Consequently, helping a client understand and deal effectively with the fear of nonexistence is a cardinal feature of lifestyle intervention that complements the cognitive and behavioral strategies discussed in this and the previous chapter.

REINFORCING NONDRUG LIFESTYLE

If treatment gains are to be preserved, it is essential that clients find suitable replacements for their drug lifestyle. This is where the third stage of the functional model of lifestyle intervention comes into play. It is at this stage that the individual seeks, identifies, and implements a reinforcing non-drug-abusing way of life designed to replace the former reliance on drugs and drug-related activities. Of critical significance at this point are establishing, maintaining, and modifying goals for treatment in the face of a future that is fraught with the threat of relapse. The third stage of lifestyle intervention treatment is particularly beneficial to clients who wish to exit a drug lifestyle permanently; it supplies the mechanism through which a substitute set of roles, behaviors, and relationships incompatible with the drug lifestyle can be identified and actualized. This step is designed to address the third goal of functional lifestyle intervention, in which effective follow-up and community integration are emphasized. The goals that guide the initial treatment and eventual follow-up processes are vital to the future success of the individual's efforts.

Goals for Treatment

Sobell and Sobell (1973) initiated a controversy when they reported successful implementation of a controlled drinking approach with alcoholic patients. This finding was subsequently replicated by Caddy, Addington, and Perkins (1978), who found moderation goals to be better predictive of long-term abstinence than strict abstinence goals. Several investigators took issue with the Sobells' conclusions, and a 10-year follow-up allegedly found many of their subjects rehospitalized for alcohol abuse problems within a year of release from the research project (Pendery, Maltzman, & West, 1982). Charges of fraud and unprofessional conduct were levied against the Sobells (see Pendery et al., 1982) but subsequently found to be without merit (Marlatt, 1983). Although the results of several studies support the superiority of abstinence over controlled drinking goals (Hall, Havassy, & Wasserman, 1990), many more studies reveal controlled drinking strategies to be equivalent (Booth, Dale, Slade, & Dewey, 1992; Miller, Leckman, Delaney, & Tinkcom, 1992; Rychtarik, Foy, Scott, Lokey, & Prue, 1987), if not superior (Alden, 1988; Nordstrom & Berglund, 1987), to abstinence strategies in the prevention of substance abuse relapse. Even more controversial are reports suggesting that controlled heroin use is possible, with or without the aid of methadone maintenance (Bianchi, Maremmani, Meloni, & Tagliamonte, 1992).

Because there is evidence that strict adherence to a philosophy of abstinence may promote, rather than inhibit, relapse (Heather, Rollnick, & Winston, 1983), Marlatt and Gordon (1985) have proposed the possibility of an Abstinence Violation Effect (AVE). The AVE is most common in clients adhering to a strict goal of abstinence because such persons view lapses as incongruent with their self-image as abstainers. Any lapse, therefore, creates tension and self-attributions of weakness that individuals attempt to alleviate by ingesting various chemical substances. Like research comparing abstinence and controlled drug use, research addressing the validity of the AVE has been inconclusive. Hence, although several studies enlist support for an AVE (Collins & Lapp, 1991; Curry, Marlatt, & Gordon, 1987), other studies fail to confirm the tenets of Marlatt and Gordon's hypothesis (Birke, Edelmann, & Davis, 1990; Brandon, Tiffany, & Baker, 1986). Despite the ambiguous nature of these data, it is certainly possible that AVE-related influences may increase the odds of relapse in a subset of drug abusers. For this reason, the AVE should be discussed openly with clients, and this discussion should be accompanied by a review of client options.

As some investigators have postulated (see Jessor & Jessor, 1977), experimental use of drugs appears to be normative. It may therefore be more appropriate and practical to direct treatment resources into reducing drug use escalation rather than worry about the treatment implications of initial drug use. Research suggests that behavioral self-control training may be highly efficacious in preventing alcohol use from escalating into alcohol abuse for groups of high-risk juveniles (Carpenter, Lyons, & Miller, 1985) and that a goal of moderation may be more practical than total abstinence for adolescents who refuse to give up marijuana entirely (Smith, 1983). It has also been noted that controlled drinking strategies may be more sensible for youthful heavy drinkers who have not yet experienced the physical and psychological deterioration that normally occurs after many years of drug and alcohol use (Miller & Hester, 1986). There are additional data to suggest that older individuals who have begun to "mature out" of a drug lifestyle may be better candidates for controlled drug use than younger individuals who have yet to achieve "maturity" (Fillmore, 1974). Accordingly, persons functioning at a pre-abuse stage of drug lifestyle development or who have entered the burnout/maturity stage are probably better risks for a controlled drinking program than persons functioning at an early or advanced stage of drug lifestyle involvement.

The severity of drug use is another factor that should be taken into account in determining whether stringent abstinence or controlled drug use goals should be pursued. Results from the Rand report (Polich, Armor, & Braiker, 1982) indicate that relapse rates are higher in heavy drinkers who abide by moderation goals than in heavy drinkers who profess total abstinence; however, younger, unmarried alcohol abusers who follow moderation goals fare better than younger, unmarried alcohol abusers who adhere to a goal of strict abstinence. Miller and Hester (1986) found that younger drinkers with less serious alcohol abuse histories were better able to refrain from abusive drinking after completing a controlled drinking program than older individuals with more severe drinking histories. Collecting follow-up data at 3.5, 5, 7, and 8 years, Miller et al. (1992) were able to show that asymptomatic or controlled drinking was possible for subjects with backgrounds of severe alcohol abuse but was most realistically attainable for clients with less serious drinking histories. Other studies, however, have failed to uncover a meaningful connection between controlled drinking outcomes and the severity of alcohol abuse (Rychtarik et al., 1987).

The existence of past attempts at controlled drinking should also be taken into account when selecting goals for treatment. This caveat is based on the oft repeated and empirically substantiated psychological adage that the best predictor of future behavior is past behavior. If a client has successfully been able to moderate intake in the past, as represented by a long history of moderate drinking or drug use bordered by much briefer periods of abuse, then controlled drinking or drug use may be a reasonable alternative. If, on the other hand, the client's past attempts at moderation have been marked by failure, or the client has never experienced a period of controlled drinking, then the therapist should probably conclude that abstinence is the more appropriate treatment goal (Marlatt & Gordon, 1985). Prior success at moderate substance use appears to be a better indicator for controlled drug use than failed attempts at moderation or no prior experience in controlling the use of alcohol and other drugs. This is one of a number of factors, therefore, that must be taken into account when formulating treatment goals for persons previously involved in chemical abuse.

The outcome of studies on controlled drinking and drug use indicate that a goal of controlled drug use is most reasonable in situations where the client is entering or preparing to exit the drug lifestyle, presents few signs of severe substance abuse, and has successfully moderated use of drugs in the past. It is vital, however, that, just as Zinberg discovered in his group of stabilized heroin users (Zinberg & Jacobson, 1976), clear rules for the "appropriate" use of substances be established and meticulously followed. Therapists should encourage clients to consider whether future use of drugs is worth running the risk of reactivating old thinking and behavioral patterns. Because the drug lifestyle is characterized by social rule breaking and bending activities, it stands to reason that someone previously committed to such a lifestyle could experience marked difficulty following rules unless they were made simple and concrete (e.g., "Don't use drugs"). Under such circumstances, abstinence goals may be the more reasonable alternative, although the derivation of treatment goals should be a collaborative effort between therapist and client rather than something that is decreed. For younger clients who have not progressed into the more advanced stages of a drug lifestyle, controlled drug use may be possible, or even advisable, provided the client is able to establish reasonable rules for substance use and possesses the requisite abilities and commitment to abide by them.

In formulating goals for intervention, a great deal depends on how relapse and recovery are defined. A reduction in drug use or abandoning one drug (heroin) in favor of a presumably less harmful substance (marijuana) may reflect a modicum of success. Although supporters of self-help groups may not agree, it appears that the accomplishments of programs like Alcoholics Anonymous (AA) and Narcotics Anonymous (NA) can be attributed, in part, to the fact that clients are provided with a substitute addiction. Instead of being addicted to alcohol, cocaine, or heroin, the individuals turn to the AA/disease-model philosophy and engage in a variety of substitute "addictive" activities that may include smoking cigarettes, drinking coffee, and compulsively attending AA/NA meetings (see Vaillant & Milofsky, 1982). Hence, even though moderate use of marijuana or heavy consumption of legalized stimulant drugs like tobacco and coffee are not goals for which a client should be encouraged to strive, they do reflect a change that, while less than ideal, is clearly in the right direction. In other words, therapists, counselors, and clients must be realistic in evaluating the success of a particular intervention, to guard against the possibilities of change agent burnout and client demoralization.

When it comes to selecting treatment goals, lifestyle theory considers two primary factors. First, the therapist must prepare the client for the likelihood of slip-ups (although in some cases these lapses may be nothing more than an unchallenged drug-oriented thought) and tutor the client in the skills needed to cope with them effectively. The client should be made aware that successful adaptation requires that one demonstrate respect for oneself, others, and nature. Second, the therapist must underscore the fact that the client has choices in establishing goals for treatment and recovery and may select from a variety of treatment options, under the watchful eye of an astute and patient therapist. The question the client should be asking is whether future involvement in drug use is worth the risk (and this risk will vary depending on a combination of factors, several of which were discussed earlier in this section) of reviving drug-oriented thoughts that may, in turn, lead him or her back into a drug lifestyle.

CONCLUSION

The lifestyle approach to intervention considers both the structural and functional features of lifestyle patterns of adjustment and behavior. The structural model provides an overview of the major skill areas that need to be addressed and, in the case of deficiencies, taught and reinforced. The functional model supplies the therapist with a blueprint of how treatment should proceed and brings the developmental roots of intervention into focus. Individual skills and issues are more or less important during different stages of the treatment process.

The functional model's strongest quality may be its ability to keep the treatment process in perspective. With all of the strategies and techniques discussed in this and the previous chapter, it is easy to miss the forest for the trees. The functional model reminds therapists that they are instructing clients in skills for the purpose of augmenting their adaptive resources and decreasing their reliance on drug lifestyle activities in the face of existential fear. In so doing, it is important for therapists to keep in mind that the stages of functional lifestyle intervention, although they have been presented in a particular order here, need to be continually reworked and reexamined. Accordingly, these stages should be seen as interdependent rather than independent, and every effort must be directed at routinely updating and reinforcing previously negotiated stages.

Due to the interrelated nature of the three stages of functional lifestyle intervention, it is essential that the foundation be continually reinforced to support each client's overall program of vehicles of change and alternate activities. By the same token, the foundation should be the stage at which intervention begins. It has been my observation that many clients attempt to maneuver their way around the foundation or bypass it altogether because it provokes uncomfortable feelings they would prefer to ignore. Neglecting to lay the foundation, however, simply strengthens lifestyle-based thinking by reinforcing the cognitively indolent belief that one can solve problems and manage feelings by taking a passive approach to life. Before long-term change can take place, clients must come to realize that the remnants of a drug lifestyle survive well beyond the point at which they stopped imbibing drugs. For this reason, clients should remain ever vigilant to the resurfacing of old drug-oriented thoughts, even in the absence of drug use. The foundation for change helps maintain this attitude of attentive introspection by continually reminding individuals of the enormity of the task before them and the likely consequences of not meeting the challenge through failure to attain access to and control over their thoughts and actions.

Chapter 11

Prevention

INTRODUCTION

There are two ways by which historical-developmental conditions can be managed: cognitive reorientation and primary prevention. Although it is true that one cannot effect change in conditions that already exist, the perspective one chooses to adopt toward these conditions is clearly amenable to change; consequently, a therapist may employ a cognitive technique like rational restructuring or cognitive reframing (see Chapter 9) to assist a client in changing his or her attitude toward a particular previous life event or condition. Another method for managing historical-developmental conditions is via primary prevention: If the historical-developmental precursors of a drug lifestyle can be identified, a certain percentage of high-risk individuals may be prevented from drifting into serious drug use if these conditions are changed. Of course, there is no way of realistically preventing all forms of drug abuse, even if every "controlling" risk factor could be identified, because individual choice exerts a powerful influence over lifestyle development.

Although, as noted above, primary prevention is no panacea for drug abuse, it may nonetheless prove effective in reducing the number of high-risk persons entering into the early stages of a drug lifestyle. The first order of business in establishing an effective program of primary and secondary prevention concerns the delineation of historical-developmental conditions that require remediation. Lifestyle theory maintains that there are several important classes of conditions that place an individual at risk for drug abuse outcomes (see conclusion of Chapter 4). Other than biology-based factors like heightened natural tolerance and autonomic hypersensitivity, there are five conditions that seem to be of primary etiological significance in the development of a drug lifestyle: sociocultural influences, family factors, peer influence, low self-esteem, and early antisocial behavior. Sociocultural conditions suggest the need for media-based prevention campaigns; family factors and early antisocial behavior signal the need for family-based preventive activities; and peer factors and low self-esteem identify the need for school-based prevention. Hence, three primary methods of drug abuse prevention are examined in this chapter: media-based strategies, family-based strategies, and school-based strategies.

MEDIA-BASED PREVENTIVE STRATEGIES

Black (1991), in reviewing survey research on the Partnership for a Drug-Free America media campaign, states that positive attitudes toward and self-reported use of marijuana and cocaine evidenced greater reductions in areas receiving high, as opposed to low, levels of media saturation. However, the majority of studies probing the utility of media-based anti-drug or antismoking educational campaigns have concluded that such programs rarely effect long-term behavioral change (Goodstadt, 1986; Kinder, Pape, & Walfish, 1980). This failure may be explained, in part, by the fact that antidrug campaigns have often exaggerated the harmfulness of drug use, encouraging viewers to discount even the factual information provided and possibly leading to their increased drug involvement (Murphy, Reinarman, & Waldorf, 1989). It is also possible that antidrug campaigns are just unable to compete with the seemingly contradictory and often potent commercial messages put out by national advertising agencies, in which the use of alcohol and other legal drugs is promoted and glamorized (Carroll, 1986).

Media-based programs appear to be the primary prevention strategy for enhancing drug awareness, and perhaps even for changing attitudes toward drug use, because of the wide audience they are able to reach. However, research indicates that if such programs are to affect awareness and attitudes, they must be combined with other preventive strategies, such as those that target parents or provide training through school curricula (Flay & Pentz, 1985). In a longitudinal investigation of 16 Kansas City, MO, communities, Johnson et al. (1990) observed that a media-based drug prevention campaign enjoyed only modest success in reducing adolescent drug use, although its effectiveness was increased by the addition of parent- and school-based training. The results of an Australian study suggest that media-based educational campaigns can be made more effective by the introduction of supplemental interventions designed to alert the viewing public to the campaign's initiation and apprise them of the program's intent and rationale (Barber, Bradshaw, & Walsh, 1989). For these reasons, additional components must be included in a comprehensive program of primary prevention, two of which—parent-based and school-based preventive strategies—work their way into the present discussion.

FAMILY-BASED PREVENTIVE STRATEGIES

Because research indicates that family factors are crucial in the development of a drug lifestyle (see Chapter 4), it stands to reason that the family should assume some degree of prominence in a program of preventive intervention. Epidemiological analyses suggest that the risk of alcoholism and other forms of drug abuse is low in children whose parents make a clear distinction between drinking and drunkenness, integrate drinking with other activities, and endow their children with effective problem-solving and social communication skills (Schoefer, 1981). Baumrind (1985) studied the relationship between parenting and child behavior and determined that authoritative parents (firm but consistent) produce children who are more friendly, self-controlled, and self-reliant than the children of authoritarian (harsh and domineering) and permissive (nondemanding and noncontrolling) parents. Authoritarian and permissive parenting styles have also been found to be associated with an earlier onset of drug and alcohol use in adolescent males and females (Baumrind, 1985), whereas families that provide their members with a sense of self-efficacy through love, support, and discipline tend to produce significantly fewer drug-dependent offspring (Blum, 1972).

Many parents, however, require training in how to stimulate feelings of self-efficacy in their children. Poor parenting skills tend to be passed down from one generation to the next, and research shows that parenting skills predict a child's propensity to engage in deviant behavior, whether the parenting skills measured are those of the parents or those of the grandparents (Patterson, 1986). Thus it may be difficult for parents to teach their children something that they themselves have never learned.

Family management training has been implemented at the Oregon Learning Center in Eugene (Patterson, 1980) and at the University of Utah in Salt Lake City (Alexander & Parsons, 1973). Although aggression and delinquency are the behaviors most commonly measured in program evaluations of parenting skills training (Barton, Alexander, Waldron, Turner, & Warbuton, 1985), there is some indication that such programs may be useful in reducing subsequent drug use as well (Klein, Alexander, & Parsons, 1977). Given the results of several investigations suggesting that the parents of drug-using adolescents often possess weak disciplinary and family management skills (Coombs & Paulson, 1988), instruction in child rearing and parenting appears to be a potentially important avenue of preventive intervention. More research is required, not only to determine the preventive value of these programs, but also to develop means of buttressing their effectiveness and counteracting any influences that may disrupt training.

The social isolation of single-parent families, poor financial status, and a general absence of social support are other factors that potentially interfere with effective parenting (Dumas, 1986). Dadds and McHugh (1992) incorporated an ally support procedure into a 6-week child management training program for parents of misbehaving children and contrasted this group of parents with another group of parents who received the 6-week child management training program without ally support. Results indicated that both groups showed significant improvement in parenting skills, child compliance, and social support, and that these gains continued to hold 6 months after treatment. Although there were no significant outcome differences between children whose parents received the child management training package with the ally support component and those whose parents received child management training alone, better outcomes were observed in children whose parents reported higher levels of social support. This finding underscores the contributions of social support to the ultimate success of child management training and the potential problems clinicians face in incorporating such support into a formal program of preventive intervention.

Studies indicate that, although behavioral management strategies like cognitive reframing and positive interpretation are capable of preventing substance abuse in adolescents who have minor experience with drugs (Stanton, Todd, Steir, Van Deusen, & Cook, 1982), there is some question as to how efficacious these techniques are for use with individuals already heavily involved in abuse of mind-altering substances (Alexander, Waldron, Barton, & Mas, 1989).

There is a positive side to these findings, however, that should not be overlooked. Behavioral family management training may be more effective if used as a primary prevention tool rather than as a secondary or tertiary prevention strategy. The nontargeted siblings of conduct-disordered and drug-using adolescents, in fact, have been shown to profit incidentally from their parents' involvement in child management training, as represented by a reduced level of subsequent drug use and delinquency, even though they were never the target of intervention (Humphreys, Forehand, McMahon, & Roberts, 1978; Klein, Alexander, & Parsons, 1977). Hence, parenting skills training is probably most effective as a prevention strategy when conducted early in or prior to the development of a drug lifestyle.

In situations where drug abuse has progressed beyond where such training can be expected to be of much use, other forms of family intervention should be entertained. Altering the relational atmosphere of the home through strategic family therapy and other forms of intervention offers some hope for families with members functioning at early to advanced stages of drug lifestyle commitment (Piercy, Volk, Trepper, Sprenkle, & Lewis, 1991). There is evidence, in fact, that strategic family therapy may lend both support and leverage to families interested in managing the behavior of a family member preoccupied with drugs (Lewis, Piercy, Sprenkle, & Trepper, 1990). Strategic family interventions are designed to take the focus away from the identified patient (drug abuser) and redirect it toward the pathological family interactions and alliances that allow the abuser's behavior to continue. Even when the family is not the sole or primary cause of a member's drug abuse, problematic drug use encourages the configuration of relationships in which the family focuses undue attention on the problem behavior of one member, to the detriment of family members' understanding of the patterns that may be unwittingly reinforcing this behavior.

A component analysis of the skills, attitudes, and procedures taught in these programs is the next logical step in evaluating the overall effectiveness of family-based prevention. Such an approach may eventually supply researchers with a method by which the more cogent and dynamic attributes of drug abuse prevention programs may be identified and emphasized. Bry (1988) writes that child management training normally covers five basic skill areas: parent contingency management (discipline), communication, problem solving, behavioral contracting, and self-management. Fraser, Hawkins, and Howard (1988) attribute the success of child management training programs to the teaching of contingency management and contingency contracting skills, and state that training in problem solving, negotiation skills, behavioral self-management, and effective communication are of secondary importance in preventing drug abuse and delinquency. Unfortunately, Fraser et al. fail to provide anything more than anecdotal evidence in support of their claims. For this reason, rigorous empirical component analysis of these training programs is needed.

SCHOOL-BASED PREVENTIVE STRATEGIES

Alcohol and drug education programs have been instituted in many primary and secondary schools with varying degrees of success. Change agents for these programs have ranged from teachers (Mitchel, Hu, McDonnell, & Swisher, 1984), to peers (Carpenter, Lyons, & Miller, 1985), to college students (Hurd, Johnson, Pechacheck, Jacobs, & Luepker, 1980), to supervising adults (Williams, Ward, & Gray, 1985). Behaviors and areas targeted for change have encompassed self-reported drug use (Mitchel et al., 1984), knowledge about and attitudes toward drugs (Carpenter et al., 1985), and various "objective" measures, such as breathalyzer tests to detect alcohol (Carpenter et al., 1985) or blood carbon monoxide level tests to discern use of tobacco (Perry, Killen, Telch, Slinkard, & Danaher, 1980). The consensus of research conducted on traditional school-based drug information programs is that they often expand participants' drug knowledge but fail to produce a salubrious effect on subjects' decision-making skills or actual use of substances (Abbey, Oliansky, Stilianos, Hohlstein, & Kaczynski, 1990).

In direct contrast to the information dissemination approach adopted by the media and many school systems, the social competency model of preventive intervention instructs children in ways to resist the peer pressure that often fosters initial drug use. Evans' (1976) resistance skills model of drug abuse prevention comprises three stages: (a) *inoculation*, when the child is exposed to arguments in favor of drug use; (b) *antithesis*, when the child is exposed to strong counterarguments against drug use; and (c) *skill development*, when the child is taught and provided an opportunity to practice the skills required to resist social pressure to use drugs. The resistance skills approach has been found to be effective in preventing cigarette smoking in adolescents (Dielman et al., 1985; Perry et al., 1980), but its results are equivocal in preventing adolescent alcohol (Gersick, Grady, & Snow, 1988; Hansen, Malotte, & Fielding, 1988) and other drug (Pentz et al., 1989) use. However, many of the studies in this area are plagued by methodological shortcomings and conceptual oversights (Shope, Dielman, Butchart, Campanelli, & Kloska, 1992).

Attempting to control for many of the methodological problems in extant social competency research on alcohol use prevention, Shope et al. (1992) randomly assigned 213 Michigan classrooms of fifth and sixth graders to one of three conditions: social pressure resistance training (four sessions), social pressure resistance training (four sessions) plus booster (three sessions), and no-contact control. After 26 months, subjects in both social pressure resistance groups displayed greater understanding of alcohol's effects and increased awareness of the role social pressure plays in a person's decision to use alcohol than did subjects in the control group (this effect being somewhat stronger in subjects afforded the three booster sessions). While there were no significant group differences in subsequent use and misuse of alcohol, the resistance training sessions were found to be more effective than the control sessions in limiting the alcohol intake of sixth graders who had prior experience with alcohol. This outcome was interpreted by Shope et al. (1992) as supporting the hypothesis that social pressure resistance training may be unnecessary for children who have no prior experience with alcohol but may prove valuable in preventing further alcohol use in persons previously exposed to it.

The Life Skills Training (LST) program (Botvin, 1983) is a treatment package containing 12 curriculum modules to be taught over 15 class sessions. The LST is designed to furnish students with basic personal and social skills for coping with the pressure/desire to use cigarettes, alcohol, and other drugs. Skills taught as part of the LST experience include evaluating and resisting advertising pressure, asserting one's rights and ideas, communicating effectively with others, forming positive interpersonal relationships, and feeling good about oneself in the face of pressure to use drugs. Instruction is provided by teachers who are trained by project staff in the proper use of program materials. A 3-year study conducted with 56 schools in New York State disclosed that schools using LST programming experienced significant reductions in student cigarette smoking, marijuana use, and heavy alcohol consumption relative to no-contact control schools (Botvin, Baker, Dusenbury, Tortu, & Botvin, 1990). This effect held whether teachers were initially instructed in program procedures and goals through a 1-day workshop or simply supplied with written instructions and a 2-hour videotape training session. Programs such as the LST hold promise for preventing substance abuse problems and warrant additional study in a number of different primary prevention settings.

Botvin and Wills (1985) offer several recommendations for research and program development in social skills training for prevention of substance abuse problems. One recommendation made by these authors is to include process variables in the program evaluation so that the impact of these programs on specific skills, attitudes, and behaviors can be gauged. Second, Botvin and Wills advocate use of component analysis procedures to identify and promote the program components most responsible for the positive outcomes enjoyed by social competency programs. They report that many of these programs teach assertiveness, general social skills, anxiety/stress management, decision making/problem solving, and information related to substance abuse. The question is whether all five components are necessary and, if not, which ones can be deleted from the curriculum without detracting from the overall effectiveness of the program. Botvin and Wills also advise that increased attention should be paid to the external factors (trainers, format, school atmosphere) that either enhance or interfere with the effective implementation of skill-based programming. Finally, they urge researchers to conduct large-scale "clinical" trials on a wide cross-section of student groups so that the generalizability of outcomes obtained in earlier studies can be properly evaluated.

CONCLUSION

There are three principal targets of drug prevention programs: awareness/ knowledge, attitudes, and behavior. Media-based strategies and traditional informational school-based programs, if properly implemented, can increase awareness, foster knowledge, and perhaps assist in changing attitudes. These procedures must be coupled with parent-based and social competency school-based preventive programs if drug use is to be meaningfully reduced, however. These findings help explain why scare tactics and cliché-based programs often fail to effect long-term behavioral changes in youthful viewers. With respect to scare tactics, the messenger rapidly loses credibility with the audience as soon as he or she describes a consequence of drug use the listener knows from personal experience is either false or greatly exaggerated. Cliché-based programs may also inadvertently encourage drug use if not reinforced with vigorous and relevant skills training. Exposing children to the dangers of drug use or imploring them to "just say no" is very different from instructing them in ways of coping with the social pressure that often gives rise to drug experimentation. If a child instructed to say no to drugs does not possess effective refusal skills, then he or she may actually fare worse than a child given no such advice because of the conflict and guilt engendered when such a child finds him- or herself unable to resist the social pressure to use drugs.

It may be useful, from a clinical management standpoint, to group youthful clients into three general categories of risk/need: (a) persons at low risk for drug involvement, who have a low need for intervention; (b) persons at high risk for drug involvement, or currently functioning at an embryonic stage of drug involvement, who have a high need for intervention; and (c) persons who have progressed beyond an incipient stage of drug involvement, who have a high need for intervention. The second group should receive priority for participating in school-based preventive programs, because students at low risk for drug use may not require intensive formal assistance (Shope et al., 1992), and also because research indicates that parenting skills programming may be a more effective prevention strategy with low-risk individuals. School officials should invest their limited resources in procedures that provide high-risk and initially involved students with the skills necessary to avoid (in the case of high-risk students) or escape (in the case of initially involved students) problematic drug use. Persons already committed to a drug lifestyle, on the other hand, require direct treatment services aimed at the current-contextual conditions, choices, and cognitions that support their continued drug involvement.

The future of drug use prevention rests with its ability to provide integrated programs that impart practical knowledge, encourage a more positive attitudinal state, and teach basic social and coping skills. Johnson et al. (1990) implemented such a program in eight Kansas City communities and discovered that this approach proved effective. Supplying students with resistance skills training conducted through the schools, instructing parents in how to communicate with their children, raising the awareness of community leaders, administering an antidrug media campaign, and incorporating each of these components into a single intervention package led to significant reductions in tobacco and marijuana use after 3 years, but failed to affect rates of alcohol consumption. The outcome was commensurate for persons at high and low risk for substance abuse problems, perhaps because of the counterbalancing effect of parent-based (most effective with low-risk children) and school-based (most effective with high-risk children) programming.

The challenge, as always, is to balance efficiency with comprehensiveness. This objective can best be accomplished by addressing key conditional parameters (i.e., sociocultural milieu, family factors, peer relations), forming valid risk categories from these parameters, and then matching these risk categories with specific prevention strategies.

Chapter 12

Case Studies

INTRODUCTION

In this chapter, four case studies are examined in an effort to identify ways by which the principles described in this book can be applied to individual clients. The first three case studies are of inmates with whom the author is personally familiar by virtue of their involvement in the Lifestyle Change program offered at the correctional institution at which the author works. Information for the fourth case study, of a 19-year-old female substance abuser, was derived from the files of a university-based psychology clinic to demonstrate the applicability of the lifestyle concept to subjects with no history of criminal involvement. Each case study is divided into four sections—background, Drug Lifestyle Screening Interview (DLSI) evaluation, treatment plan, and outcome—for the purpose of clarifying pivotal clinical issues in the treatment of clients preoccupied with drug use and committed to a drug lifestyle.

FRANK

This first case report details the story of a 43-year-old white male who reportedly began using substances and engaging in criminal activity at age 7. Although the subject's stated drug of choice is heroin, he, like two of the other cases profiled in this chapter, has used and abused a variety of substances. In fact, he describes himself as a "garbage addict," because he has used and abused whatever substances have been available to him. This statement implies that the lifestyle of drug abuse may be more important than the specific drug of abuse in explaining Frank's behavior and that of the other two inmates presented in this section.

Background

Raised the eighth of 10 children in a lower-middle-class home environment, Frank was introduced to drugs and crime at an early age. He states that by age 7 he was committing burglaries at the prodding of several older brothers, who would jimmy open a window or knock out the lower section of a door and then squeeze Frank through the small opening. Frank also began experimenting with alcohol around age 7 and recalls being picked up by the police after getting drunk on vodka given to him by the boyfriend of an older sister. No stranger to the mood-altering effects of alcohol and other drugs, Frank grew up in a home with an alcoholic father and several older siblings who were well acquainted with the use of alcohol and other substances. By age 9, Frank was transporting alcohol and marijuana to school for the express purpose of getting high and "turning on" his friends. His adjustment at school was poor, and his problems there increased as his drug use escalated. These problems eventually led to expulsion from school midway through the 10th grade. Frank reasoned that joining the military might provide him with the direction his life so sorely lacked.

His time spent in the military did little to curb Frank's growing appetite for abusable substances, and it was during this period that Frank was most heavily addicted to alcohol and barbiturates. Just prior to his discharge, however, Frank quit drinking, only to replace alcohol with heroin. For the next 22 years he used cocaine, LSD, mescaline, marijuana, and dilaudid, but clearly preferred heroin. A consummate con artist, Frank was able to deceive even his wife about his drug use, living a double life for 7 years, acting one way with his spouse and her family and a very different way with the drug users he hung around with on the streets. He developed an interest in cocaine relatively late in life and typically used this substance in combination with heroin in what is commonly referred to as a "speed-ball." Frank lived for heroin, and crime became a means of financing his drug use activities and lifestyle. The majority of Frank's criminal convictions were for possession of controlled substances and petty larceny, but he sometimes bypassed the middleman to go right to the source, robbing and burglarizing pharmacies for controlled substances like dilaudid and morphine. Eventually, he grew desperate, and at age 40 he robbed a bank. Within minutes he was apprehended, and he was sentenced to 4 years in federal prison.

Frank has been enrolled in a number of treatment programs, but his longest period of drug-free living since age 9 (other than his most recent incarceration) was 78 days. At age 27 he entered a VA hospital detoxification center because he believed his use of heroin had gotten out of control. However, he left 16 hours later because he did not like the answers the doctors were giving him: namely, that he needed to stop using drugs. Shortly thereafter, he enrolled in an outpatient substance abuse treatment program, where he received methadone and individual counseling. He states that he was making good progress when his therapist resigned to take another job. Angry and hurt, he vowed never to trust mental health professionals again. Eight years later, Frank completed a 7-day detoxification program and began attending AA and NA. This is the point at which he enjoyed the 78-day stretch of sobriety. Frank attributes his relapse on the 79th day to the craving evoked by the vivid recollections of heroin addicts describing the preparation and use of opiates. Several other brief hospitalizations ensued in the years that followed, and although Frank often took the methadone he was prescribed by clinic personnel, he continued using heroin, ingesting as much as $1500 to $2500 worth each day in combination with a healthy dose (90 mg) of methadone.

DLSI Evaluation

The DLSI evaluation yields a total score of between 0 and 20, with contributions of between 0 and 5 from each of the four subscales. The DLSI profile obtained from an interview with Frank is displayed in Table 12-1. Several points need to be made with respect to this profile. First, a total score of 16 (standard cutting score = 10) indicates a strong prior identi-

Table 12-1 DLSI Scores for Frank

Scale	Score
Irresponsibility/pseudoresponsibility	4
Stress-coping imbalance	4
Interpersonal triviality	3
Social rule breaking/bending	5
Total DLSI score	16

fication with the drug lifestyle and suggests that Frank will require a great deal of assistance in remaining drug-free upon his release from custody. Second, Frank reports problems in all four areas diagnostic of drug lifestyle preoccupation (i.e., irresponsibility/pseudoresponsibility, stress-coping imbalance, interpersonal triviality, and social rule breaking/bending). The fact that Frank scores 5 on social rule breaking/bending implies that a major component of any treatment he receives should include a consideration of rules and problem solving designed to instruct him in how to achieve his goals in a more socially acceptable manner than has been the case in the past.

Treatment Plan

When working with someone involved in more than one lifestyle, as Frank is, it is imperative to explore and clarify the relationship between these lifestyles. Frank's involvement with the drug and criminal lifestyles is complex and variable. In some ways, his preoccupations with drugs and crime have developed independently, although they clearly parallel one another in timing and motivation. There also appears to be evidence that his preoccupation with drugs has precipitated specific criminal acts (burglarizing pharmacies) and that certain crimes may have inspired him to expand his use of substances (i.e., periods of increased prosperity realized through successful criminal ventures may have caused escalated drug use). Frank must therefore be made to realize that, while many of his legal problems can be traced to his preoccupation with drugs, he will probably continue experiencing problems of a social rule-breaking nature if his criminal lifestyle is not also addressed. Consequently, both drug and criminal issues should be included in any program of relapse prevention for Frank and others like him.

The conditions that most closely tie into Frank's use of substances and his potential for relapse include association with drug-using friends and family and the craving evoked by drug-related cues. The former might be handled through geographic relocation, the latter through cue exposure training. Frank relates that at age 22 he and his wife moved from New York to North Carolina, where he was no longer exposed to old drug associates and environmental cues. The hiatus in heavy drug use that followed this transfer was cut short when he decided to return to New York out of boredom with rural life. Substitution and priority realignment, as well as geographic relocation and cue exposure training, are therefore critical to a program of relapse prevention for someone like Frank. Several drug- and crime-based cognitive patterns also figure prominently in Frank's treatment needs. The mollification ("I took money from groups rather than individual people"), sentimentality ("I'd provide dope to addicts who didn't have anything"), and discontinuity ("For the first 7 years of using heroin I lived a double life") that characterize Frank's thinking must be delimited, challenged, and altered if he is to have any chance of remaining drug- and crime-free upon his release from prison.

The structural features of intervention—conditions, choice, cognitions—are not the only factors that must be considered in formulating a plan of intervention; the functional features must also be addressed. The functional aspect of Frank's preoccupation with drugs and crime that is most in need of remediation is his self-identity. Frank suffers from low self-esteem and displays minimal confidence in his ability to refrain from future drug use. The fact that he commonly refers to himself as a "dope fiend" or "garbage addict" implies that he lacks self-efficacy in the face of high-risk drug-using situations and perceives himself to be a victim rather than an active decision maker. This attitude also reflects an identification with the drug lifestyle that may be difficult to overcome unless the issue of self-identity is handled in an aggressive manner by the therapist. Treatment should be directed at assisting Frank in developing his abilities and attributes and expanding his repertoire of behaviors, toward a goal of forming a more positive self-image and a prosocial self-identity.

Outcome

Frank enrolled in the Lifestyle Change program offered at the federal correctional institution at which the author works. After showing an initial burst of interest, he gradually grew bored and attended fewer and fewer sessions. Whenever present, Frank was very active in group discussions; however, he was given to long tirades that frequently failed to come to a discernable resolution and sometimes seemed to make comments simply for the purpose of hearing himself talk. This behavior reflects his ongoing problem with discontinuity. There is a manipulative flavor to Frank's interactions with authority figures, and on several occasions he has attempted to maneuver the therapist into giving him a certificate for classes for which he did not complete all the requirements. The odds that Frank will be able to avoid future drug use opportunities on his release from custody are not good, although they might be improved through geographic relocation and the construction of an active network of family and community support.

ROBERTO

The next case study describes the background and present-day functioning of Roberto, a 31-year-old Hispanic male who was heavily involved in the use of crack cocaine and alcohol until his arrest for bank robbery 4 years ago. Unlike Frank, who exhibits parallel development of the drug and criminal lifestyles, Roberto exhibits antisocial behavior that seems to be largely a function of his involvement and preoccupation with drugs.

Background

Roberto was brought up by his grandmother after a judge ruled that his parents were unfit to raise him because of irresponsibility, fighting, and alcoholism. The subject's own use of chemical substances began at around age 8, when he started sneaking drinks from the family punch bowl during holiday celebrations. His use escalated to the point where at age 13 he was smoking marijuana daily and getting drunk on the weekends. Roberto states that he ran away from home when he was 16 because he had trouble getting along with an aunt who had moved in with him and his grandmother, and also because he wanted to be with his girlfriend who had also just run away. It is at this point that Roberto began committing various petty crimes (e.g., shoplifting) to support himself and his girlfriend. He returned home at age 17 to a situation that was much improved. Besides being able to get along better with his aunt, Roberto was able to limit his use of marijuana and alcohol and secure steady employment. At age 20, Roberto married a woman he had known since childhood. This union produced one son, presently age 9, but ended in divorce 4 years later.

The divorce was devastating for Roberto, who reacted to the ensuing stress, anger, and depression by withdrawing into himself and consuming large quantities of liquor. Shortly thereafter, he was introduced to cocaine by a coworker. The cocaine seemed to relieve him of his daily worries and feelings of inadequacy but also contributed to a long-term buildup of stress. Aggression toward objects increased as his preoccupation with cocaine grew, although Roberto states that he was rarely physically aggressive toward people, even when heavily addicted to cocaine. Roberto's criminality, which seemed to have gone into hibernation after his return home at age 17, reawakened with a vengeance. No longer satisfied with petty crimes like shoplifting, Roberto was stealing large sums of money from the cash register at work and contemplating robbing other people to support his expanding drug habit. This situation continued for several months, until he could no longer maintain employment. Desperate for money to support his dependence on cocaine and his rapidly growing family (girlfriend, her son, and his son), he left home, vowing never to return until he had sufficient money to take care of all his worries. He bought a gun and a week later robbed a bank. Because Roberto collected only $3,000 from this crime, it was only a matter of time before he "needed" to rob another bank. This pattern continued until his arrest for multiple bank robberies 7 months later.

Of the factors that contributed to Roberto's drug use, stress and mood management are at the top of the list. Roberto states that he was always a rather uptight, anxious teenager and that marijuana made him feel "mellow." Alcohol did much the same thing, but it also released pent-up anger that frequently spilled over into violence. Cocaine, on the other hand, seemed to evoke a calm reassurance that enabled Roberto to self-medicate depression and anxiety while simultaneously providing him with an avenue of escape from an existence he saw as humdrum and unexciting. This drug, however, only led to more problems, medical as well as interpersonal. Roberto states that he began by snorting cocaine but switched to smoking crack when he started experiencing nosebleeds. He indicates further that he did not initially like the high he got from smoking crack but forced himself to adapt to the experience. Cocaine use also interfered with Roberto's job performance; he was fired from nearly every job he ever held after his exposure to cocaine, because the drug made him so paranoid that he would walk off the job for fear of being surveilled. Roberto's use of drugs was mixed with a strong interest in pornography, sex, and masturbation, all of which indicate a struggle to reduce uncomfortable feelings of tension, fear, and self-denigration.

DLSI Evaluation

A total score of 14 on the DLSI indicates that Roberto has exhibited strong identification with the drug lifestyle ideal in the past (see Table 12-2). Analysis of the subscale scores reveals that irresponsibility/pseudoresponsibility, stress-coping imbalance, and interpersonal triviality are probably of greater concern than social rule breaking and bending in this case. What these results mean, behaviorally, is that on release Roberto is likely to have little trouble following rules provided he can learn to be more responsible, stress-coping efficient, and interpersonally skillful. The single most important area of concern in counseling someone like Roberto, although the DLSI fails to discriminate between his three highest subscales, is the stress-coping imbalance, according to both personal history and the

Table 12-2   DLSI Scores for Roberto

Scale	Score
Irresponsibility/pseudoresponsibility	4
Stress-coping imbalance	4
Interpersonal triviality	4
Social rule breaking/bending	2
Total DLSI score	14

subject's self-report. In fact, during the interview, Roberto displayed teeth-grinding and other facial signs of tension when rehashing the events of his past life. Treatment must therefore center on stress and mood management to be effective.

Treatment Plan

Whereas Frank demonstrates parallel development of the drug and criminal lifestyles, Roberto exhibits a clear pattern of stress and negative affect, followed by drug use, followed by crime. Thus, although Roberto clearly realized secondary gain from his criminal activities—a fact that would not be lost on the astute therapist—the bulk of intervention for Roberto and clients like him should be directed at their maladaptive response to stress. Historically, Roberto has escaped from stress through drug use or some other ineffective form of coping (e.g., throwing objects against the wall, withdrawing socially). For this reason, the conditions-based branch of intervention must converge around the issue of stress management. As far as choice-based intervention is concerned, Roberto notes that his life lacked direction until just recently. Consequently, goal setting and values clarification should serve as powerful vehicles for change. The thinking patterns that need to be addressed with respect to Roberto's past use of drugs and involvement with crime are cutoff (he regularly used drugs prior to committing a crime), superoptimism (he believed he could continue ingesting cocaine and escape any serious repercussions), and power orientation (he used drugs as a way of gaining control over his seemingly out-of-control affective state).

The functional features of lifestyle intervention for Roberto, as is the case for many clients who have had problems with drugs in the past, congregate around the issue of existential fear. Roberto acknowledges that while he pursued hedonistic aims he never really liked or respected himself. He now understands that a change in lifestyle requires that he confront his negative behavior, rather than run away from his fears and concerns by embracing a lifestyle of drug abuse or crime. Ways to accomplish this objective include individual therapy, experiential group interactions, and a variety of self-help programs. Roberto demonstrates a desire to be of assistance to others and has reestablished ties with his religious heritage, roots that were severed after his divorce and years of heavy cocaine use. Although these are useful goals, Roberto, like many persons recovering from a drug problem, has to realize that he must concentrate on his own behavior and thinking before he can hope to be of assistance to others. Long-term change, therefore, requires that Roberto learn to manage existential fear by becoming more adaptive, rather than fleeing from fear through involvement in lifestyle activities that only mask the fear.

Outcome

Roberto has been involved in the Lifestyle Change program since his arrival at the author's institution approximately 2 years ago. His participation was spotty and diffident at first, but gradually grew as he became more comfortable with the group format and lifestyle concept. Roberto's attitude toward religion has also matured as his involvement with the Lifestyle Change program has grown; he no longer appears to invest all his aspirations for change in his religious beliefs. Instead, he has worked diligently to integrate his commitment to religious values with such lifestyle concepts as adaptability and choice. It should be noted that Roberto's capacity for stress management, which appears to have improved since his enrollment in the program, may serve as a useful barometer of his eventual success on the streets, given the importance of stress and negative affect in the genesis of his difficulties with drugs and crime.

CARL

In contrast to Frank, for whom drug use and crime exist as parallel lifestyles, and Roberto, whose criminal activities appear to stem largely from his use of drugs, Carl, a 29-year-old single black male, displays a pattern in which crime and delinquent activity have tended to precede and in many ways inspire his use of drugs.

Background

Carl was raised as the oldest of three children by a mother and father who lived together but never married. His parents separated when he was 12 years old, and he was sent to live with his mother. The subject's mother and father offer contrasting pictures of social adjustment. Carl's mother currently leads a productive and law-abiding life despite having served 6 months in jail for selling drugs as a young adult. Carl's father, on the other hand, was an alcoholic who was in and out of jail and who eventually died at age 51 of a stroke brought on by high blood pressure and heavy drinking. Drawn to the excitement of his father's lifestyle and the prospect of doing whatever he wanted whenever he wanted, Carl ran away from home at age 14 so that he could be with his father. Asked by the judge where he wanted to live, Carl replied that he preferred living with his father. In light of the father's extensive criminal record, the judge thought it best that Carl be raised by the paternal grandmother. The problem with this arrangement was that now the father had ready access to Carl and it was not long before Carl was living with his father full time. It was at this point that Carl's criminal and drug use behavior commenced.

From the day he went to live with his father, Carl began "hanging out" with a group of older juveniles who had formed their own neighborhood gang. Carl demonstrated a bravado that endeared him to his law-breaking buddies, and he rapidly moved up the gang hierarchy. He seemed willing to do just about anything, from vandalizing soda machines, to stealing cars, to breaking into people's homes. He recalls the sense of power and control that came over him as he robbed an adult gas station attendant of $20 at the tender age of 14 and the sense of daring and exhilaration he experienced upon getting away with the crime. Around this same time, he began drinking alcohol (given to him by his father) and smoking marijuana. His father allowed him to use marijuana in the home because he preferred that his son stay at home to smoke rather than run the streets with his gangster friends. The only rules Carl was willing to follow, however, were his own, and so although he smoked marijuana at home, he was unwilling to abandon life on the streets. After a handful of juvenile court appearances, Carl was adjudged a delinquent and sent to a boy's reformatory at age 15. Released several months later, he was recommitted to the reformatory twice more before turning 18. His entrance into adulthood only solidified his commitment to criminal goals and the desire to follow in his father's footsteps. The number of adult convictions currently stands at 12, including one state incarceration and his current federal imprisonment for drug distribution.

Although Carl had imbibed alcohol and smoked marijuana in the past, he did not develop a serious problem with drugs, in this case cocaine, until he was 26 year old, 6 months before his arrest for cocaine distribution. His dependency on cocaine can be attributed to the fact that he had access to large amounts of it (which he was selling) and associated with several female customers who were heavily involved in its use. His rising preoccupation with cocaine interfered with his ability to manage his drug distribution business effectively and alienated him from his drug-dealing peers, who reminded him that dipping into his own "stash" was a sure-fire way of winding up dead or in prison. Incapable of exercising rational judgment and plagued by a growing paranoia, Carl was arrested for selling cocaine to an undercover detective. The crime to drug use progression occurred again several years later, when Carl was in prison. Approached by an individual who wanted to trade him a bag of cocaine for a portion of the marijuana Carl had been selling to other inmates, Carl acquiesced because he wanted to determine whether he could use cocaine without getting paranoid. Shortly after ingesting the cocaine, however, he became so paranoid that his behavior came to the attention of unit staff, who promptly had him locked up in Segregation. A urine test revealed the presence of cocaine, and Carl was subsequently transferred to another institution.

DLSI Evaluation

Results from Carl's DLSI (see Table 12-3) indicate that he was strongly committed to the drug lifestyle while on the streets (total DLSI score = 15). Subscale analyses show irresponsibility and social rule breaking (but not social rule bending) as the two most prominent features of Carl's identification with the drug lifestyle. It is certainly no coincidence that irresponsibility and social rule breaking are also two behavioral styles that help link the drug and criminal lifestyles. Because both the DLSI evaluation and the subject's history suggest that the majority of Carl's drug-related difficulties are attributable to his preoccupation with power, control, and other features of a criminal lifestyle, effective intervention demands that the treatment plan emphasize Carl's past antisocial behavior and current criminal thinking and identification. Carl's long-term recovery hinges on implementation of a treatment program that addresses the relapse-promoting roots of irresponsibility and social rule breaking, but also covers other major elements of a criminal lifestyle, including self-indulgence and interpersonal intrusiveness.

Treatment Plan

It seems that Carl's commitment to the criminal lifestyle caricature preceded and precipitated his involvement with drugs. Therefore, the focus of Carl's treatment should be on the criminal lifestyle, although overlapping and other relevant drug issues should not be ignored. The problem with clients like Carl is that the professionals who work with them often become preoccupied with the drug issue because this aspect of a drug-involved offender's behavior is often more pronounced and accessible to treatment than the criminal features. The emphasis of treatment with a client like Carl, however, must be on the criminal lifestyle, with a secondary focus on drug-related problems. In tackling the criminal identity (functional intervention) that formed from Carl's emulation of his father and neighbor-

Table 12-3   DLSI Scores for Carl

Scale	Score
Irresponsibility/pseudoresponsibility	5
Stress-coping imbalance	3
Interpersonal triviality	3
Social rule breaking/bending	4
Total DLSI score	15

hood pals, the therapist may hold the mother up as a role model, as someone who despite a record of criminality is currently leading a law-abiding, productive life. The contrast in identities provided by the mother and father can serve as a powerful therapeutic tool for directing and encouraging Carl to enter into the identity transformation process. Tackling Carl's drug use without first challenging the criminal thinking and identity that apparently support it is doomed to failure from the start.

Condition-based intervention with Carl should be engineered to limit his access to drugs and opportunities for crime (e.g., avoiding certain people, places, and situations likely to bring him into conflict with the law, such as carrying a weapon) and also to avoid previous drug associates. Choice-based interventions a therapist might choose to employ with a client like Carl include problem-solving training, educational/occupational enrichment, and instruction in goal setting. Cognition-based intervention holds great promise for aiding Carl's desistance from crime and drug abuse because he has relied so heavily on mollification, cutoff, power orientation, and cognitive indolence in the past. Drug use, in fact, has served to potentiate the thinking patterns originally devised to support the subject's criminal activities. Carl recalls that the lazy, shortcut thinking that characterized his criminal lifestyle increased two- or threefold after he started smoking marijuana. The most pronounced feature of Carl's thinking, however, is a monumental power orientation, which not only encouraged Carl to engage in crime as a means of achieving control, but also influenced his choice of cocaine as his preferred substance of abuse. Although cocaine gave him an initial feeling of power and control, it eventually led to problems with judgment, paranoia, and incarceration.

Outcome

Given the fact Carl had only a short amount of time left on his sentence when he arrived at the author's institution, his programming was accelerated. From the very beginning, Carl's contributions to group discussion were substantial, and he displayed a unique ability to challenge his own and others' thinking without being self-derogatory or imperious. Carl had been enrolled in treatment before, but this was the first time he had ever completed a program. His change in attitude can be ascribed, at least in part, to the fact that this was the first time therapy had meaningfully addressed the criminal features of Carl's drug problem. Consequently, Carl was able to see the relevance of the lifestyle concept to himself and the problems he had been experiencing both in prison and on the streets. Continued avoidance of drug and criminal opportunities will require that Carl transform his identity from that of stand-up convict and loyal gang member to that of law-abiding citizen, perhaps using his mother as a role model and his fiancee as a source of moral support and feedback.

MARY

Mary is a 19-year-old single white female college student who sought treatment at a university-based psychology clinic for depression and substance abuse. Unlike Frank, Roberto, and Carl, Mary has no prior history of criminal involvement.

Background

Mary was raised the oldest of three children in an upper-middle-class home. She describes her father, a physician, as cold, aloof, and demanding, and characterizes their relationship as strained and conflicted. Although she enjoyed a better relationship with her mother, there was cross-generational blurring in that the two behaved more as friends than as mother and daughter. In many ways, Mary derived emotional strength from her mother, whose self-confidence contrasted sharply with Mary's uneasiness and self-doubt. In fact, after visiting her mother in the hospital where the older woman was recovering from breast surgery, Mary was struck by how weak and vulnerable her mother appeared as she lay in the hospital bed. This event challenged the subject's already tenuous sense of stability, previously held together by her identification with her mother, and helped precipitate the depression for which she was seeking treatment. Even though the mother eventually recovered, Mary never did. Still upset about the experience 2 years later, she frequently voiced obsessive concern for her mother's health and well-being during therapy sessions. This concern contributed to an already high level of anxiety, stress, and psychological discomfort that Mary attempted to alleviate by ingesting drugs and entering into a series of short-term sexual liaisons.

Mary was born in Germany and lived there until the age of 10; she experienced disaffection and alienation when she and her family subsequently moved to the United States. The demand for increased social relatedness that normally occurs when youngsters enter adolescence was truly frightening to Mary, who responded by walling off her feelings and retreating into a world of her own. The majority of interpersonal transactions she engaged in during this period were shallow, superficial, and short-term, frequently centering around sex or the use of drugs. Her relationships with males, most of whom were 5 to 10 years her senior, were largely sexual in nature, and she reports feeling guilt over having entered into affairs with men she hardly knew. One way by which she managed the guilt and other negative feelings that occurred as a result of her sexual indiscretions was to use drugs. The record indicates that Mary began drinking alcohol at age 12, smoking marijuana at age 13, and consuming LSD at age 16. However, the drugs provided only momentary respite from the guilt and negative feelings that now plagued her daily. Taking a retrospective view of her situation, Mary came to realize that she sought the comfort of superficial relationships because she feared intimacy and commitment. In fact, she broke off the only meaningful relationship she had ever experienced because she was frightened about the prospect of sharing her thoughts and feelings with another person.

At college, Mary acquired the nickname "space cadet," which she wore with a certain degree of pride despite her protests that she did not appreciate the term's connotations. A perfectionist by nature, she frequently set unrealistic goals for herself, as was clearly the case with academics. When she enrolled in treatment at the psychology clinic, Mary was maintaining a 3.0 grade point average, which is quite remarkable given the struggle she was having with depression, substance abuse, and confusion. Anything less than an A, however, was totally unacceptable to her. She would spend hours studying but complained of poor concentration and remarked that this only added to her frustration. It was no secret that Mary was dissatisfied with nearly every aspect of her life and that she used drugs to allay the frustration and stress that ensued when she was unable to meet her perfectionist expectations. Mary's abuse of alcohol, marijuana, and LSD appeared to have begun as an attempt on her part to self-medicate against negative affect, self-doubt, and low self-esteem. However, these drug use behaviors became reinforcing in and of themselves, and it was not long before Mary found herself using these substances both to alleviate negative feelings and to promote positive ones. It was clear that something had to be done if Mary was to avoid a life of drug abuse and unrelenting misery.

A psychiatric evaluation was conducted to determine whether Mary's depression could be treated with psychotropic drugs. A consultation revealed the presence of clinically significant levels of depression, anxiety, and obsessional thinking. Consequently, Mary was placed on Prozac, an antidepressant medication. Although her depression lifted after several months of treatment with Prozac, Mary's drug use was unaffected. It is speculated that although Mary's use of substances may have stemmed from her efforts to self-medicate her depression, a metamorphosis of sorts took place that found drug use evolving into a self-reinforcing pattern of behavior functionally independent of its self-medicating origins.

DLSI Evaluation

A total score of 10 on the DLSI indicates that Mary demonstrates a predilection for drug lifestyle activities and probably seizes on drug use opportunities (see Table 12-4). However, her identification with the drug lifestyle falls short of the level attained by the three male subjects whose case histories were reviewed previously. This factor, in conjunction with Mary's age and background, suggests that she may still be functioning at a relatively early stage of drug lifestyle development. Unless the cognitive and behavioral errors that support Mary's commitment to a drug lifestyle are corrected, however, she will likely progress further in the lifestyle developmental sequence. Subscale analysis highlights stress-coping imbalance and interpersonal triviality as the two most prominent features of Mary's commitment to a drug lifestyle. Although she displays irresponsibility, pseudoresponsibility, and social rule bending, there is no evidence of social rule breaking on the DLSI—a finding that supports the observation that, unlike the previous three subjects, Mary possesses no criminal record. In short, the DLSI results show that Mary's drug lifestyle is expressed principally in her use of drugs as stress reducers and in her propensity to gravitate toward shallow, drug-centered interpersonal relationships.

Treatment Plan

The structural features of a treatment plan for a client like Mary should probably emphasize stress management and social skills training. Because Mary's drug use seems linked to, and is probably triggered by, stress and frustration, she must be instructed in more effective ways to manage these conditions. Furthermore, because Mary's social-interpersonal difficulties can be ascribed, at least in part, to several social skill deficits, she may benefit from enrollment in a communication skills group where she can learn to become more assertive, interpersonally responsive, and self-confident. Thinking patterns that need to be addressed with Mary include entitlement ("I need to use drugs to handle the stress in my life"), superoptimism ("I don't have a drug problem; I can stop any time I want"), and discontinuity ("I have trouble following through on initially good intentions").

Whereas the structural features of intervention for Mary should focus on stress management, social skills training, and cognitive restructuring,

Table 12-4   DLSI Scores for Mary

Scale	Score
Irresponsibility/pseudoresponsibility	2
Stress-coping imbalance	4
Interpersonal triviality	3
Social rule breaking/bending	1
Total DLSI score	10

the functional features should be more attuned to existential fear and self-identity. Mary should be encouraged to explore the various fears that lie behind the panoply of defenses she employs. The issue of self-identity should also be addressed with Mary, because her self-identity is what makes it so difficult for her to abandon the drug lifestyle. Her ambivalence about her nickname is a result of the fact that it furnishes her with a unique identity, which she has craved since childhood, but also alienates her from others and reinforces her negative self-view. Identity transformation must take place if Mary is to have any chance of relinquishing the drug lifestyle in favor of a more satisfying way of life.

Outcome

Early in treatment it became apparent that Mary's self-identity as a "space cadet" interfered with her ability to change because it allowed her to avoid others and discount her own feelings. A social-communication skills group was helpful in eliminating some of the barriers Mary had constructed to prevent others from getting close to her. As Mary acquired social skills, small interpersonal successes, and a sense of mastery over her feelings, her interpersonal relationships and view of herself improved. After several counseling sessions, it became apparent that Mary's various fears, ranging from a fear of intimacy to a fear of failure, had a common ancestry in the existential fear of nonexistence and change. Mary was subsequently encouraged to explore these feelings with an eye toward understanding their evolution and gaining a sense of mastery over them.

These identity changes showed signs of becoming stable and self-reinforcing until Mary's therapist left the clinic because of a change in clinical rotations. The new therapist took a psychodynamic approach in working with her, which not only confused Mary but also encouraged her to drop out of treatment. At last count, Mary had left college and was working for a travel agency, and although she still had problems forming stable interpersonal relationships, she was no longer using drugs to sedate her feelings, and she was looking forward to enrolling in technical school in the fall.

Chapter 13

Redirecting the Ripples

While it is evident that the ripple patterns of a drug lifestyle are for the most part pernicious, it does not necessarily follow that all ripples are negative. Just as the destructive repercussions of a drug lifestyle can exert an adverse effect on the lives of others, positive reverberations can also spill over into adjoining ponds (or lives) to yield beneficial results. Lifestyle theory maintains that we humans are social animals who seek interpersonal contact, even though in the case of a drug lifestyle such interaction tends to be superficial and often exploitative. The interdependence of humans is demonstrated wherever people congregate, whether at work or play. Individuals must possess the capacity to engage in social interaction effectively or risk being drawn into a vortex of alienation and despair. They must be able to adapt to their surroundings and learn from their environment. According to the tenets of lifestyle theory, adaptation is the key to change, growth, and long-term satisfaction. As such, it merits a brief description and a discussion of its role in lifestyle theory.

As previously mentioned in the chapter on motivation (Chapter 5), three factors determine the adaptive value of a particular behavior: respect for oneself, respect for others, and respect for nature. The preeminence of these criteria is revealed in their ability to discriminate between short-term, lifestyle-based "adaptations" and genuine adaptation, in which both short- and long-term goals are taken into account. Substance abusers who conform to the treatment environment by parroting back whatever they believe their counselor wants to hear are no more adaptive in the long run than government employees who handle the pressures of their jobs by becoming "mindless" bureaucrats. Such patterns of so-called adaptation are geared toward short-term gain while overlooking the negative long-term consequences of a particular course of action. Consequently, they reflect a lifestyle, rather than an adaptive, mode of adjustment and problem resolution. Each of the three goals of adaptation must be taken into account and satisfied before a behavior can qualify as adaptive, and only then can the process of converting negative ripples into positive ripples begin.

Lifestyle theory starts with the individual and moves outward, based on the realization that one must love and respect oneself before one can love and respect others. The well functioning individual must put him- or herself first, not in an egocentric, selfish way, but in a self-reflective way. Many people who enroll in drug treatment programs are there because they have been coerced into seeking treatment by a well-meaning parent, spouse, employer, or judge. A certain portion of this group, although they enter treatment for the wrong reasons, will learn that they must change for themselves, not anyone else. Clients who never achieve this insight are at risk for relapse because their foundation for change is weak, in that they tend to divert attention away from their own problems by their concern about what others are doing. These individuals must learn that they can never be of assistance to others until they straighten out their own behavior, and this means making themselves their own primary motivator for change. Nature also holds little value for persons who have insufficient regard for themselves. Self-respect thus precedes and complements respect for others and respect for nature by calling attention to the primary agent of change: namely, the individual.

Before moving into a discussion of how respect for others is formed, it is essential to discriminate between self-indulgence and self-respect. No matter how self-indulgent or self-centered a person engaged in a drug lifestyle may at first appear, such an individual lacks genuine concern for him- or herself; someone with true self-respect would never be willing to trade life, health, or psychological well-being for the short-term pleasure provided by drugs, as persons committed to a drug lifestyle do daily. Furthermore, therapy frequently reveals that persons committed to a drug lifestyle use drugs to fill the psychological void that underlies their behavior.

Although drug use may provide short-term relief from psychological pain, it does not satiate the psychological hunger that gnaws at them as they deal with the problems created by their mishandling of existential fear. It is these clients' persistent efforts to fill the void with drugs and drug-related activities that gives rise to the driven quality of a drug lifestyle.

Once clients' actions have been demonstrated to be guided by respect for themselves, the next step is to determine whether they respect other people. *Social interest* is a term originally coined by the psychodynamic theorist Alfred Adler (1927) to demonstrate the importance of social issues in human behavior and motivation. Adler maintained that a vigorous interest in social relationships and responsibilities increases personal productivity and directs one toward activities on the "useful side of life." Lifestyle theory considers social interest and interpersonal investment to be of key etiological significance in the formation of an adaptive approach to fear management. Someone who manages fear through adaptation considers the long- and short-term ramifications of any action, with particular emphasis on how the behavior could affect others; someone who relies on the lifestyle method of fear management is willing to violate the rights or dignity of others in the service of short-sighted, self-serving goals. Investment in social relations and commitments is therefore of cardinal significance in defining adaptation.

The final criterion used to determine whether a behavior is adaptive or lifestyle-driven involves the capacity to express respect for nature. The environment comprises a wide assortment of living organisms as well as inanimate objects. A person's nonsocial environment, which includes the creatures of the earth, myriad plant life, and the natural and manmade physical environment, must also be considered whenever the topic of adaptation is broached. Defacing other people's personal property, torturing animals, or destroying miles of forest land in return for a quick financial payoff suggests movement toward a lifestyle approach to fear management.

Likewise, groups and nations that fail to achieve harmony with nature are sacrificing long-term satisfaction and success for short-term gratification. To destroy the natural environment is to destroy potential solutions to many of humankind's problems. The tropical rain forest, for example, is thought to hold many secrets, some of which may eventually lead to cures for such devastating conditions as AIDS and cancer. Considering the fact that thousands upon thousands of acres of rain forest are lost each year to various economic interests, one begins to see how failure to heed and respect nature can lead to a person's, group's, or culture's eventual demise.

In discussing the nature of adaptation and the interaction of positive and negative ripples, it is important to keep in mind that a society affects the behavior of each one of its members. Societies that provide their citizens with clear-cut criteria and guidelines for proper behavior have traditionally encountered fewer problems with substance abuse than societies plagued by nebulous or inconsistent prescriptions for the proper use of alcohol and other chemicals. Such guidelines exert a profound influence on the smaller social units found in a society, particularly on the nuclear family. Clear, consistent social prescriptions lower societal drug use by guiding the socialization process through which children begin to form and internalize certain values and beliefs, whereas ambiguous prescriptions can interfere with parents' ability to socialize their children. Society therefore has an obligation to provide its members with clear prescriptions for appropriate behavior, to support the smaller social units more intimately involved in the socialization process.

Along with lack of guidelines, another antisocialization influence is the transformation of social issues like drug abuse and crime into political issues. In the United States, drug abuse historically has been used as a political tool for the advancement of certain groups that have coveted power and distracted the public from more pressing social issues by playing to the fears of the average citizen. Society must have the courage to consider alternative strategies for managing social problems, some of which may not be particularly appealing to those intent on being elected to political office. Drug legalization and decriminalization, for instance, are two alternative strategies in the "war" on drugs that receive scant attention from social policymakers in this country. By framing the American drug situation as a social, rather than a legal or medical, problem and by emphasizing education and treatment over enforcement and interdiction, decision makers might conceivably be able to construct a more rational and effective drug policy. Such innovation would be an adaptive response, potentially capable of limiting the negative ripples of a drug lifestyle and promoting the positive ripples of adaptive living.

Before concluding this chapter, it seems advisable to consider the parallels that appear to exist between lifestyle theory and the procedures used in its derivation. Lifestyle theory was originally framed as an effort to explain serious patterns of criminal behavior. It has its origins not in traditional theories of crime or delinquency, but in the interactions that took place between the author and persons intimately familiar with the criminal lifestyle, that is, hardened criminal offenders. This inquiry began about 10 years ago and continues to mature as a consequence of feedback supplied by the client groups to which lifestyle theory has been applied. Although the theory has been refined with the aid of research and other scholarly pursuits, the single greatest source of information still comes from persons who have lived the lifestyle. Hence, lifestyle theory is an evolving, rather than static, model of human behavior that adjusts to new information—just as clients are encouraged to adapt in response to new information accrued through their interaction with the environment. Not all information, whether directed at lifestyle theory or at an individual client, is worthwhile, and so the theory and the individual must be in a position to evaluate it both logically and empirically. What this ultimately means is that adaptation and theory development are both never-ending processes that respond to feedback from the social and nonsocial environments.

The reader should keep in mind that true adaptation calls for adjustment based on feedback gleaned from an individual's interaction with the environment. This adjustment should not be confused with the superficial bantering observed in a drug lifestyle. There is clearly a false sense of adaptation in persons who engage in drug lifestyle activities. The actions, scams, and hustles of streetwise drug addicts may appear ingenious to the outside observer; however, the reader must realize that these actions are designed to protect the lifestyle and are therefore directed at short-term goals.

The intent of lifestyle intervention is to help clients blend and balance short- and long-term expectancies, mindful of the effect their actions may have on themselves, other people, and the natural environment. This approach improves chances for survival, whether for a species or for an individual client's emotional well-being—which, after all, is the overriding objective of adaptation. Lifestyle theory holds adaptation to be the single most efficient response to existential fear and the goal of lifestyle intervention. This is also how lifestyle theory was constructed; its value lies in its ability to evolve, expand, and become more adaptive as new information comes to light. Without new knowledge there would be no growth, and without growth there would be little hope of taking the negative ripples of a drug lifestyle and transforming them into the positive ripples of adaptive living.

References

Abbey, A., Oliansky, D., Stilianos, K., Hohlstein, L. A., & Kaczynski, R. (1990). Substance abuse prevention for second graders: Are they too young to benefit? *Journal of Applied Developmental Psychology, 11*, 149–162.

Abramson, L. Y., Seligman, M. E. P., & Teasdale, J. D. (1978). Learned helplessness in humans: Critique and reformulation. *Journal of Abnormal Psychology, 87*, 49–74.

Adesso, V. J. (1985). Cognitive factors in alcohol and drug use. In M. Galizio & S. A. Maisto (Eds.), *Determinants of substance abuse: Biological, psychological, and environmental factors* (pp. 179–208). New York: Plenum.

Adler, A. (1927). *The practice and theory of individual psychology*. New York: Harcourt, Brace, & World.

Aghajanian, G. K. (1985). The neurobiology of opiate withdrawal: Receptors, second messengers, and ion channels. *Fair Oaks Hospital Psychiatry Letter, 3*, 57–60.

Ahmed, S. W., Bush, P. J., Davidson, F. R., & Ionnotti, R. J. (1984). *Predicting children's use and intentions to use abusable substances*. Paper presented at the Annual Meeting of the American Psychological Association, Washington, DC.

Ainsworth, M. D. S. (1979). Infant-mother attachment. *American Psychologist, 34*, 932–937.

Ainsworth, M. D. S. (1989). Attachments beyond infancy. *American Psychologist, 44*, 709–716.

Akers, R. L. (1984). Delinquent behavior, drugs, and alcohol— What is the relationship? *Today's Delinquent, 3,* 19–47.

Alden, L. (1988). Behavioral self-management controlled-drinking strategies in a context of secondary prevention. *Journal of Consulting and Clinical Psychology, 56,* 280–286.

Alexander, B. K. (1990). The empirical and theoretical bases of an adaptive model of addiction. *Journal of Drug Issues, 20,* 37–65.

Alexander, J. F., & Parsons, B. V. (1973). Short-term behavioral intervention with delinquent families: Impact on family process and recidivism. *Journal of Abnormal Psychology, 81,* 219–225.

Alexander, J. F., Waldron, H. B., Barton, C., & Mas, C. H. (1989). The minimizing of blaming attributions and behaviors in delinquent families. *Journal of Consulting and Clinical Psychology, 57,* 19–24.

Alkana, R. L., Parker, E. S., Cohen, H. B., Birch, H., & Nobel, E. P. (1976). Reversal of ethanol intoxication in humans: An assessment of the efficacy of propranolol. *Psychopharmacology, 51,* 29–38.

Amit, Z., Levitan, D. E., & Lindros, K. O. (1976). Suppression of ethanol intake following administration of dopamine-beta- hydroxylase inhibitors in rats. *Archives of International Pharmacodynamic Therapy, 223,* 114–119.

Andrucci, G. L., Archer, R. P., Pancoast, D. L., & Gordon, R. A. (1989). The relationship of MMPI and sensation-seeking scales to adolescent drug use. *Journal of Personality Assessment, 53,* 253–266.

Anglin, M. D., Brecht, M. L., Woodward, J. A., & Bonett, D. G. (1986). An empirical study of maturing out: Conditional factors. *International Journal of the Addictions, 21,* 233–246.

Annis, H. M. (1982). *Inventory of drinking situations.* Toronto: Addiction Research Foundation.

Annis, H. M., & Davis, C. S. (1988). Self-efficacy and the prevention of alcoholic relapse: Initial findings from a treatment trial. In T. B. Baker & D. S. Cannon (Eds.), *Assessment and treatment of addictive disorders* (pp. 88–111). New York: Praeger.

Aronson, H., & Gilbert, A. (1963). Preadolescent sons of alcoholics. *Archives of General Psychiatry, 8,* 235–241.

Azrin, N. H., Sisson, R. W., Meyers, R. E., & Godley, M. (1982). Alcoholism treatment by disulfiram and community reinforcement therapy. *Journal of Behavior Therapy and Experimental Psychiatry, 13,* 105–112.

Bachman, J. G., Johnston, L. D., & O'Malley, P. M. (1981). *Monitoring the future: Questionnaire responses from the nations' high school seniors 1980.* Ann Arbor, MI: Institute for Social Research.

Baer, J. S., Holt, C. S., & Lichtenstein, E. (1986). Self- efficacy and smoking reexamined: Construct validity and clinical utility. *Journal of Consulting and Clinical Psychology, 54,* 846–852.

Baer, J. S., Marlatt, G. A., Kivlahan, D. R., Fromme, K., Larimer, M. E., & Williams, E. (1992). An experimental test of three methods of alcohol risk reduction with young adults. *Journal of Consulting and Clinical Psychology, 60,* 974–979.

Baker, B. L. (1969). Symptom treatment and symptom substitution in enuresis. *Journal of Abnormal Psychology, 74,* 42–49.

Bales, R. F. (1946). Cultural differences in rates of alcoholism. *Quarterly Journal of Studies on Alcohol, 6,* 480–489.

Balster, R. L., Kilbey, M. M., & Ellinwood, E. H. (1976). Methamphetamine self-administration in the cat. *Psychopharmacologia, 46,* 229–233.

Balster, R. L., & Woolverton, W. L. (1980). Continuous-access phencyclidine self-administration by rhesus monkeys leading to physical dependence. *Psychopharmacology, 70*, 5–10.

Bandura, A. (1977). *Social learning theory.* Englewood Cliffs, NJ: Prentice-Hall.

Bandura, A. (1982). Self-efficacy mechanism in human agency. *American Psychologist, 37*, 122–147.

Barber, J. G., Bradshaw, R., & Walsh, C. (1989). Reducing alcohol consumption through television advertising. *Journal of Consulting and Clinical Psychology, 57*, 613–618.

Barrett, M. E., Joe, G. W., & Simpson, D. D. (1990). Availability of drugs and psychological proneness in opioid addiction. *International Journal of the Addictions, 25*, 1211–1226.

Barton, C., Alexander, J. F., Waldron, H., Turner, C. W., & Warbuton, J. (1985). Generalizing treatment effects of functional family therapy: Three replications. *American Journal of Family Therapy, 13*, 16–26.

Bates, J. E., Maslin, C. A., & Frankel, K. A. (1985). Attachment security, mother-child interaction, and temperament as predictors of behavior-problem ratings at age three years. *Monographs of the Society for Research in Child Development, 50*, (1–2, Serial No. 209).

Baumann, D. J., Obitz, F., & Reich, J. W. (1982). Attribution theory: A fit with problems of substance abuse. *International Journal of the Addictions, 17*, 295–303.

Baumrind, D. (1985). Familial antecedents of adolescent drug use: A developmental perspective. *NIDA Research Monograph Series, 56*, 13–44.

Beck, A. T. (1976). *Cognitive therapy and mental disorders.* New York: International Universities Press.

Becker, G. S. (1968). Crime and punishment: An economic approach. *Journal of Political Economy, 76*, 169–217.

Becker, H. S. (1953). Becoming a marijuana user. *American Journal of Sociology, 59*, 235–243.

Beecher, H. K. (1959). *Measurement of subjective responses: Quantitative effects of drugs.* New York: Oxford University Press.

Begleiter, H., Porjesz, B., Bihari, B., & Kissin, B. (1984). Event-related potentials in boys at risk for alcoholism. *Science, 225*, 1493–1496.

Bell, R. Q. (1979). Parent, child, and reciprocal influences. *American Psychologist, 34*, 821–826.

Bennett, T. (1986). A decision-making approach to opioid addiction. In D. B. Cornish & R. V. Clarke (Eds.), *The reasoning criminal: Rational choice perspectives on offending* (pp. 83–103). New York: Springer-Verlag.

Berg, G., Laberg, J. C., Skutle, A., & Ohman, A. (1981). Instructed versus pharmacological effects of alcohol in alcoholics and social drinkers. *Behavior, Research, and Therapy, 19*, 55–66.

Bianchi, E., Maremmani, I., Meloni, D., & Tagliamonte, A. (1992). Controlled use of heroin in patients on methadone maintenance treatment. *Journal of Substance Abuse Treatment, 9*, 383–387.

Bidlack, J. M., Frey, D. K., Seyed-Mozaffari, A., & Archer, S. (1990). Irreversible affinity ligands for Mu opioid receptors. *NIDA Research Monograph Series, 95*, 296.

Bigelow, G. E., Griffiths, R. R., & Liebson, I. A. (1976). Effects of response requirement upon human sedative self- administration and drug seeking behavior. *Pharmacology, Biochemistry and Behavior, 5*, 681–685.

Bigelow, G. E., Griffiths, R. R., & Liebson, I. A. (1977). Pharmacological influences upon ethanol self-administration. In M. M. Gross (Ed.), *Alcohol intoxication and withdrawal* (Vol. 3B, pp. 523–538). New York: Plenum.

Bigelow, G. E., & Preston, K. L. (1989). Drug discrimination: Methods for drug characterization and classification. *NIDA Research Monograph Series, 92*, 101–122.

Bigelow, G. E., Stitzer, M. L., Griffiths, R. R., & Liebson, I. A. (1981). Contingency management approaches to drug self- administration and drug abuse: Efficacy and limitations. *Addictive Behaviors, 6*, 241–252.

Binkoff, J. A., Monti, P. M., Zwick, W., Abrams, D. B., Pedraza, M., & Monroe, S. (1986). *Relationship between problem drinkers' performance in alcohol-specific role plays and post- treatment drinking.* Poster presented at the 7th Annual Meeting of the Society of Behavioral Medicine, San Francisco, CA.

Birke, S. A., Edelmann, R. J., & Davis, P. E. (1990). An analysis of the abstinence violation effect in a sample of illicit drug users. *British Journal of Addiction, 85*, 1299–1307.

Black, G. S. (1991, January). *Partnership for a Drug-Free America attitude tracking study.* Paper presented at the NIDA National Conference on Drug Abuse Research and Practice, Washington, DC.

Blakey, R., & Baker, R. (1980). An exposure approach to alcohol abuse. *Behaviour Research and Therapy, 18*, 319–325.

Blehar, M. C., Lieberman, A. F., & Ainsworth, M. D. S. (1977). Early face-to-face interaction and its relation to later infant-mother attachment. *Child Development, 48*, 182–194.

Block, J. (1971). *Lives through time.* Berkeley, CA: Bancroft.

Blum, K., Eubanks, J. D., Wallace, J. E., Schwertner, H., & Morgan, W. W. (1976). Possible role of tetrahydroisoquinoline alkaloids in post-alcohol intoxication states. *Annals of the New York Academy of Sciences, 273*, 234–246.

Blum, K., Noble, E. P., Sheridan, P. J., Montgomery, A., Richie, T., Jagadeeswaran, P., Nogami, H., Briggs, A. H., & Cohn, J. B. (1990). Allelic association of human dopamine D_2 receptor gene in alcoholism. *Journal of the American Medical Association, 263*, 2055–2060.

Blum, R. (1972). *Horatio Alger's children: The role of the family in the origin and prevention of drug risk.* San Francisco: Jossey-Bass.

Bohman, M. (1978). Some genetic aspects of alcoholism and criminality: A population of adoptees. *Archives of General Psychiatry, 35*, 269–276.

Bohman, M., Sigvardsson, S., & Cloninger, C. R. (1981). Maternal inheritance of alcohol abuse: Cross-fostering analysis of adopted women. *Archives of General Psychiatry, 38*, 965–969.

Booth, B. M., Russell, D. W., Soucek, S., & Laughlin, P. R. (1992). Social support and outcome of alcoholism treatment: An exploratory analysis. *American Journal of Drug and Alcohol Abuse, 18*, 87–101.

Booth, P. G., Dale, B., Slade, P. D., & Dewey, M. E. (1992). A follow-up study of problem drinkers offered a goal choice option. *Journal of Studies on Alcohol, 53*, 594–600.

Borkovec, T. D. (1970). Autonomic reactivity to sensory stimulation in psychopathic, neurotic, and normal juvenile delinquents. *Journal of Consulting and Clinical Psychology, 35*, 217–222.

Botvin, G. J. (1983). *Life skills training: Teachers manual.* New York: Smithfield Press.

Botvin, G. J., Baker, E., Dusenbury, L., Tortu, S., & Botvin, E. M. (1990). Preventing adolescent drug abuse through a multimodal cognitive-behavioral approach: Results of a 3-year study. *Journal of Consulting and Clinical Psychology, 58*, 437–446.

Botvin, G. J., & Wills, T. A. (1985). Personal and social skills training: Cognitive-behavioral approaches to substance abuse prevention. *NIDA Research Monograph Series, 63*, 8–49.

Bowlby, J. (1982). *Attachment and loss: Volume 1. Attachment.* New York: Basic Books (originally published in 1969).

Bradley, B. P., Gossop, M., Brewin, C. R., Phillips, G., & Green, L. (1992). Attribution and relapse in opiate addicts. *Journal of Consulting and Clinical Psychology, 60,* 470–472.

Bradley, B. P., Phillips, G., Green, L., & Gossop, M. (1989). Circumstances surrounding the initial lapse to opiate use following detoxification. *British Journal of Psychiatry, 154,* 354–359.

Brady, J. V., & Griffiths, R. R. (1977). Drug maintained performance and the analysis of stimulant reinforcing effects. In E. H. Ellinwood & M. M. Kilbey (Eds.), *Cocaine and other stimulants* (pp. 599–613). New York: Plenum.

Brandon, T. H., Tiffany, S. T., & Baker, T. B. (1986). The process of smoking relapse. *NIDA Research Monograph Series, 72,* 104–117.

Brennan, P. L., & Moos, R. H. (1990). Life stressors, social resources, and later life problem drinking. *Psychology and Aging, 5,* 491–501.

Briddle, D. W., Rimm, D. C., Caddy, G. R., Krawitz, G., Sholis, D., & Wunderlin, R. J. (1978). The effects of alcohol and cognitive set on sexual arousal to deviant stimuli. *Journal of Abnormal Psychology, 87,* 418–430.

Brook, J. S., Brook, D. W., Gordon, A. S., Whiteman, M., & Cohen, P. (1990). The psychosocial etiology of adolescent drug use: A family interactional approach. *Genetic, Social, and General Psychology Monographs, 116* (2).

Brook, J. S., Cohen, P., Whiteman, M., & Gordon, A. S. (1992). Psychosocial risk factors in the transition from moderate to heavy use or abuse of drugs. In M. Glantz & R. Pickens (Eds.), *Vulnerability to drug abuse* (pp. 359–388). Washington, DC: American Psychological Association.

Brook, J. S., Whiteman, M., Gordon, A. S., & Brook, D. W. (1983). Paternal correlates of adolescent marijuana use in the context of the mother-son and parental dyads. *Genetic Psychology Monographs, 108,* 197–213.

Brown, H. P., & Peterson, J. H. (1990). Rationale and procedural suggestions for defining and actualizing spiritual values in the treatment of dependency. *Alcoholism Treatment Quarterly, 7,* 17–46.

Brown, R. A. (1980). Conventional education and controlled drinking education courses with convicted drunken drivers. *Behavior Therapy, 11,* 632–642.

Brown, S. A., Vik, P. W., McQuaid, J. R., Patterson, T. L., Irwin, M. R., & Grant, I. (1990). Severity of psychosocial stress and outcome of alcoholism treatment. *Journal of Abnormal Psychology, 99,* 344–348.

Bry, B. H. (1988). Family-based approaches to reducing adolescent substance use: Theories, techniques, and findings. *NIDA Research Monograph Series, 77,* 39–68.

Budney, A. J., Higgins, S. T., Delaney, D. D., Kent, L., & Bickel, W. K. (1991). Contingent reinforcement of abstinence with individuals abusing cocaine and marijuana. *Journal of Applied Behavior Analysis, 24,* 657–665.

Burling, T. A., Reilly, P. M., Moltzen, J. O., & Ziff, D. C. (1989). Self-efficacy and relapse among inpatient drug and alcohol abusers: A predictor of outcome. *Journal of Studies on Alcohol, 50,* 354–360.

Bush, J. (1983). Criminality and psychopathology: Treatment for the guilty. *Federal Probation, 47,* 44–49.

Butcher, J. N., Dahlstrom, W. G., Graham, J. R., Tellegen, A., & Kaemmer, B. (1989). *Minnesota Multiphasic Personality Inventory-2 (MMPI-2): Manual for administration and scoring.* Minneapolis, MN: University of Minnesota Press.

Caddy, G. R., Addington, H. J., & Perkins, D. (1978). Individualized behavior therapy for alcoholics: A third year independent double-blind follow-up. *Behaviour Research and Therapy, 16,* 345–362.

Cadoret, R. J., & Gath, A. (1978). Inheritance of alcoholism in adoptees. *British Journal of Psychiatry, 132,* 252–258.

Cadoret, R. J., Troughton, E., O'Gorman, T. W., & Heywood, E. (1986). An adoption study of genetic and environmental factors in drug abuse. *Archives of General Psychiatry, 43,* 1131–1136.

Caetano, R., & Medina-Mora, M. E. (1988). Acculturation and drinking among people of Mexican descent in Mexico and the United States. *Journal of Studies on Alcohol, 49,* 462–471.

Cahalan, D., Cisin, I. H., & Crossley, H. M. (1969). *American drinking practices: A natural study of drinking behavior and attitudes* (Monograph No. 6). New Brunswick: NJ: Rutgers Center for Alcohol Studies.

Cahalan, C., & Room, R. (1974). *Problem drinking among American men.* New Brunwick, NJ: Rutgers Center for Alcohol Studies.

Calsyn, D. A., Roszell, D. K., & Chaney, E. F. (1989). Validation of MMPI profile subtypes among opioid addicts who are beginning methadone maintenance treatment. *Journal of Clinical Psychology, 45,* 991–998.

Cannon, S. R. (1976). *Social functioning patterns in families receiving treatment for drug abuse.* Roslyn Heights, NY: Libra.

Carpenter, R., Lyons, C., & Miller, W. (1985). Peer-managed self-control program for prevention of alcohol abuse in American Indian high school students. *International Journal of the Addictions, 20,* 299–310.

Carroll, J. K. (1986). Secondary prevention: A programmatic approach to the problem of substance abuse among adolescents. In I. Beschner & A. I. Friedman (Eds.), *Teen drug use.* Lexington, MA: Lexington Books.

Castaneda, R., Galanter, M., & Franco, H. (1989). Self- medication among addicts with primary psychiatric disorders. *Comprehensive Psychiatry, 30,* 80–83.

Chait, L. D., Uhlenhuth, E. H., & Johanson, C. E. (1986). The discriminative stimulus and subjective effects of *d*- amphetamine, phenmetrazine and fenfluramine in humans. *Psychopharmacology, 89,* 301–306.

Chaney, E. F., O'Leary, M. R., & Marlatt, G. A. (1978). Skill training with alcoholics. *Journal of Consulting and Clinical Psychology, 46,* 1092–1104.

Chaney, E. F., Roszell, D. K., & Cummings, C. (1982). Relapse in opiate addicts: A behavioral analysis. *Addictive Behaviors, 7,* 291–297.

Chein, I., Gerard, D. L., Lee, R. S., & Rosenfeld, E. (1964). *The road to H: Narcotics, delinquency, and social policy.* New York: Basic Books.

Childress, A. R., McLellan, A. T., Ehrman, R., & O'Brien, C. P. (1987). Extinction of conditioned responses in abstinent cocaine or opioid users. *NIDA Research Monograph Series, 76,* 189–195.

Childress, A. R., McLellan, A. T., Ehrman, R., & O'Brien, C. P. (1988). Classically conditioned responses in opioid and cocaine dependence: A role in relapse? *NIDA Research Monograph Series, 84,* 25–43.

Childress, A. R., McLellan, A. T., & O'Brien, C. P. (1986). Conditioned responses in a methadone population: A comparison of laboratory, clinical, and natural setting. *Journal of Substance Abuse Treatment, 3,* 173–179.

Christiansen, B. A., & Goldman, M. S. (1983). Alcohol-related expectancies versus demographic/background variables in the prediction of adolescent drinking. *Journal of Consulting and Clinical Psychology, 51,* 249–257.

Christiansen, B. A., & Teahan, J. E. (1987). Cross-cultural comparisons of Irish and American adolescent drinking practices and beliefs. *Journal of Studies on Alcohol, 48,* 558–562.

Church, A. C., Fuller, J. L., & Dudek, B. C. (1976). Salsolinol differentially affects mice selected for sensitivity to alcohol. *Psychopharmacology*, *47*, 49–52.

Cinquemani, D. K. (1975). *Drinking and violence among Middle American Indians*. Unpublished dissertation, Columbia University, New York.

Ciraulo, D. A., Barnhill, J. G., Ciraulo, A. M., Greenblatt, D. J., & Shader, R. I. (1989). Parental alcoholism as a risk factor in benzodiazepine abuse: A pilot study. *British Journal of Psychiatry*, *146*, 1333–1335.

Clayton, R. R. (1992). Transitions in drug use: Risk and protective factors. In M. Glantz & R. Pickens (Eds.), *Vulnerability to drug abuse* (pp. 15–51). Washington, DC: American Psychological Association.

Cloninger, C. R. (1987). Neurogenetic adaptive mechanisms in alcoholism. *Science*, *236*, 410–416.

Cloninger, C. R., Bohman, M., & Sigvardsson, S. (1981). Inheritance of alcohol abuse: Cross-fostering analysis of adopted men. *Archives of General Psychiatry*, *38*, 861–868.

Coggans, N., & Davies, J. B. (1988). Explanations for heroin use. *Journal of Drug Issues*, *18*, 457–465.

Collier, H. O. J. (1980). Cellular site of opiate dependence. *Nature*, *283*, 625–629.

Collins, R. L., & Lapp, W. M. (1991). Restraint and attributions: Evidence of the abstinence violation effect in alcohol consumption. *Cognitive Therapy and Research*, *15*, 69–84.

Condiotte, M. M., & Lichtenstein, E. (1981). Self-efficacy and relapse in smoking cessation programs. *Journal of Consulting and Clinical Psychology*, *49*, 648–658.

Connell, D. B. (1976). *Individual differences in attachment: An investigation into stability, implications, and relationships to the structure of early language development*. Unpublished doctoral dissertation, Syracuse University.

Coombs, R. H., & Paulson, M. J. (1988). Contrasting family patterns of adolescent drug users and nonusers. *Journal of Chemical Dependency Treatment*, *1*, 59–72.

Coombs, R. H., Paulson, M. J., & Richardson, M. A. (1991). Peer vs. parental influence in substance use among hispanic and anglo children and adolescents. *Journal of Youth and Adolescence*, *20*, 73–88.

Cooney, N. L., Baker, L., & Pomerleau, O. F. (1983). Cue exposure for relapse prevention in alcohol treatment. In R. J. McMahon & K. D. Craig (Eds.), *Advances in clinical therapy* (pp. 174–210). New York: Brunner/Mazel.

Cooper, M. L., Russell, M., Skinner, J. B., & Windle, M. (1992). Development and validation of a three-dimensional measure of drinking motives. *Psychological Assessment*, *4*, 123–132.

Cooper, S. E. (1983). The influence of self-concept outcomes of intensive alcoholism treatment. *Journal of Studies on Alcohol*, *44*, 1087–1092.

Corbin, R. M. (1980). Decisions that might not get made. In T. S. Wallsten (ed.), *Cognitive processes in choice and decision behavior*. Hillsdale, NJ: Erlbaum.

Craig, R. J., & Olson, R. (1992). MMPI subtypes for cocaine abusers. *American Journal of Drug and Alcohol Abuse*, *18*, 197–205.

Critchlow, B. (1986). The powers of John Barleycorn: Beliefs about the effects of alcohol on social behavior. *American Psychologist*, *41*, 751–764.

Crowley, T. J. (1988). Learning and unlearning drug abuse in the real world: Clinical treatment and public policy. *NIDA Research Monograph Series*, *84*, 100–121.

Curry, S., Marlatt, G. A., & Gordon, J. R. (1987). Abstinence violation effect: Validation of an attributional construct with smoking cessation. *Journal of Consulting and Clinical Psychology*, *55*, 145–149.

Cushman, P. (1974). Detoxification of rehabilitated methadone patients: Frequency and predictors of long term success. *American Journal of Drug and Alcohol Abuse*, *1*, 393–408.

Cutter, H., Maloof, B., Kurtz, N., & Jones, W. (1976). Feeling no pain: Differential responses to pain by alcoholics and nonalcoholics before and after drinking. *Journal of Studies on Alcohol, 37*, 273–277.

Dackis, C. A., & Gold, M. S. (1988). Psychopharmacology of cocaine. *Psychiatric Annals, 18*, 528–530.

Dadds, M. R., & McHugh, T. A. (1992). Social support and treatment outcome in behavioral family therapy for child conduct problems. *Journal of Consulting and Clinical Psychology, 60*, 252–259.

Daitzman, R., & Zuckerman, M. (1980). Disinhibitory sensation seeking, personality and gonadal hormones. *Personality and Individual Differences, 1*, 103–110.

Dalgard, O. S., & Kringlen, E. (1976). A Norwegian twin study of criminality. *British Journal of Criminology, 16*, 213–232.

Davidson, R., & Schwartz, G. (1976). The psychobiology of relaxation and related states: A multi-process theory. In D. I. Motofsky (Ed.), *Behavior control and the modification of physiological activity* (pp. 399–442). New York: Prentice-Hall.

Davison, G. C., Tsujimoto, R., & Glaros, A. (1973). Attribution and the maintenance of behavior change in falling asleep. *Journal of Abnormal Psychology, 82*, 124–135.

de Bono, E. (1981). *CoRT thinking program*. Toronto: Pergamon.

Deitrich, R. A., & Spuhler, K. (1984). Genetics of alcoholism and alcohol actions. In R. Smart & E. M. Sellers (Eds.), *Research advances in alcohol and drug problems* (Vol. 8, pp. 47–98). New York: Plenum.

de Lint, J. (1976). The etiology of alcoholism with specific reference to sociocultural factors. In M. W. Everett, J. O. Waddell, & D. B. Heath (Eds.), *Cross-cultural approaches to the study of alcohol: An introductory perspective* (pp. 323–339). Paris: Mouton.

Denney, M. R., Baugh, J. L., & Hardt, H. D. (1991). Sobriety outcome after alcoholism treatment with biofeedback participation: A pilot inpatient study. *International Journal of the Addictions, 26*, 335–341.

de Wit, H., & McCracken, S. G. (1990). Preference for ethanol in males with or without an alcoholic first degree relative. *NIDA Research Monograph Series, 95*, 374–375.

de Wit, H., Pierri, J., & Johanson, C. E. (1989). Reinforcing and subjective effects of diazepam in nondrug-abusing volunteers. *Pharmacology, Biochemistry and Behavior, 33*, 205–213.

de Wit, H., Uhlenbuth, E. H., Pierri, J., & Johanson, C. E. (1987). Individual differences in behavioral and subjective responses to alcohol. *Alcoholism, 11*, 52–59.

Dielman, T. E., Lorenger, A. T., Leech, S. L., Lyons, A. L., Klos, D. M., & Horvath, W. J. (1985). Fifteen-month follow-up results of an elementary school based smoking prevention project: Resisting pressures to smoke. *Hygiene, 4*, 28–35.

Dishion, T. J., Patterson, G. R., & Reid, J. R. (1988). Parent and peer factors associated with sampling in early adolescence: Implications for treatment. *NIDA Research Monograph Series, 77*, 69–93.

Dishion, T. J., Stouthamer-Loeber, M., & Patterson, G. R. (1984). *The monitoring construct* [OSLC technical report]. (Available from OSLC, 207 East 5th, Suite 202, Eugene, OR 97401).

Dobson, K. S., & Block, L. (1988). Historical and physiological bases of the cognitive-behavioral therapies. In K. S. Dobson (Ed.), *Handbook of cognitive-behavioral therapies* (pp. 3–38). New York: Guilford.

Donovan, J. E., Jessor, R., & Jessor, L. (1983). Problem drinking in adolescence and young adulthood: A follow-up study. *Journal of Studies on Alcohol, 44*, 109–137.

Donovan, J. M. (1986). An etiologic model of alcoholism. *American Journal of Psychiatry, 143*, 1–11. Drake, R. E., & Wallach, M. A. (1989). Substance abuse among the chronically mentally ill. *Hospital and Community Psychiatry, 40*, 1041–1046.

Dumas, J. E. (1986). Parental perception of treatment outcome in families of aggressive children: A causal model. *Behavior Therapy, 17*, 420–432.

Dusenbury, L., & Botvin, G. J. (1992). Substance abuse prevention: Competence enhancement and the development of positive life options. *Journal of Addictive Diseases, 11*, 29–45.

D'Zurilla, T. J., & Goldfried, M. R. (1971). Problem-solving and behavior modification. *Journal of Abnormal Psychology, 78*, 107–126.

Earlywine, M., & Finn, P. R. (1991). Sensation seeking explains the relation between behavioral disinhibition and alcohol consumption. *Addictive Behaviors, 16*, 123–128.

Eastman, C., & Norris, H. (1982). Alcohol dependence, relapse, and self-identity. *Journal of Studies on Alcohol, 43*, 1214–1231.

Eikelboom, R., & Stewart, J. (1979). Conditioned temperature effects using morphine as the unconditioned stimulus. *Psychopharmacology, 61*, 31–38.

Einhorn, H. J., & Hogarth, R. M. (1978). Confidence in judgment: Persistence in the illusion of validity. *Psychological Review, 85*, 395–416.

Ellickson, P. L., Hays, R. D., & Bell, R. M. (1992). Stepping through the drug use sequence: Longitudinal scalogram analysis of initiation and regular use. *Journal of Abnormal Psychology, 101*, 441–451.

Elliott, D. S., Huizinga, D., & Ageton, S. S. (1985). *Explaining delinquency and drug use.* Beverly Hills, CA: Sage.

Ellis, A. (1970). *The essence of rational psychotherapy: A comprehensive approach to treatment.* New York: Institute of Rational Living.

Emmelkamp, P. M. G. (1986). Behavior therapy with adults. In S. L. Garfield & A. E. Bergin (Eds.), *Handbook of psychotherapy and behavior change* (3rd. ed., pp. 385–442). New York: John Wiley.

Emmelkamp, P. M. G., & Herres, H. (1988). Drug addiction and parental rearing style: A controlled study. *International Journal of the Addictions, 23*, 207–216.

Eriksen, L., Bjornstad, S., & Gertestam, K. G. (1986). Social skills training in groups for alcoholics: One-year treatment outcome for groups and individuals. *Addictive Behaviors, 11*, 309–329.

Evans, R. I. (1976). Smoking in children: Developing a social psychological strategy of deterrence. *Preventive Medicine, 5*, 122–127.

Fanselow, M. S., & German, C. (1982). Explicitly unpaired delivery of morphine and the test situation: Extinction and retardation of tolerance to the suppressing effects of morphine on locomotor activity. *Behavior and Neural Biology, 35*, 231–241.

Farley, F. (1986). The big T in personality. *Psychology Today, 20*, 44–52.

Farrell, A. D., Danish, S. J., & Howard, C. W. (1992). Relationship between drug use and other problem behaviors in urban adolescents. *Journal of Consulting and Clinical Psychology, 60*, 705–712.

Fattah, E. H. (1982). A critique of deterrence research with particular reference to the economic approach. *Canadian Journal of Criminology, 24*, 79–90.

Faupel, C. E. (1985). A theoretical model for socially oriented drug treatment policy. *Journal of Drug Education, 15*, 189–203.

Faupel, C. E. (1987). Heroin use and criminal careers. *Qualitative Sociology, 10*, 115–131.

Faupel, C. E., & Klockars, C. B. (1987). Drugs-crime connections: Elaborations from the life histories of hard-core heroin addicts. *Social Problems, 34*, 54–68.

Feigelman, W., Hyman, M. M., Amann, K., & Feigelman, B. (1990). Correlates of persisting drug use among former youth multiple drug abuse patients. *Journal of Psychoactive Drugs, 22*, 63–75.

Fenley, J. M., & Williams, J. E. (1991). A comparison of perceived self among drug addicts and nonaddicts. *International Journal of the Addictions, 26*, 973–979.

Fillmore, K. M. (1974). Drinking and problem drinking in early adulthood and middle age: An exploratory 20 year follow-up study. *Quarterly Journal of Studies on Alcohol, 35*, 819–840.

Fillmore, K. M. (1988). *Alcohol use across the life course: A critical review of 70 years of international research.* Toronto: Addiction Research Foundation.

Filskov, S. B., & Goldstein, S. G. (1974). Diagnostic validity of the Halstead-Reitan Neuropsychological Battery. *Journal of Consulting and Clinical Psychology, 42*, 382–388.

Finn, P. R., & Pihl, R. O. (1987). Men at high risk for alcoholism: The effect of alcohol on cardiovascular response to unavoidable shock. *Journal of Abnormal Psychology, 96*, 230–236.

Fischman, M. W., & Rachlinski, J. J. (1989). *Cocaine self- administration in humans: A laboratory analysis.* Unpublished manuscript, John Hopkins University School of Medicine.

Fischman, W. M., & Schuster, C. R. (1982). Cocaine self- administration in humans. *Federation Proceedings, 41*, 241–246.

Fischman, M. W., Schuster, C. R., & Rajfer, S. (1983). A comparison of the subjective and cardiovascular effects of procaine and cocaine in humans. *Pharmacology, Biochemistry and Behavior, 18*, 711–716.

Fisher, J. D., & Farina, A. (1979). Consequences of beliefs about the nature of mental disorders. *Journal of Abnormal Psychology, 88*, 320–327.

Fisher, L. A., & Bauman, K. E. (1988). Influence and selection in the friend-adolescent relationship: Findings from studies of adolescent smoking and drinking. *Journal of Applied Social Psychology, 18*, 289–314.

Flay, B. R., & Pentz, M. A. (1985). Reaching children with mass media health promotion programs: The relative effectiveness of an advertising campaign, a community-based program, and a school-based program. In D. S. Leathar (Ed.), *Health education and the media* (Vol. 2, pp. 149–154). Oxford: Pergamon.

Folkins, C. H., & Sime, W. E. (1981). Physical fitness training and mental health. *American Psychologist, 36*, 373–389.

Forsterling, F. (1985). Attributional training: A review. *Psychological Bulletin, 98*, 495–512.

Frankl, V. E. (1984). *Man's search for meaning: An introduction to Logotherapy* (3rd ed.). New York: Simon & Schuster.

Fraser, M. W., Hawkins, J. D., & Howard, M. O. (1988). Parent training for delinquency prevention. *Family Perspectives in Child and Youth Services, 11*, 93–125.

Friedman, A. S., Pomerance, E., Sanders, R., Santo, Y., & Utada, A. (1980). The structure and problems of the families of adolescent drug abusers. *Contemporary Drug Problems, 9*, 327–356.

Friedman, A. S., Utada, A., & Morrissey, M. R. (1987). Families of adolescent drug abusers are "rigid:" Are these families either "disengaged" or "enmeshed," or both? *Family Process, 26*, 131–148.

Froman, R. D., & Owen, S. V. (1989). Infant care self-efficacy. *Scholarly Inquiry for Nursing Practice, 3*, 199–211.

Fromme, K., & Dunn, M. E. (1992). Alcohol expectancies, social and environmental cues as determinants of drinking and perceived reinforcement. *Addictive Behaviors, 17*, 167–177.

Frykholm, B. (1979). Termination of the drug career: An interview study of 58 ex-addicts. *Acta Psychiatrica Scandinavica, 59*, 370–380.

Fuller, R. K. (1984). A critical analysis of the efficacy and toxicity of alcohol sensitising drugs. In G. Edwards & J. Littleton (Eds.), *Pharmacological treatments for alcoholism* (pp. 559–571). New York: Methuen, Inc.

Gabrielli, W. F., Mednick, S. A., Volavka, J., Pollock, V. E., Schulsinger, F., & Itil, T. M. (1982). Electroencephalograms in children of alcoholic fathers. *Psychophysiology, 19,* 404–407.

Gelernter, J., Goldman, D., & Risch, N. (1993). The A1 allele at the D_2 dopamine receptor gene and alcoholism: A reappraisal. *Journal of the American Medical Association, 269,* 1673–1677.

Gendreau, P., & Gendreau, L. P. (1970). The "addiction-prone" personality: A study of Canadian heroin addicts. *Canadian Journal of Behavioral Science, 2,* 18–25.

Gersick, K. E., Grady, K., & Snow, D. L. (1988). Social- cognitive skill development with sixth graders and its initial impact on substance use. *Journal of Drug Education, 18,* 55–70.

Gianoulakis, C., & Gupta, A. (1986). Inbred strains of mice with variable sensitivity to ethanol exhibit differences in the content and processing of B-endorphin. *Life Sciences, 39,* 2315–2325.

Gillmore, M. R., Catalano, R. F., Morrison, D. M., Wells, E. A., Iritani, B., & Hawkins, J. D. (1990). Racial differences in acceptability and availability of drugs and early initiation of substance use. *American Journal of Drug and Alcohol Abuse, 16,* 185–206.

Ginsberg, I. J., & Greenely, J. R. (1978). Competing theories of marijuana use: A longitudinal study. *Journal of Health and Social Behavior, 19,* 22–34.

Glassner, B., & Laughlin, J. (1987). *Drugs in adolescent worlds: Burnouts to straights.* New York: St. Martin's Press.

Goldberg, S. R., & Schuster, C. R. (1970). Conditioned nalorphine-induced abstinence changes: Persistence in post morphine dependent monkeys. *Journal of the Experimental Analysis of Behavior, 14,* 33–46.

Goldfried, M. R., & Robins, C. (1982). On the facilitation of self-efficacy. *Cognitive Therapy and Research, 6,* 361–380.

Goldsmith, H. H., & Alansky, J. A. (1987). Maternal and infant temperamental predictors of attachment: A meta-analytic review. *Journal of Consulting and Clinical Psychology, 55,* 805–816.

Goldsmith, H. H., Bradshaw, D. L., & Rieser-Danner, L. A. (1986). Temperamental dimensions as potential developmental influences on attachment. In J. V. Lerner & R. M. Lerner (Eds.), *New directions for child development: Temperament and psychosocial interaction in infancy and childhood* (pp. 5–34). San Francisco: Jossey-Bass.

Goldsmith, H. H., & Campos, J. J. (1982). Toward a theory of infant temperament. In R. N. Emde & R. J. Harmon (Eds.), *The development of attachment and affiliative systems* (pp. 161–193). New York: Plenum.

Goldstein, J. W., & Sappington, J. (1977). Personality characteristics of students who become heavy drug users: An MMPI study of an avant-garde. *American Journal of Drug and Alcohol Abuse, 4,* 401–412.

Goodstadt, M. S. (1986). School-based drug education in North America: What is wrong? What can be done? *Journal of School Health, 56,* 278–281.

Goodwin, D. W. (1989). The gene for alcoholism. *Journal of Studies on Alcohol, 50,* 397–398.

Goodwin, D. W., Schulsinger, F., Hermansen, L., Guze, S. B., & Winokur, G. (1973). Alcohol problems in adoptees raised apart from alcoholic biological parents. *Archives of General Psychiatry, 28,* 238–243.

Goodwin, D. W., Schulsinger, F., Hermansen, L., Guze, S. B., & Winokur, G. (1975). Alcoholism and the hyperactive child syndrome. *Journal of Nervous and Mental Diseases, 160,* 349–353.

Gottfredson, M. R., & Hirschi, T. (1990). *A general theory of crime.* Stanford, CA: Stanford University Press.

Grant, B. F., Harford, T. C., & Grigson, M. B. (1988). Stability of alcohol consumption among youth: A national longitudinal survey. *Journal of Studies on Alcohol, 49,* 253–260.

Greene, R. L. (1991). *The MMPI-2/MMPI: An interpretive manual.* Boston: Allyn & Bacon.

Greene, R. L., & Garvin, R. D. (1988). Substance abuse/ dependence. In R. L. Greene (Ed.), *The MMPI: Use with specific populations* (pp. 159–197). Philadelphia: Grune & Stratton.

Greene, R. L., & Nichols, D. S. (1987). *Replicability and validity of the 2–8-7–4 codetype: A comment and some data.* Unpublished manuscript, Texas Tech University.

Greenfield, T. K., Guydish, J., & Temple, M. T. (1989). Reasons students give for limiting drinking: A factor analysis with implications for research and practice. *Journal of Studies on Alcohol, 50,* 108–115.

Griffiths, R. R., Bigelow, G. E., & Henningfield, J. E. (1980). Similarities in animal and human drug-taking behavior. In N. K. Mello (Ed.), *Advances in substance abuse* (Vol. 1, pp. 1–90). Greenwich, CT: JAI Press.

Griffiths, R. R., Bigelow, G. E., & Liebson, I. A. (1976). Human sedative self-administration: Effects of interingestion interval and dose. *Journal of Pharmacology and Experimental Therapeutics, 197,* 488–494.

Griffiths, R. R., Bigelow, G. E., Liebson, I. A., & Kaliszak, J. E. (1980). Drug preference in humans: Double-blind choice comparison of pentobarbital, diazepam, and placebo. *Journal of Pharmacology and Experimental Therapeutics, 215,* 649–661.

Griffiths, R. R., McLeod, D. R., Bigelow, G. E., Liebson, I. A., Roache, J. D., & Nowowieski, P. (1984). Comparison of diazepam and oxazepam: Preferences, liking and extent of abuse. *Journal of Pharmacology and Experimental Therapeutics, 229,* 501–507.

Gruder, C. L., Mermelstein, R. J., Kirkendol, S., Hedeker, D., Wong, S. C., Schreckengost, J., Warnecke, R. B., Burzette, R., & Miller, T. Q. (1993). Effects of social support and relapse prevention training as adjuncts to a televised smoking- cessation intervention. *Journal of Consulting and Clinical Psychology, 61,* 113–120.

Gurling, H. M. D., Murray, R. M., & Clifford, C. A. (1981). Investigations into the genetics of alcohol dependence and into its effects on brain function. In *Twin research 3: Epidemiology and clinical studies* (pp. 77–87). New York: Liss.

Gutierres, S. E., & Reich, J. W. (1988). Attributional analysis of drug abuse and gender: Effects of treatment and relationship to rehabilitation. *Journal of Social and Clinical Psychology, 7,* 176–191.

Haertzen, C. A., Kocher, T. R., & Miyasato, K. (1983). Reinforcements from the first drug experience can predict later drug habits and/or addiction: Results with coffee, cigarettes, alcohol, barbiturates, minor and major tranquilizers, stimulants, marijuana, hallucinogens, heroin, opiates and cocaine. *Drug and Alcohol Dependence, 11,* 147–165.

Hagnell, O., Lanke, J., Rorsman, B., & Ohman, R. (1986). Predictors of alcoholism in the Lundby study: II. Personality traits as risk factors for alcoholism. *European Archives of Psychiatry and Neurological Science, 235,* 192–196.

Hall, S. M., Havassy, B. E., & Wasserman, D. A. (1990). Commitment to abstinence and acute stress in relapse to alcohol, opiates, and nicotine. *Journal of Consulting and Clinical Psychology, 58,* 175–181.

Hansen, W. B., Malotte, C. K., & Fielding, J. E. (1988). Evaluation of a tobacco and alcohol abuse prevention curriculum for adolescents. *Health Education Quarterly, 15,* 93–114.

Hanson, S. L., & Ginsburg, A. L. (1988). Gaining ground: Values and high school success. *American Educational Research Journal, 25,* 334–365.

Harachkiewicz, J. M., Sansone, C., Blair, L. W., Epstein, J. A., & Manderlink, G. (1987). Attributional processes in behavior change and maintenance: Smoking cessation and continued abstinence. *Journal of Consulting and Clinical Psychology*, *55*, 372–378.

Harbin, H., & Maziar, H. (1975). The families of drug abusers: A review. *Family Process*, *14*, 411–431.

Harburg, E., DiFranceisco, W., Webster, D. W., Gleiberman, L., & Schork, A. (1990). Familial transmission of alcohol use: II. Imitation of and aversion to parent drinking (1960) by adult offspring (1977)—Tecumseh, Michigan. *Journal of Studies on Alcohol*, *51*, 245–256.

Hare, R. D., & McPherson, L. M. (1984). Psychopathy and perceptual asymmetry during verbal dichotic listening. *Journal of Abnormal Psychology*, *93*, 141–149.

Harford, T. C., & Grant, B. F. (1987). Psychosocial factors in adolescent drinking contexts. *Journal of Studies on Alcohol*, *48*, 551–557.

Harlow, H. F. (1959). Love in infant monkeys. *Scientific American*, *200*, 68–86.

Harris, K. B., & Miller, W. R. (1990). Behavioral self-control training for problem drinkers: Components of efficacy. *Psychology of Addictive Behaviors*, *4*, 82–90.

Hawkins, J. D., Catalano, R. F., Gillmore, M. R., & Wells, E. A. (1989). Skills training for drug abusers: Generalization, maintenance, and effects on drug use. *Journal of Consulting and Clinical Psychology*, *57*, 559–563.

Hawkins, J. D., Lishner, D. M., & Catalano, R. F. (1985). Childhood predictors and the prevention of adolescent substance abuse. In C. L. Jones & R. J. Battjes (Eds.), *Etiology of drug abuse: Implications for prevention* (pp. 75–120). Washington, DC: U.S. Government Printing Office.

Hazan, C., & Shaver, P. (1987). Romantic love conceptualized as an attachment process. *Journal of Personality and Social Psychology*, *52*, 511–524.

Heath, A. C., Jardine, R., & Martin, N. G. (1989). Interactive effects of genotype and social environment on alcohol consumption in female twins. *Journal of Studies on Alcohol*, *50*, 38–48.

Heather, N., Rollnick, S., & Winston, M. A. (1983). A comparison of objective and subjective measures of alcohol dependence as predictors of relapse following treatment. *British Journal of Clinical Psychology*, *22*, 11–17.

Heller, M. C., & Krauss, H. H. (1991). Perceived self-efficacy as a predictor of aftercare treatment entry by the detoxification patient. *Psychological Reports*, *68*, 1047–1052.

Henningfield, J. E., Chait, L. D., & Griffiths, R. R. (1983). Cigarette smoking and subjective responses in alcoholics: Effects of pentobarbital. *Clinical Pharmacology and Therapeutics*, *33*, 806–812.

Henningfield, J. E., & Goldberg, S. R. (1983). Control of behavior by intravenous nicotine injections in human subjects. *Pharmacology, Biochemistry and Behavior*, *19*, 1021–1026.

Henningfield, J. E., & Griffiths, R. R. (1980). Effects of ventilated cigarette holders on cigarette smoking by humans. *Psychopharmacology*, *68*, 115–119.

Herbert, M., Sluckin, W., & Sluckin, A. (1984). Mother-to-infant "bonding." *Annual Progress in Child Psychiatry and Child Development*, 63–84.

Hermalin, J., Husband, S. D., & Platt, J. J. (1990). Reducing costs of employee alcohol and drug abuse: Problem-solving and social skills training for relapse prevention. *Employee Assistance Quarterly*, *6*, 11–25.

Hermos, J. A., Locastro, J. S., Glynn, R. J., Bouchard, G. R., & DeLabry, L. O. (1988). Predictors of reduction and cessation of drinking in community-dwelling men: Results from the normative aging study. *Journal of Studies on Alcohol*, *49*, 363–368.

Hesselbrock, V., Stabenau, J., & Hesselbrock, M. (1985). Minimal brain dysfunction and neuropsychological test performance in offspring of alcoholics. In M. Galanter (Ed.), *Recent developments in alcoholism* (Vol. 3, pp. 65–82). New York: Plenum.

Hesselbrock, V., Stabenau, J., Hesselbrock, M., Meyer, R., & Babor, T. (1982). The nature of alcoholism in patients with different family histories of alcoholism. *Progress in Neuropsychopharmacological Biological Psychiatry*, *6*, 607–614.

Higuchi, S., Parrish, K. M., Dufour, M. C., Towle, L. H., & Harford, T. C. (1992). The relationship between three subtypes of the flushing response and DSM-III alcohol abuse in Japanese. *Journal of Studies on Alcohol*, *53*, 553–560.

Hill, H. E., Haertzen, C. A., & Davis, H. (1962). An MMPI factor analytic study of alcoholics, narcotic addicts and criminals. *Quarterly Journal of Studies on Alcohol*, *23*, 411–431.

Hill, S. Y. (1974). Intraventricular injection of 5-hydroxytryptamine and alcohol consumption in rats. *Biological Psychiatry*, *8*, 151–158.

Hinson, R. E., Poulos, C. X., Thomas, W., & Cappell, H. (1986). Pavlovian conditioning and addictive behavior: Relapse to oral self-administration of morphine. *Brain Neuroscience*, *100*, 368–375.

Hirschi, T. (1969). *Causes of delinquency*. Berkeley, CA: University of California Press.

Hodo, G. L., & Fowler, R. D. (1976). Frequency of MMPI two-point codes in a large alcoholic sample. *Journal of Clinical Psychology*, *32*, 487–489.

Horgan, J. (1993). Eugenics revisited: Trends in behavioral genetics. *Scientific American*, 122–131.

Hover, S., & Gaffney, L. R. (1991). The relationship between social skills and adolescent drinking. *Alcohol and Alcoholism*, *26*, 207–214.

Hrubec, Z., & Omenn, G. S. (1981). Evidence of genetic predisposition to alcoholic cirrhosis and psychosis: Twin concordance for alcoholism and its biological end points by zygosity among veterans. *Alcoholism: Clinical and Experimental Research*, *5*, 207–215.

Hser, Y., Anglin, M. D., & McGlothlin, W. H. (1987). Sex differences in addict careers: I. Initiation of use. *American Journal of Drug and Alcohol Abuse*, *13*, 33–57.

Huba, G. J., Newcomb, M. D., & Bentler, P. M. (1986). Adverse drug experiences and drug use behavior: A one-year longitudinal study of adolescents. *Journal of Pediatric Psychology*, *11*, 203–219.

Hudleby, J. D. (1986). Personality and the prediction of delinquency and drug use. *British Journal of Criminology*, *26*, 129–146.

Hughes, S. O., Power, T. G., & Francis, D. J. (1992). Defining patterns of drinking in adolescence: A cluster analytic approach. *Journal of Studies on Alcohol*, *53*, 40–47.

Humphreys, L., Forehand, R., McMahon, R., & Roberts, M. (1978). Parent behavioral training to modify child noncompliance: Effects on untreated siblings. *Journal of Behavior Therapy and Experimental Psychiatry*, *9*, 235–238.

Hunt, W. A., & Dalton, T. K. (1976). Regional brain acetylcholine levels in rats acutely treated with ethanol or rendered ethanol-dependent. *Brain Research*, *109*, 628–631.

Hurd, P. D., Johnson, C. A., Pechacheck, T., Jacobs, D. R., & Luepker, R. V. (1980). Prevention of cigarette smoking in seventh grade students. *Journal of Behavioral Medicine*, *3*, 15–28.

Huselid, R. F., Self, E. A., & Gutierres, S. E. (1991). Predictors of successful completion of a halfway-house program for chemically-dependent women. *American Journal of Drug and Alcohol Abuse*, *17*, 89–101.

Hutzell, R. R. (1984). Logonanalysis for alcoholics. *International Forum for Logotherapy*, *7*, 40–45.

Hutzell, R. R., & Eggert, M. A. (1989). *A workbook to increase your meaningful and purposeful goals*. Saratoga, CA: Institute of Logotherapy Press.

Iso-Abola, S. E. (1985). Conceptual and methodological problems in the analysis of self-serving causal attributions of success and failure. *Scandinavian Journal of Psychology*, *26*, 2–11.

Janoff-Bulman, R. (1979). Characterological versus behavioral self-blame. *Journal of Personality and Social Psychology*, *37*, 1798–1809.

Jellinek, E. M. (1960). *The disease concept of alcoholism.* New Haven, CT: United Printing Services.

Jessor, R., & Jessor, S. L. (1977). *Problem behavior and psychosocial development: A longitudinal study of youth.* San Diego: Academic Press.

Jessor, R., Jessor, S. L., & Finney, J. (1973). A social psychology of marijuana use: Longitudinal studies of high school and college youth. *Journal of Personality and Social Psychology*, *26*, 1–15.

Johanson, C. E. (1988). Behavioral studies of the reinforcing properties of cocaine. *NIDA Research Monograph Series*, *88*, 107–124.

Johanson, C. E., & de Wit, H. (1989). The use of choice procedures for assessing the reinforcing properties of drugs in humans. *NIDA Research Monograph Series*, *92*, 171–209.

Johanson, C. E., & Uhlenhuth, E. H. (1980a). Drug preference and mood in humans: *d*-amphetamine. *Psychopharmacology*, *71*, 275–279.

Johanson, C. E., & Uhlenhuth, E. H. (1980b). Drug preference and mood in humans: Diazepam. *Psychopharmacology*, *71*, 269–273.

Johnson, C. A., Pentz, M. A., Weber, M. D., Dwyer, J. H., Baer, N., MacKinnon, D. P., Hansen, W. B., & Flay, B. R. (1990). Relative effectiveness of comprehensive community programming for drug abuse prevention with high-risk and low-risk adolescents. *Journal of Consulting and Clinical Psychology*, *58*, 447–456.

Johnson, R. E., Marcos, A. C., & Bahr, S. J. (1987). The role of peers in the complex etiology of adolescent drug use. *Criminology*, *25*, 323–340.

Johnson, R. S., Tobin, J. W., & Cellucci, T. (1992). Personality characteristics of cocaine and alcohol abusers: More alike than different. *Addictive Behaviors*, *17*, 159–166.

Johnston, L. D., O'Malley, P. M., & Bachman, J. G. (1991). *Drug use among American high school seniors, college students and young adults 1975–1990.* Washington, DC: U.S. Government Printing Office.

Jones, B. E., & Prada, J. A. (1975). Drug-seeking behavior during methadone maintenance. *Psychopharmacologia*, *41*, 7–10.

Jones, M. (1968). Personality correlates and antecedents of drinking patterns in adult males. *Journal of Consulting and Clinical Psychology*, *32*, 2–12.

Jonsson, E., & Nilsson, T. (1968). Alcoholism in monozygotic and dizygotic twins. *Nordsk Hygienisk Tidskrift*, *49*, 21–25.

Kaij, L. (1960). *Studies on the etiology and sequels of abuse of alcohol.* Lund, Sweden: University of Lund.

Kandel, D. B. (1978). Convergencies in prospective longitudinal surveys of drug use in normal populations. In D. B. Kandel (Ed.), *Longitudinal research on drug use: Empirical findings and methodological issues* (pp. 3–38). Washington, DC: Hemisphere-Wiley.

Kandel, D. B. (1982). Epidemiological and psychosocial perspectives on adolescent drug use. *Journal of the American Academy of Child Psychiatry*, *21*, 328–347.

Kandel, D. B. (1984). Marijuana users in young adulthood. *Archives of General Psychiatry*, *41*, 200–209.

Kandel, D. B., & Davies, M. (1992). Progression to regular marijuana involvement: Phenomenology and risk factors for near-daily use. In M. Glantz & R. Pickens (Eds.), *Vulnerability to drug abuse* (pp. 211–253). Washington, DC: American Psychological Association.

Kandel, D. B., Kessler, R. C., & Margulies, R. Z. (1978). Antecedents of adolescent initiation into stages of drug use: A developmental analysis. *Journal of Youth and Adolescence*, *7*, 13–40.

Kandel, D. B., Simcha-Fagan, O., & Davies, M. (1986). Risk factors for delinquency and illicit drug use from adolescence to young adulthood. *Journal of Drug Issues, 16*, 67–90.

Kandel, D. B., Yamaguchi, K., & Chen, K. (1992). Stages of progression in drug involvement from adolescence to adulthood: Further evidence for the gateway theory. *Journal of Studies on Alcohol, 53*, 447–457.

Kaplan, H. B. (1980). *Deviant behavior in defense of self.* New York: Academic Press.

Kaplan, H. B., & Johnson, R. J. (1992). Relationships between circumstances surrounding initial illicit drug use and escalation of drug use: Moderating effects of gender and early adolescent experiences. In M. Glantz & R. Pickens (Eds.), *Vulnerability to drug abuse* (pp. 299–358). Washington, DC: American Psychological Association.

Kaplan, H. B., Johnson, R. J., & Bailey, C. A. (1986). Self- rejection and the explanation of deviance: Refinement and elaboration of a latent structure. *Social Psychology Quarterly, 49*, 110–128.

Kaplan, H. B., Martin, S. S., & Robbins, C. (1984). Pathways to adolescent drug use: Self-derogation, peer influence, weakening social control, and early substance use. *Journal of Health and Social Behavior, 25*, 270–289.

Kaprio, J., Koskenuuo, M., Langinvainio, H., Romanov, K., Sarna, S., & Rose, R. J. (1987). Genetic influences on use and abuse of alcohol: A study of 5638 adult Finnish twin brothers. *Alcoholism: Clinical and Experimental Research, 11*, 349–356.

Kellam, S. G., & Brown, H. (1982). *Social adaptational and psychological antecedents of adolescent psychopathology ten years later.* Baltimore: John Hopkins University Press.

Kelley, H. (1973). The process of causal attribution. *American Psychologist, 28*, 107–128.

Khantzian, E. J. (1985). The self-medication hypothesis of addictive disorders: Focus on heroin and cocaine dependence. *American Journal of Psychiatry, 142*, 1259–1264.

Khatami, M., Mintz, J., & O'Brien, C. P. (1978). Biofeedback mediated relaxation in narcotic addicts. *Behavior Therapy, 9*, 968–969.

Kiianmaa, K. (1976). Alcohol intake in the rat after lowering brain 5-hydroxytryptamine content by electrolytic midbrain raphe lesions, 5,6-dihydroxytryptamine or p- chloro-phenylalanine. *Medical Biology, 54*, 203–209.

Kinder, B. N., Pape, N. E., & Walfish, S. (1980). Drug and alcohol education programs: A review of outcome studies. *International Journal of the Addictions, 15*, 1035–1054.

Kirschenbaum, D. S., & Tomanken, A. J. (1982). On facing the generalization problem: The study of self-regulatory failure. In P. C. Kendall (Ed.), *Advances in cognitive-behavioral research and therapy* (Vol. 1, pp. 119–200). New York: Academic Press.

Kissin, B., Schenker, V., & Schenker, A. (1959). The acute effects of ethyl alcohol and chlorpromazine on certain physiological functions in alcoholics. *Quarterly Journal of Studies on Alcohol, 20*, 480–492.

Kitano, H. H. L., Chi, I., Rhee, S., Law, C. K., & Lubben, J. E. (1992). Norms and alcohol consumption: Japanese in Japan, Hawaii and California. *Journal of Studies on Alcohol, 53*, 33–39.

Klein, N. C., Alexander, J. F., & Parsons, B. V. (1977). Impact of family system intervention on recidivism and sibling delinquency: A model of primary prevention and program evaluation. *Journal of Consulting and Clinical Psychology, 45*, 469–474.

Klepping, J., Guilland, J.-C., Didier, J.-P., Klepping, C., & Malval, M. (1976). Alcooh: Facteur de stress ou tranquillisant? *Revue de l'alcoolisme, 22*, 5–14.

Knop, J., Goodwin, D., Teasdale, T. W., Mikkelsen, U., & Schulsinger, F. (1984). A Danish perspective study of young males at high risk for alcoholism. In D. W. Goodwin, D. Teilmann Van Dusen, & S. A. Mednick, (Eds.), *Longitudinal research in alcoholism* (pp. 107–124). Boston: Kluwer-Nijhoff.

Kozlowski, L. T., & Harford, M. R. (1976). On the significance of never using a drug: An example from cigarette smoking. *Journal of Abnormal Psychology, 85,* 433–434.

Kranzler, H. R., & Orrok, B. (1989). The pharmacology of alcoholism. In A. Tasman, R. E. Hales, & A. J. Frances (Eds.), *Review of psychiatry* (Vol. 8, pp. 359–379). Washington, DC: American Psychiatric Press.

Kuehnle, J. C., Anderson, W. H., & Chandler, E. (1974). First drinking experience in addictive and nonaddictive drinkers. *Archives of General Psychiatry, 31,* 521–523.

Kutner, G., & Zahourek, R. P. (1989). Relaxation and imagery groups for alcoholics. *Advances, 6,* 57–64.

Labouvie, E. W., & McGee, C. R. (1986). Relation of personality to alcohol and drug use in adolescence. *Journal of Consulting and Clinical Psychology, 54,* 289–293.

Lang, A. R., Goeckner, D. J., Adesso, V. J., & Marlatt, G. A. (1975). The effects of alcohol and aggression in male social drinkers. *Journal of Abnormal Psychology, 84,* 505–518.

Larsen, D. E., & Abu-Laban, B. (1968). Norm qualities and deviant drinking behavior. *Social Problems, 15,* 441–450.

Lehman, W. E. K., Barrett, M. E., & Simpson, D. D. (1990). Alcohol use by heroin addicts 12 years after drug abuse treatment. *Journal of Studies on Alcohol, 51,* 233–244.

Leigh, B. C. (1989). In search of the seven dwarves: Issues of measurement and meaning in alcohol expectancy research. *Psychological Bulletin, 105,* 361–373.

Leigh, B. C., & Stacy, A. W. (1993). Self-generated alcohol outcome expectancies in four samples of drinkers. *Addictive Research.*

Levenson, M. R. (1990). Risk taking and personality. *Journal of Personality and Social Psychology, 58,* 1073–1080.

Levinson, D., Darrow, C., Klein, E., Levinson, M., & McKee, B. (1978). *The seasons of a man's life.* New York: Knopf.

Lewis, C. E., Rice, J. P., & Helzer, J. E. (1983). Psychiatric diagnostic interactions: Alcoholism and antisocial personality. *Journal of Nervous and Mental Disease, 171,* 105–113.

Lewis, M., & Brooks, J. (1978). Self-knowledge and emotional development. In M. Lewis & L. A. Rosenblum (Eds.), *The development of affect* (pp. 205–226). New York: Plenum.

Lewis, M., Feiring, C., McGuffog, C., & Jaskir, J. (1984). Predicting psychopathology in six-year-olds from early social relations. *Child Development, 55,* 123–136.

Lewis, R. A., Piercy, F., Sprenkle, D., & Trepper, T. (1990). The Purdue brief family therapy model for adolescent substance abusers. In T. Todd & M. Selekman (Eds.), *Family therapy approaches with adolescent substance abusers* (pp. 29–48). New York: Human Sciences Press.

Linkenbach, J. (1990). Adlerian techniques for substance abuse prevention and intervention. *Individual Psychology: Journal of Adlerian Theory, Research, and Practice, 46,* 203–207.

Linquist, C. M., Lindsay, T. S., & White, G. D. (1979). Assessment of assertiveness in drug abusers. *Journal of Clinical Psychology, 35,* 676–679.

Liskow, B. I., & Goodwin, D. W. (1987). Pharmacological treatment of alcohol intoxication, withdrawal and dependence: A critical review. *Journal of Studies on Alcohol, 48,* 356–370.

Litman, G. K., Stapleton, J., Oppenheim, A. N., Peleg, M., & Jackson, P. (1983). Situations related to alcoholism relapse. *British Journal of Addiction, 78,* 381–389.

Loeber, R. (1990). Development and risk factors of juvenile antisocial behavior and delinquency. *Clinical Psychology Review, 10,* 1–41.

Loeber, R., & Dishion, T. (1983). Early predictors of male delinquency: A review. *Psychological Bulletin, 94,* 68–99.

Lolli, G., Schesler, E., & Golder, G. (1960). Choice of alcoholic beverage among 105 alcoholics in New York. *Quarterly Journal of Studies on Alcohol, 21,* 475–482.

Ludwig, A. M. (1985). Cognitive processes associated with "spontaneous" recovery from alcoholism. *Journal of Studies on Alcohol, 46,* 53–58.

Ludwig, A. M., Cain, R. B., Wikler, A., Taylor, R. M., & Bendfeldt, F. (1977). Physiologic and situational determinants of drinking behavior. In M. M. Gross (Ed.), *Alcohol intoxication and withdrawal—IIIb: Studies in alcohol dependence* (pp. 589–600). New York: Plenum.

Ludwig, A. M., & Wikler, A. (1974). Craving and relapse to drink. *Quarterly Journal of Studies on Alcohol, 35,* 108–130.

Lukas, S. E., Mendelson, J. H., Amass, L., & Benedikt, R. (1990). Behavioral and EEG studies of acute cocaine administration: Comparisons with morphine, amphetamine, pentobarbital, nicotine, ethanol, and marijuana. *NIDA Research Monograph Series, 95,* 146–151.

Lund, C., & Landesmann-Dwyer, S. (1979). Predelinquent and disturbed adolescents: The role of parental alcoholism. In M. Galanter (Ed.), *Currents in alcoholism* (Vol. 5, pp. 339–348). New York: Grune & Stratton.

MacAndrew, C., & Edgerton, R. B. (1969). *Drunken comportment: A social explanation.* New York: Aldine.

Maddux, J. F., & Desmond, D. P. (1980). New light on the maturing out hypothesis in opioid dependence. *Bulletin on Narcotics, 32,* 15–25.

Maddux, J. F., & Desmond, D. P. (1982). Residence relocation inhibits opioid dependence. *Archives of General Psychiatry, 39,* 1313–1317.

Maddux, J. F., & Desmond, D. P. (1989). Family and environment in the choice of opioid dependence or alcoholism. *American Journal of Drug and Alcohol Abuse, 15,* 117–134.

Magnusson, D. (1988). *Individual development from an interactional perspective: A longitudinal study.* Hillsdale, NJ: Erlbaum.

Main, M., Kaplan, N., & Cassidy, J. (1985). Security in infancy, childhood, and adulthood: A move to the level of representation. *Monographs of the Society for Research in Child Development, 50,* (1–2, Serial No. 209).

Main, M., Tomasini, L., & Tolan, W. (1979). Differences among mothers of infants judged to differ in security. *Developmental Psychology, 15,* 472–473.

Mann, L. M., Chassin, L., & Sher, K. J. (1987). Alcohol expectancies and the risk of alcoholism. *Journal of Consulting and Clinical Psychology, 55,* 411–417.

Marcos, A. C., Bahr, S. J., & Johnson, R. E. (1986). Test of a bonding/association theory of adolescent drug use. *Social Forces, 65,* 135–161.

Marlatt, G. A. (1978). Craving for alcohol, loss of control, and relapse: A cognitive behavioral analysis. In P. E. Nathan, G. E. Marlatt, & T. Løberg (Eds.), *Alcoholism: New directions in behavioral research and treatment.* New York: Plenum.

Marlatt, G. A. (1983). The controlled-drinking controversy: A commentary. *American Psychologist, 38,* 1097–1110.

Marlatt, G. A. (1985). Cognitive factors in the relapse process. In G. A. Marlatt & J. R. Gordon (Eds.), *Relapse prevention: Maintenance strategies in the treatment of addictive behaviors* (pp. 128–200). New York: Guilford.

Marlatt, G. A., Demming, B., & Reid, J. B. (1973). Loss of control drinking in alcoholics: An experimental analogue. *Journal of Abnormal Psychology, 81,* 223–241.

Marlatt, G. A., & Gordon, J. R. (1980). Determinants of relapse: Implications for the maintenance of behavior change. In P. O. Davidson & S. M. Davidson (Eds.), *Behavioral medicine: Changing health lifestyles* (pp. 410–472). New York: Brunner/Mazel.

Marlatt, G. A., & Gordon, J. R. (Eds.). (1985). *Relapse prevention: Maintenance strategies in the treatment of addictive behaviors.* New York: Guilford.

Marlatt, G. A., Kosturn, C. F., & Lang, A. R. (1975). Provocation to anger and opportunity for retaliation as determinants of alcohol consumption in social drinkers. *Journal of Abnormal Psychology*, *84*, 652–659.

Marlatt, G. A., & Marques, J. K. (1977). Meditation, self- control and alcohol abuse. In R. B. Stuart (Ed.). *Behavioral self-management: Strategies, techniques and outcomes* (pp. 117–153). New York: Brunner/Mazel.

Marlatt, G. A., & Rohsenow, D. R. (1980). Cognitive processes in alcohol use: Expectancy and the balanced placebo design. In N. K. Mello (Ed.), *Advances in substance abuse* (pp. 155–199). Greenwich, CT: JAI Press.

Maslow, A. H. (1969). Toward a humanistic biology. *American Psychologist*, *24*, 734–735.

Maultsby, M. C. (1975). *Help yourself to happiness through rational self-counseling*. New York: Institute for Rational Living.

May, R. (1967). *Psychology and the human dilemma*. Princeton, NJ: Van Nostrand.

Mayo Clinic. (1976). *Clinical examinations in neurology*. Philadelphia: Saunders.

McAuliffe, W. E. (1982). A test of Wikler's theory of relapse due to conditioned withdrawal sickness. *International Journal of the Addictions*, *17*, 19–33.

McAuliffe, W. E., & Ch'ien, J. M. N. (1986). Recovery training and self-help: A relapse-prevention program for treated opiate addicts. *Journal of Substance Abuse Treatment*, *3*, 9–20.

McCaul, M. E., Svikis, D. S., Turkkan, J. S., Bigelow, G. E., & Cromwell, C. C. (1990). Degree of familial alcoholism: Effects on substance use by college males. *NIDA Research Monograph Series*, *95*, 372–373.

McCord, J. (1988). Identifying developmental paradigms as leading to alcoholism. *Journal of Studies on Alcohol*, *49*, 357–362.

McCraken, S. G., de Wit, H., Uhlenhuth, E. H., & Johanson, C. E. (1990). Preference for diazepam in anxious adults. *Journal of Clinical Pharmacology*, *10*, 190–196.

McCusker, C. G., & Brown, K. (1990). Alcohol-predictive cues enhance tolerance to and precipitate "craving" for alcohol in social drinkers. *Journal of Studies on Alcohol*, *51*, 494–499.

McGee, L., & Newcomb, M. D. (1992). General deviance syndrome: Expanded hierarchical evaluations at four ages from early adolescence to adulthood. *Journal of Consulting and Clinical Psychology*, *60*, 766–776.

McKay, J. R., Murphy, R. T., McGuire, J., Rivinus, T. R., & Maisto, S. A. (1992). Incarcerated adolescents' attributions for drug and alcohol use. *Addictive Behaviors*, *17*, 227–235.

McKenna, T., & Pickens, R. (1983). Personality characteristics of alcoholic children of alcoholics. *Journal of Studies on Alcohol*, *44*, 688–700.

McLellan, A. T., & Druley, K. A. (1977). Non-random relation between drugs of abuse and psychiatric diagnosis. *Journal of Psychiatric Research*, *13*, 179–184.

McLeod, D. R., & Griffiths, R. R. (1983). Human progressive- ratio performance: Maintenance by pentobarbital. *Psychopharmacology*, *79*, 4–9.

McMurran, M., & Whitman, J. (1990). Strategies of self-control in male young offenders who have reduced their alcohol consumption without formal intervention. *Journal of Adolescence*, *13*, 115–128.

McNeal, E. T., & Cimbolic, P. (1986). Antidepressants and biochemical theories of depression. *Psychological Bulletin*, *99*, 361–374.

Mednick, S. A. (1983, May). *Subjects at risk for alcoholism: Recent reports*. Paper presented at the 14th annual medical scientific conference of the National Alcoholism Forum, Research Society on Alcoholism, Houston, TX.

Mednick, S. A., & Kandel, E. S. (1988). Congenital determinants of violence. *Bulletin of the American Academy of Psychiatry and the Law*, *16*, 101–109.

Meichenbaum, D. H. (1974). *Cognitive behavior modification.* Morristown, NJ: General Learning Press.

Meier, R. F., Burkett, S. R., & Hickman, C. A. (1984). Sanctions, peers and deviance: Preliminary models of a social control process. *Sociological Quarterly, 25,* 67–82.

Mello, N. K., & Mendelson, J. H. (1972). Drinking patterns during work-contingent and non-contingent alcohol acquisition. *Psychosomatic Medicine, 34,* 139–164.

Mello, N. K., & Mendelson, J. H. (1985). Operant acquisition of marijuana by women. *Journal of Pharmacology and Experimental Therapeutics, 235,* 162–171.

Mello, N. K., Mendelson, J. H., Kuehnle, J. C., & Sellers, M. (1978). Human polydrug use: Marijuana and alcohol. *Journal of Pharmacology and Experimental Therapeutics, 207,* 922–935.

Menard, S., & Huizinga, D. (1989). Age, period, and cohort size effects on self-reported alcohol, marijuana, and polydrug use: Results from the National Youth Survey. *Social Science Research, 18,* 174–194.

Mendelson, J. H., & Mello, N. K. (1984). Reinforcing properties of oral Δ⁹-tetrahydrocannabinol, smoked marijuana, and nabilone: Influence of previous marijuana use. *Psychopharmacology, 83,* 351–356.

Meyer, R. E., & Mirin, S. M. (1979). *The heroin stimulus: Implications for a theory of addiction.* New York: Plenum.

Miller, D., & Jang, M. (1977). Children of alcoholics: A 20-year longitudinal study. *Social Work Research Abstracts, 13,* 23–29.

Miller, F. T., Busch, F., & Tannebaum, J. H. (1989). Drug abuse in schizophrenia and bipolar disorder. *American Journal of Drug and Alcohol Abuse, 15,* 291–295.

Miller, L., (1991). Predicting relapse and recovery in alcoholism and addiction: Neuropsychology, personality, and cognitive style. *Journal of Substance Abuse Treatment, 8,* 277–291.

Miller, L. D., & Osmunson, S. (1989). Reframing. *Journal of Human Behavior and Learning, 6,* 32–38.

Miller, N. S., & Gold, M. S. (1990). The disease and adaptive models of addiction: A re-evaluation. *Journal of Drug Issues, 20,* 29–35.

Miller, P. M., & Eisler, R. M. (1977). Assertive behavior of alcoholics: A descriptive analysis. *Behavior Therapy, 8,* 146–149.

Miller, W. R., & Hester, R. K. (1986). Matching problem drinkers with optimal treatments. In W. R. Miller & N. Heather (Eds.), *Treating addictive behaviors: Processes of change* (pp. 175–203). New York: Plenum.

Miller, W. R., Leckman, A. L., Delaney, H. D., & Tinkcom, M. (1992). Long-term follow-up of behavioral self-control training. *Journal of Studies on Alcohol, 53,* 249–261.

Mirin, S. M., Meyer, R. E., & McNamee, H. B. (1976). Psychopathology and mood during heroin use. *Archives of General Psychiatry, 33,* 1503–1508.

Mirin, S. M., Weiss, R. D., Sollogub, A., & Michael, J. (1984). Psychopathology in the families of drug abusers. In S. M. Mirin (Ed.), *Substance abuse and psychopathology* (pp. 79–106). Washington, DC: American Psychiatric Press.

Mischel, W. (1969). Continuity and change in personality. *American Psychologist, 24,* 1012–1018.

Mitchel, M., Hu, T., McDonnell, M., & Swisher, J. (1984). Cost-effectiveness evaluation of an educational drug-abuse prevention program. *Journal of Drug Education, 14,* 271–292.

Monti, P. M., Abrams, D. B., Binkoff, J. A., & Zwick, W. R. (1986). Social skills training and substance abuse. In C. R. Hollin & P. Trower (Eds.), *Handbook of social skills training* (pp. 111–142). New York: Pergamon.

Monti, P. M., Abrams, D. B., Binkoff, J. A., Zwick, W. R., Liepman, M. R., Nirenberg, T. D., & Rohsenow, D. J. (1990). Communication skills training, communication skills training with family and cognitive behavioral mood management training for alcoholics. *Journal of Studies on Alcohol, 51*, 263–270.

Moore, M. (Guest), with Wilson, J. Q. (Moderator). (1984). *National Institute of Justice Crime File: Drinking and crime* [Film]. Washington, DC: National Institute of Justice.

Morey, L. C., & Blashfield, R. K. (1981). Empirical classification of alcoholism: A review. *Journal of Studies on Alcohol, 42*, 925–937.

Morgan, E. P., & Phillis, J. W. (1975). The effects of ethanol on acetylcholine release from the brain of unanaesthetized cats. *General Pharmacology, 6*, 281–284.

Moskalenko, V. D., Vanyukov, M. M., Solovyova, Z. V., Rakhmanova, T. V., & Vladimirsky, M. M. (1992). A genetic study of alcoholism in the Moscow population: Preliminary findings. *Journal of Studies on Alcohol, 53*, 218–224.

Mulford, H. A., Ledolter, J., & Fitzgerald, J. L. (1992). Alcohol availability and consumption: Iowa sales data revisited. *Journal of Studies on Alcohol, 53*, 487–494.

Murphy, C. A., Coover, D., & Owen, S. V. (1989). Development and validation of the Computer Self-Efficacy Scale. *Educational and Psychological Measurement, 49*, 893–899.

Murphy, J. M., McBride, W. J. Lumeng, L., & Li, T.-K. (1982). Regional brain levels of monoamines in alcohol-preferring and -nonpreferring lines of rats. *Pharmacology, Biochemistry and Behavior, 16*, 145–149.

Murphy, J. M., McBride, W. J., Lumeng, L., & Li, T.-K. (1987). Contents of monoamines in forebrain regions of alcohol- preferring (P) and -nonpreferring (NP) lines of rats. *Pharmacology, Biochemistry and Behavior, 26*, 389–392.

Murphy, S. B., Reinarman, C., & Waldorf, D. (1989). An 11-year follow-up of a network of cocaine users. *British Journal of Addiction, 84*, 427–436.

Murphy, T. J., Pagano, R. R., & Marlatt, G. A. (1986). Lifestyle modification with heavy alcohol drinkers: Effects of aerobic exercise and meditation. *Addictive Behaviors, 11*, 175–186.

Myers, R. D. (1978). Psychopharmacology of alcohol. *Annual Review of Pharmacological Toxicology, 18*, 125–144.

Myers, R. D. (1989). Emerging biochemical theories of alcoholism. *Resident and Staff Physician, 35*, 89–93.

Myers, R. D., & Melchior, G. E. (1975). Dietary tryptophan and the selection of ethyl alcohol in different strains of rats. *Psychopharmacologia, 42*, 109–115.

Nakken, C. (1988). *The addictive personality: Roots, rituals, and recovery*. Center City, MN: Hazelden.

Napier, T. L., Goe, R., & Bachtel, D. C. (1984). An assessment of the influence of peer association and identification on drug use among rural high school students. *Journal of Drug Education, 14*, 227–248.

Nathan, P. E. (1988). The addictive personality is the behavior of the addict. *Journal of Consulting and Clinical Psychology, 56*, 183–188.

Nathan, P. E., & O'Brien, J. S. (1971). An experimental analysis of the behavior of alcoholics and nonalcoholics during prolonged experimental drinking: A necessary precursor of behavior therapy. *Behavior Therapy, 2*, 455–476.

Needle, R., Lavec, Y., Su, S., Brown, P., & Doherty, W. (1988). Familial, interpersonal, and intrapersonal correlates of drug use: A longitudinal comparison of adolescents in treatment, drug-using adolescents not in treatment, and non-drug-using adolescents. *International Journal of the Addictions, 23*, 1211–1240.

Newcomb, M. D. (1992). Understanding the multidimensional nature of drug use and abuse: The role of consumption, risk factors, and protective factors. In M. Glantz & R. Pickens

(Eds.), *Vulnerability to drug abuse* (pp. 255–297). Washington, DC: American Psychological Association.

Newcomb, M. D., & Bentler, P. M. (1988). *Consequences of adolescent drug sue: Impact on the lives of young adults*. Beverly Hills, CA: Sage.

Newcomb, M. D., & Bentler, P. M. (1990). Antecedents and consequences of cocaine use: An eight-year study from early adolescence to young adulthood. In L. Robins & M. Rutter (Eds.), *Straight and devious pathways from childhood to adulthood* (pp. 158–181). Cambridge, England: Cambridge University Press.

Newcomb, M. D., & McGee, L. (1989). Adolescent alcohol use and other delinquent behaviors: A one-year longitudinal analysis controlling for sensation seeking. *Criminal Justice and Behavior, 16*, 345–369.

Newlin, D. B. (1984, June). *Human conditioned response to alcohol cues*. Paper presented at the Second Congress of the International Society for Biomedical Research on Alcoholism, Sante Fe, NM.

Newlin, D. B., Pretorius, M. D., & Jaffe, J. H. (1990). Pavlovian conditioning to morphine in opiate abusers. *NIDA Research Monograph Series, 95*, 390–391.

Nichols, J. R., & Hsiao, S. (1967). Addiction liability of albino rats: Breeding for qualitative differences in morphine drinking. *Science, 157*, 561–563.

Nordstrom, G., & Berglund, M. (1987). A prospective study of successful long-term adjustment in alcohol dependence. *Journal of Studies on Alcohol, 48*, 95–103.

Novaco, R. (1975). *Anger control: The development and evaluation of an experimental treatment*. Lexington, MA: D.C. Heath.

Obitz, F. W., Cooper, K., & Madeiros, D. C. (1974). General and specific perceived locus of control in heroin addicts. *International Journal of the Addictions, 9*, 757–760.

O'Brien, C. P., Childress, A. R., McLellan, A. T., Ehrman, R. & Ternies, J. W. (1988). Types of conditioning found in drug-dependent humans. *NIDA Research Monograph Series, 84*, 44–61.

O'Brien, C. P., Childress, R., McLellan, T., & Ehrman, R. (1990). Integrating systematic cue exposure with standard treatment in recovery drug dependent patients. *Addictive Behaviors, 15*, 355–365.

O'Brien, C. P., Greenstein, R., Ternies, J., McLellan, A. T., & Grabowski, J. (1980). Unreinforced self-injections: Effects on rituals and outcome in heroin addicts. *NIDA Research Monograph Series, 27*, 275–281.

O'Brien, C. P., Testa, T., O'Brien, T. J., Brady, J. P., & Wells, B. (1977). Conditioned narcotic withdrawal in humans. *Science, 195*, 1000–1002.

O'Connor, L. E., Berry, J. W., Morrison, A., & Brown, S. (1992). Retrospective reports of psychiatric symptoms before, during, and after drug use in a recovering population. *Journal of Psychoactive Drugs, 24*, 65–68.

O'Connor, S., Hesselbrock, V., & Tasman, A. (1986). Correlates of increased risk for alcoholism in young men. *Progress in Neuropsychopharmacological Biological Psychiatry, 10*, 211–218.

Oetting, E. R., & Beauvais, F. (1987). Common elements in youth drug abuse: Peer clusters and other psychosocial factors. *Journal of Drug Issues, 17*, 133–151.

Olson, D. H., Portner, J., & Bell, R. (1982). *FACES II*. St. Paul, MN: University of Minnesota.

O'Malley, S. S., & Maisto, S. A. (1985). The effects of family drinking history on responses to alcohol: Expectancies and reactions to intoxication. *Journal of Studies on Alcohol, 46*, 289–297.

Orcutt, J. D. (1987). Differential association and marijuana use: A closer look at Sutherland (with a little help from Becker). *Criminology, 25*, 341–358.

Ornstein, A. F., & Manning, W. H. (1985). Self-efficacy scaling by adult stutterers. *Journal of Communication Disorders, 18,* 313–320.

Overall, J. E. (1973). MMPI personality patterns of alcoholics and narcotic addicts. *Quarterly Journal of Studies on Alcohol, 34,* 104–111.

Pandina, R. J., & Johnson, V. (1990). Serious alcohol and drug problems among adolescents with a family history of alcoholism. *Journal of Studies on Alcohol, 51,* 278–282.

Pandina, R. J., Johnson, V., & Labouvie, E. W. (1992). Affectivity: A central mechanism in the development of drug dependence. In M. Glantz & R. Pickens (Eds.), *Vulnerability to drug abuse* (pp. 179–209). Washington, DC: American Psychological Association.

Panella, D. H., Cooper, P. F., & Henggeler, S. W. (1982). Peer relations in adolescence. In S. W. Henggeler (Ed.), *Delinquency and adolescent psychopathology: A family ecological systems approach* (pp. 139–161). Littleton, MA: Wright-PSG.

Park, J. Y., Huang, Y.-H., Nagoshi, C. T., Yuen, S., Johnson, R. C., Ching, C. A., & Bowman, K. S. (1984). The flush response to alcohol use among Koreans and Taiwanese. *Journal of Studies on Alcohol, 45,* 481–485.

Partanen, J., Brunn, K., & Markkanen, T. (1966). *Drinking behavior: A study on intelligence, personality, and use of alcohol of adult twins.* Helsinki: Finnish Foundation for Alcohol Studies.

Paternoster, R. (1989). Decisions to participate in and desist from four types of common delinquency: Deterrence and the rational choice perspective. *Law and Society Review, 23,* 7–40.

Patterson, G. R. (1980). Treatment for children with conduct problems: A review of outcome studies. In S. Feshbach & A. Fraczek (Eds.), *Aggression and behavior change: Biological and social processes* (pp. 83–132). New York: Praeger.

Patterson, G. R. (1986). Performance models for antisocial boys. *American Psychologist, 41,* 432–444.

Pavlov, I. P. (1927). *Conditioned reflexes* (G. V. Anrep, Trans.). London: Oxford University Press.

Pearce, J., & Garrett, H. D. (1970). A comparison of the drinking behavior of delinquent youth versus non-delinquent youth in the states of Idaho and Utah. *Journal of School Health, 40,* 131–135.

Pedersen, W., Clausen, S. E., & Lavik, N. J. (1989). Patterns of drug use and sensation-seeking among adolescents in Norway. *Acta Psychiatrica Scandinavica, 79,* 386–390.

Pederson, N. (1981). Twin similarity for usage of common drugs. In L. Gedda, P. Parisi, & W. E. Nance (Eds.), *Twin research 3: Epidemiological and clinical studies* (pp. 55–59). New York: Alan Liss.

Peele, S. (1986). The implications and limitations of genetic models of alcoholism and other addictions. *Journal of Studies on Alcohol, 47,* 63–73.

Pendery, M. L., Maltzman, I. M., & West, L. J. (1982). Controlled drinking by alcoholics? New findings and a reevaluation of a major affirmative study. *Science, 217,* 169–175.

Penick, E. C., Powell, B. J., Bingham, S. F., Liskow, B. I., Miller, N. S., & Read, M. R. (1987). A comparative study of familial alcoholism. *Journal of Studies on Alcohol, 48,* 136–146.

Penk, W. E., Woodward, W., Robinowitz, R., & Hess, J. (1978). Differences in MMPI scores of black and white heroin users. *Journal of Abnormal Psychology, 87,* 505–513.

Penning, M., & Barnes, G. E. (1982). Adolescent marijuana use: A review. *International Journal of the Addictions, 17,* 749–791.

Pentz, M. A., Dwyer, J. H., MacKinnon, D. P., Flay, B. R., Hansen, W. B., Wang, E. Y. I., & Johnson, C. A. (1989). A multi-community trial for primary prevention of adolescent drug abuse: Effects on drug use prevention. *Journal of the American Medical Association, 261,* 3259–3266.

Perry, C. L., Killen, J., Telch, M., Slinkard, L. A., & Danaher, B. G. (1980b). Modifying smoking behavior of teenagers: A school-based intervention. *American Journal of Public Health*, *70*, 722–725.

Piaget, J. (1963). The attainment of invariants and reversible operations in the development of thinking. *Social Research*, *30*, 283–299.

Pickens, R., & Harris, W. C. (1968). Self-administration of d- amphetamine by rats. *Psychopharmacologia*, *12*, 158–163.

Pickens, R. W., & Svikis, D. S. (1988). The twin method in the study of vulnerability to drug abuse. *NIDA Research Monograph Series*, *89*, 41–51.

Pickett, C., & Clum, G. A. (1982). Comparative treatment strategies and their interaction with locus of control in the reduction of postsurgical pain and anxiety. *Journal of Consulting and Clinical Psychology*, *50*, 439–441.

Piercy, F. P., Volk, R. J., Trepper, T., & Sprenkle, D. H., & Lewis, R. (1991). The relationship of family factors to patterns of adolescent substance abuse. *Family Dynamics of Addiction Quarterly*, *1*, 41–54.

Platt, J. J., & Metzger, D. S. (1987). Cognitive interpersonal problem-solving skills and maintenance of treatment success in heroin addicts. *Psychology of Addictive Behaviors*, *1*, 5–13.

Platt, J. J., Perry, G. M., & Metzger, D. S. (1980). The evolution of a heroin addiction treatment program within a correctional environment. In R. R. Ross & P. Gendreau (Eds.), *Effective correctional treatment*. Toronto: Butterworth.

Polich, J. M., Armor, D. J., & Braiker, H. B. (1981). *The course of alcoholism: Four years after treatment*. New York: John Wiley.

Pollock, V. E., Volavka, J., Goodwin, D. W., Mednick, S. A., Gabrielli, W. F., Knop, J., & Schulsinger, F. (1983). The EEG after alcohol administration in men at risk for alcoholism. *Archives of General Psychiatry*, *40*, 857–861.

Popham, R. E. (1959). Some social and cultural aspects of alcoholism. *Canadian Psychiatric Association Journal*, *4*, 222–229.

Post, R. M., Kotin, J., & Goodwin, F. R. (1974). The effects of cocaine on depressed patients. *American Journal of Psychiatry*, *131*, 511–517.

Powell, J., Gray, J. A., Brandley, B. P., Kasvikis, Y., Strang, J., Barratt, L., & Marks, I. (1990). The effects of exposure to drug-related cues in detoxified opiate addicts: Theoretical review and some new data. *Addictive Behaviors*, *15*, 339–354.

Prendergast, T. J. (1974). Family characteristics associated with marijuana use among adolescents. *International Journal of the Addictions*, *9*, 827–840.

Preston, K. L., Bigelow, G. E., Bickel, W., & Liebson, I. A. (1987). Three-choice drug discrimination in opioid-dependent humans: Hydromorphone, naloxone and saline. *Journal of Pharmacology and Experimental Therapeutics*, *243*, 1002–1009.

Produktschap voor Gestilleerde Dranken. (1986). *How much alcoholic beverage is drunk worldwide*. Schiedam, Netherlands: Author.

Propping, P., Kruger, J., & Janah, A. (1980). Effect of alcohol on genetically determined variations of the normal electroencephalogram. *Psychiatric Research*, *2*, 85–98.

Propping, P., Kruger, J., & Norbert, M. (1981). Genetic disposition to alcoholism: An EEG study of alcoholics and their relatives. *Human Genetics*, *59*, 51–59.

Rank, O. (1929). *The trauma of birth*. New York: Harcourt Brace.

Rankin, J.-H., & Wells, L. E. (1990). The effect of parental attachments and direct control on delinquency. *Journal of Research in Crime and Delinquency*, *27*, 140–165.

Redd, W. H., Jacobsen, P. B., Die-Trill, M., Dermatis, H., McEvoy, M., & Holland, J. C. (1987). Cognitive/attentional distraction in the control of conditioned nausea in pediatric cancer patients receiving chemotherapy. *Journal of Consulting and Clinical Psychology*, *55*, 391–395.

Reed, H., & Janis, I. L. (1974). Effect of induced awareness of rationalizations on smokers's acceptance of fear-arousing warnings about health hazards. *Journal of Consulting and Clinical Psychology, 42*, 748.

Reitman, J. (1974). Without surreptitious rehearsal, information in short-term memory decays. *Journal of Verbal Learning and Verbal Behavior, 13*, 365–377.

Research Triangle Institute. (1976). *Drug use and crime: Report of the panel on drug use and criminal behavior.* Research Triangle Park, NC: Author.

Rist, F., & Watzl, H. (1983). Self assessment of relapse risk and assertiveness in relation to treatment outcome of female alcoholism. *Addictive Behaviors, 8*, 121–127.

Ritz, M. C., George, F. R., de Fiebre, C. M., & Meisch, R. A. (1986). Genetic differences in the establishment of ethanol as a reinforcer. *Pharmacology, Biochemistry and Behavior, 24*, 1089–1094.

Roache, J. D., & Griffiths, R. R. (1987). Interactions of diazepam and caffeine: Behavioral and subjective dose effects in humans, *Pharmacology, Biochemistry and Behavior, 26*, 801–812.

Robins, L. N., Davis, D. H., & Goodwin, D. W. (1974). Drug use by U.S. Army enlisted men in Vietnam: A follow-up on their return home. *American Journal of Epidemiology, 99*, 235–249.

Robins, L. N., & Przybeck, T. (1985). Age of onset of drug use as a function of drug use and other disorders. In C. L. Jones & R. Battjes (Eds.), *Etiology of drug abuse: Implications for prevention* (pp.178–192). Rockville, MD: National Institute on Drug Abuse.

Robins, L. N., West, P. A., & Herjanic, B. L. (1975). Arrests and delinquency in two generations: A study of black urban families and their children. *Journal of Child Psychology and Psychiatry, 16*, 125–140.

Robins, L. N., & Wish, E. (1977). Childhood deviance as a developmental process: A study of 223 urban Black men from birth to 18. *Social Forces, 56*, 448–471.

Rodin, J. (1976). Density, perceived choice, and response to controllable and uncontrollable outcomes. *Journal of Experimental Social Psychology, 12*, 564–578.

Roe, A., & Burks, B. (1945). Adult adjustment of children of alcoholic and psychotic parentage and the influence of the foster home. Memoirs of the Section on Alcohol Studies, Yale University. *Quarterly Journal of Studies on Alcohol*, No. 3.

Rohsenow, D. J., & Bachorowski, J. (1984). Effects of alcohol and expectancies on verbal aggression in men and women. *Journal of Abnormal Psychology, 93*, 418–432.

Rohsenow, D. J., Beach, L. R., & Marlatt, G. A. (1978, July). *A decision-theory model of relapse.* Paper presented at the Summer Conference of the Alcoholism and Drug Abuse Institute, University of Washington, Seattle, WA.

Rohsenow, D. J., & Marlatt, G. A. (1981). The balanced placebo design: Methodological considerations. *Addictive Behaviors, 6*, 107–122.

Rohsenow, D. J., Monti, P. M., Binkoff, J. A., Liepman, M. R., Nirenberg, T. D., & Abrams, D. B. (1991). Patient-treatment matching for alcoholic men in communication skill versus cognitive-behavioral mood management training. *Addictive Behaviors, 16*, 63–69.

Roizen, R., Cahalan, D., & Shanks, P. (1978). "Spontaneous remission" among untreated problem drinkers. In D. B. Kandel (Ed.), *Longitudinal research on drug use: Empirical findings and methodological issues* (pp. 197–221). New York: John Wiley.

Rokeach, M. (1983). A value approach to the prevention and reduction of drug abuse. *NIDA Research Monograph Series, 47*, 172–194.

Ross, H. E., Glaser, F. B., & Germanson, T. (1988). The prevalence of psychiatric disorders in patients with alcohol and other drug problems. *Archives of General Psychiatry, 45*, 1023–1032.

Ross, R. R., & Fabiano, E. A. (1985). *Time to think: A cognitive model of delinquency prevention and offender rehabilitation*. Johnson City, TN: Institute of Social Sciences and Art.

Ross, S. (1973). A study of living and residence patterns of former heroin addicts as a result of their participation in a methadone treatment program. In *Proceedings of the Fifth National Conference on Methadone Treatment* (pp. 554–561). New York: National Association for the Prevention of Addiction to Narcotics.

Rothman, R. B., Long, J. B., Bykov, V., Rice, K. C., & Holaday, J. W. (1990). Site-directed affinity ligands as tools to study the phenomenology and mechanisms of morphine-induced upregulation of opioid receptors. *NIDA Research Monograph Series, 95,* 192–198.

Rounsaville, B. J., Dolinsky, Z. S., Babor, T. F., & Meyer, R. E. (1987). Psychopathology as a predictor of treatment outcome in alcoholics. *Archives of General Psychiatry, 44,* 505–513.

Rounsaville, B. J., & Kleber, H. D. (1986). Untreated opiate addicts. *Archives of General Psychiatry, 42,* 1072–1077.

Rutter, M., & Giller, H. (1984). *Juvenile delinquency: Trends and perspectives*. New York: Guilford.

Rychtarik, R. G., Foy, D. W., Scott, T., Lokey, L., & Prue, D. M. (1987). Five-six-year follow-up of broad-spectrum behavioral treatment for alcoholism: Effects of training controlled drinking skills. *Journal of Consulting and Clinical Psychology, 55,* 106–108.

Rychtarik, R. G., Prue, D. M., Rapp, S. R., & King, A. C. (1992). Self-efficacy, aftercare and relapse in a treatment program for alcoholics. *Journal of Studies on Alcohol, 53,* 435–440.

Rydelius, P. A. (1983). Alcohol-abusing teenage boys. *Acta Psychiatrica Scandinavica, 68,* 368–380.

Schall, M., Kemeny, A., & Maltzman, I. (1992). Factors associated with alcohol use in university students. *Journal of Studies on Alcohol, 53,* 122–136.

Schnoll, S. H., Daghestani, A. N., & Hansen, T. R. (1984). Cocaine dependence. *Residence and Staff Physician, 30,* 24–31.

Schoefer, J. (1981). *Prevention of alcoholism*. Presentation made at the University of Nebraska.

Schuckit, M. A. (1984). Subjective responses to alcohol in sons of alcoholics and controls. *Archives of General Psychiatry, 41,* 879–884.

Schuckit, M. A. (1985). Studies of populations at high risk for alcoholism. *Psychiatric Development, 3,* 31–63.

Schuckit, M. A. (1987). Biological vulnerability to alcoholism. *Journal of Consulting and Clinical Psychology, 55,* 301–309.

Schuckit, M. A. (1989). *Drug and alcohol abuse* (3rd ed.). New York: Plenum.

Schuckit, M. A., Goodwin, D. W., Winokur, G. A. (1972). A study of alcoholism in half siblings. *American Journal of Psychiatry, 128,* 1132–1136.

Sebald, H. (1986). Adolescents' shifting orientation toward parents and peers: A curvilinear trend over recent decades. *Journal of Marriage and the Family, 48,* 5–14.

Shapiro, D. H., & Walsh, R. N. (Eds.). (1984). *Meditation: Classic and contemporary perspectives*. New York: Aldine.

Shedler, J., & Block, J. (1990). Adolescent drug use and psychological health: A longitudinal inquiry. *American Psychologist, 45,* 612–630.

Shelden, W. (1954). *Atlas of men*. New York: Harper.

Shelton, M. D., Parsons, O. A., Leber, W. R., & Yohman, J. R. (1982). Locus of control and neuropsychological performance in chronic alcoholics. *Journal of Clinical Psychology, 38,* 649–655.

Sher, K., & Levenson, R. (1982). Risk for alcoholism and individual differences in the stress response dampening effect of alcohol. *Journal of Abnormal Psychology, 91,* 350–367.

Shope, J. T., Dielman, T. E., Butchart, A. T., Campanelli, P. C., & Kloska, D. D. (1992). An elementary school-based alcohol misuse prevention program: A follow-up evaluation. *Journal of Studies on Alcohol, 53,* 106–121.

Shute, R., Pierce, R., & Lubell, E. (1981). Smoking awareness and practices of urban preschool and first grade children. *Journal of School Health, 5,* 347–351.

Sideroff, S. I., & Jarvick, M. E. (1980). Conditioned responses to video tape showing heroin related stimuli. *International Journal of the Addictions, 15,* 529–536.

Siegel, S. (1988). Drug anticipation and the treatment of dependence. *NIDA Research Monograph Series, 84,* 1–24.

Siegel, S., & Ellsworth, D. (1986). Pavlovian conditioning and death from apparent overdose of medically prescribed morphine: A case report. *Bulletin of the Psychonomic Society, 24,* 278–280.

Simo, S., & Perez, J. (1991). Sensation seeking and antisocial behavior in a junior student sample. *Personality and Individual Differences, 12,* 965–966.

Simons, R. L., Conger, R. D., & Whitbeck, L. B. (1988). A multistage social learning model of the influences of family and peers upon adolescent substance abuse. *Journal of Drug Issues, 18,* 293–315.

Simons, R. L., & Robertson, J. F. (1989). The impact of parenting factors, deviant peers, and coping style upon adolescent drug use. *Family Relations, 38,* 273–281.

Simpson, D. D., & Marsh, K. L. (1986). Relapse and recovery among opioid addicts 12 years after treatment. *NIDA Research Monograph Series, 72,* 86–103.

Sisson, R. W., & Azrin, N. H. (1986). Family-member involvement to initiate and promote treatment of problem drinkers. *Journal of Behavior Therapy and Experimental Psychiatry, 17,* 15–21.

Sitharthan, T., & Kavanagh, D. J. (1990). Role of self-efficacy in predicting outcomes from a programme of controlled drinking. *Drug and Alcohol Dependence, 27,* 87–94.

Sjoberg, L., & Johnson, T. (1978). Trying to give up smoking: A study of volitional breakdowns. *Addictive Behaviors, 3,* 149–164.

Sjoberg, L., Samsonowitz, V., & Olsson, G. (1978). Volitional problems in alcohol abuse. *Gotteberg Psychological Reports, 8,* No. 5.

Sjoquist, B., Perdahl, E., & Winblad, B. (1983). Effect of alcoholism on salsolinol and biogenic amines in human brain. *Drug and Alcohol Dependence, 12,* 15–24.

Skinner, H. A. (1982). Statistical approaches to the classification of alcohol and drug addiction. *British Journal of Addiction, 27,* 259–273.

Skutle, A., & Berg, G. (1987). Training in controlled drinking for early-stage problem drinkers. *British Journal of Addiction, 82,* 493–501.

Smart, R. G., & Fejer, D. (1972). Drug use among adolescents and their parents: Using the generation gap in mood modification. *Journal of Abnormal Psychology, 70,* 153–166.

Smith, G. M., & Fogg, C. P. (1978). Psychological predictors of early use, late use, and nonuse of marijuana among teenage students. In D. B. Kandel (Ed.), *Longitudinal research on drug use: Empirical findings and methodological issues* (pp. 101–113). Washington, DC: Hemisphere-Wiley.

Smith, T. E. (1983). Reducing adolescents' marijuana abuse. *Social Work in Health Care, 9,* 33–44.

Sobell, L. C., Sobell, M. B., Toneatto, T., & Leo, G. I. (1993). Severely dependent alcohol abusers may be vulnerable to alcohol cues in television programs. *Journal of Studies on Alcohol, 54,* 85–91.

Sobell, M. B., & Sobell, L. C. (1973). Individualized behavior therapy for alcoholics. *Behavior Therapy, 4,* 49–72.

Solomon, K. E., & Annis, H. M. (1990). Outcome and efficiency expectancy in the prediction of post-treatment drinking behavior. *British Journal of Addiction, 85,* 659–665.

Sommer, R. (1978). *The mind's eye: Imagery in everyday life.* New York: Delacorte.

Speckart, G., & Anglin, M. D. (1986). Narcotics use and crime: An overview of recent research advances. *Contemporary Drug Problems, 13,* 741–769.

Sroufe, L. A. (1983). Infant-caregiver attachment and patterns of adaptation in pre-school: The roots of maladaption and competence. In M. Perlmutter (Ed.), *Minnesota symposium on child psychiatry* (Vol. 16, pp. 41–81). Hillsdale, NJ: Erlbaum.

Stabenau, J. R. (1986). Basic research on heredity and alcohol: Implications for clinical application. *Social Biology, 32,* 297–321.

Stabenau, J., & Hesselbrock, V. (1984). Psychopathology in alcoholics and their families and vulnerability to alcoholism: A review and new findings. In S. Mirin (Ed.), *Substance abuse and psychopathology* (pp. 108–132). Washington, DC: American Psychiatric Association.

Stacy, A. W., Newcomb, M. D., & Bentler, P. M. (1991). Personality, problem drinking, and drunk driving: Mediating, moderating, and direct-effect models. *Journal of Personality and Social Psychology, 60,* 795–811.

Stall, R., & Biernacki, P. (1986). Spontaneous remission from the problematic use of substances: An inductive model derived from a comparative analysis of the alcohol, opiate, tobacco, and food/obesity literatures. *International Journal of the Addictions, 21,* 1–23.

Stanton, M. D., Todd, T. C., Steir, F., Van Deusen, J. M., & Cook, L. (1982). Treatment outcomes. In M. D. Stanton & T. C. Todd (Eds.), *Family therapy of drug abuse and addiction.* New York: Guilford.

Strassberg, D. S., & Robinson, J. S. (1974). Relationship between locus of control and other personality measures in drug use. *Journal of Consulting and Clinical Psychology, 42,* 744–745.

Strickler, D., Bigelow, G., Wells, D., & Liebson, I. (1977). Effects of relaxation instructions on the electromyographic responses of abstinent alcoholics to drinking related stimuli. *Behaviour Research and Therapy, 15,* 500–502.

Stuck, M. F., Ksander, M., Berg, B., Loughin, J., & Johnson, B. D. (1982). *The consequences of breaking the law: Perceptions of adolescents involved in serious crime.* New York: Interdisciplinary Research Center.

Sutherland, E. H. (1939). *Principles of criminology* (3rd ed.). Philadelphia: Lippincott.

Sutker, P. B., & Archer, R. P. (1979). MMPI characteristics of opiate addicts, alcoholics, and other drug abusers. In C. E. Newmark (Ed.), *MMPI: Clinical and research trends* (pp. 105–148). New York: Praeger.

Suwaki, H., & Ohara, H. (1985). Alcohol-induced facial flushing and drinking behavior in Japanese men. *Journal of Studies on Alcohol, 46,* 196–198.

Suzdak, P. D., Glowa, J. R., Crowley, J. N., Schwartz, R. D., Skolnick, P., & Paul, S. M. (1986). A selective imidazobenzodiazepine antagonist of ethanol in rats. *Science, 234,* 1243–1247.

Swadi, H. S. (1988). Adolescent drug taking: Role of family and peers. *Drug and Alcohol Dependence, 21,* 157–160.

Swaim, R. C., Oetting, E. R., Edwards, R. W., & Beauvais, F. (1989). Links from emotional distress to adolescent drug use: A path model. *Journal of Consulting and Clinical Psychology, 57,* 227–231.

Takahashi, R. N., & Singer, G. (1979). Self-administration of delta-9-tetrahydrocannabinol by rats. *Pharmacology, Biochemistry and Behavior, 11,* 737–740.

Tarbox, A. R., Weigel, J. D., & Biggs, J. T. (1985). A cognitive typology of alcoholism: Implications for treatment outcome. *American Journal of Drug and Alcohol Abuse, 11,* 91–101.

Tarter, R. E., Alterman, A. I., & Edwards, K. L. (1985). Vulnerability to alcoholism in men: A behavior-genetic perspective. *Journal of Studies on Alcohol, 46*, 329–356.

Taub, D. E., & Skinner, W. F. (1990). A social bonding-drug progression model of amphetamine use among young women. *American Journal of Drug and Alcohol Abuse, 16*, 77–95.

Teasdale, J. D. (1973). Conditioned abstinence in narcotic addicts. *International Journal of the Addictions, 8*, 273–292.

Teichman, M., Barnea, Z., & Ravav, G. (1989). Personality and substance use among adolescents: A longitudinal study. *British Journal of Addiction, 84*, 181–190.

Temple, M., & Ladouceur, P. (1986). The alcohol-crime relationship as an age-specific phenomenon: A longitudinal study. *Contemporary Drug Problems, 15*, 89–115.

Terry, J., Lolli, G., & Golder, G. (1957). Choice of alcoholic beverage among 531 alcoholics in California. *Quarterly Journal of Studies on Alcohol, 18*, 417–428.

Teuber, H. L., & Powers, E. (1953). Evaluating therapy in a delinquency prevention program. *Psychiatric Treatment, 21*, 138–147.

Thompson, R. A. (1986). Temperament, emotionality, and infant cognition. In J. V. Lerner & R. M. Lerner (Eds.), *Temperament and social interaction in infants and children* (pp. 35–53). San Francisco: Jossey-Bass.

Tiffany, S. T. (1990). A cognitive model of drug usage and drug- use behavior: Role of automatic and nonautomatic processes. *Psychological Review, 97*, 147–168.

Tuchfeld, B. S. (1981). Spontaneous remission in alcoholics: Empirical observations and theoretical implications. *Journal of Studies on Alcohol, 42*, 626–641.

Udel, M. M. (1984). Chemical abuse/dependence: Physicians' occupational hazard. *Journal of the Medical Association of Georgia, 73*, 775–778.

Ullman, A. D. (1958). Sociocultural backgrounds of alcoholism. *Annals of the American Academy of Political Social Science, 315*, 48–54.

Ullmann, L. P., & Krasner, L. (1975). *A psychological approach to abnormal behavior* (2nd ed.). Englewood Cliffs, NJ: Prentice-Hall.

U.S. Department of Health and Human Services. (1990). *National household survey on drug abuse: Main findings 1988.* Washington, DC: U.S. Government Printing Office.

Vaillant, G. E., & Milofsky, E. S. (1982). Natural history of male alcoholism: IV. Paths to recovery. *Archives of General Psychiatry, 39*, 127–133.

Venables, P. H. (1987). Autonomic nervous system factors in criminal behavior. In S. A. Mednick, T. E. Moffitt, & S. A. Stack (Eds.), *The causes of crime: New biological approaches* (pp. 110–136). New York: Cambridge University Press.

Volkow, N. D., Fowler, J. S., Wolf, A. P., Schlyer, D., Shiue, C.-Y., Alpert, R., Dewey, S. L., Logan, J., Bendriem, B., Christman, D., Hitzemann, R., & Henn, F. (1990). Effects of chronic cocaine abuse on postsynaptic dopamine receptors. *American Journal of Psychiatry, 147*, 719–724.

Waldorf, D. (1976). Life without heroin: Some social adjustments during long-term periods of voluntary abstention. In R. H. Coobs, L. J. Fry, & P. G. Lewis (Eds.), *Socialization in drug abuse* (pp. 365–384). Cambridge, MA: Schenkman.

Walters, G. D. (1990). *The criminal lifestyle: Patterns of serious criminal conduct.* Newbury Park, CA: Sage.

Walters, G. D. (1992). Drug-seeking behavior: Disease or lifestyle? *Professional Psychology: Research and Practice, 23*, 139–154.

Walters, G. D. (1993). The lifestyle approach to substance abuse. *International Forum for Logotherapy, 16*, 13–19.

Walters, G. D. (1994a). Discriminating between high and low volume substance abusers by means of the Drug Lifestyle Screening Interview. *American Journal of Drug and Alcohol Abuse, 20*, 19–33.

Walters, G. D. (1994b). The drug lifestyle: One pattern or several? *Psychology of Addictive Behaviors, 8*, 8–13.

Walters, G. D., & White, T. W. (1989). Heredity and crime: Bad genes or bad research? *Criminology, 27*, 455–485.

Walton, N. Y., & Deutsch, J. A. (1978). Self-administration of diazepam by the rat. *Behavioral Biology, 24*, 533–538.

Weary, G., Harvey, J. H., Schwieger, P., Olson, C. T., Perloff, E., & Pritchard, S. (1982). Self-presentation and the moderation of self-serving biases. *Social Cognition, 1*, 140–159.

Weaver, F. M., & Carroll, J. S. (1985). Crime perceptions in a natural setting by expert and novice shoplifters. *Social Psychology Quarterly, 48*, 349–359.

Weiner, B. (Ed.). (1974). *Achievement motivation and attribution theory*. Morristown, NJ: General Learning Press.

Weinstein, R. M. (1978). The avowal of motives for marijuana behavior. *International Journal of the Addictions, 13*, 887–910.

Weiss, R. D. (1992a). The role of psychopathology in the transition from drug use to abuse and dependence. In M. Glantz & R. Pickens (Eds.), *Vulnerability to drug abuse* (pp. 137–148). Washington, DC: American Psychological Association.

Weiss, R. D. (1992b, August). *Therapeutic approaches to alcohol and drug abuse*. Workshop presented at the Cape Cod Summer Symposia, Eastham, MA.

Weiss, R. D., Griffin, M. L., & Mirin, S. M. (1992). Drug abuse as self-medication for depression: An empirical study. *American Journal of Drug and Alcohol Abuse, 18*, 121–129.

Weiss, R. D., Mirin, S. M., Griffin, M. L., & Michael, M. L. (1988). Psychopathology in cocaine abusers: Changing trends. *Journal of Nervous and Mental Disease, 176*, 719–725.

Werch, C. E. (1990). Behavioral self-control strategies for deliberately limiting drinking among college students. *Addictive Behaviors, 15*, 119–128.

Werner, E. E. (1986). Resilient offspring of alcoholics: A longitudinal study from birth to age 18. *Journal of Studies on Alcohol, 47*, 34–40.

Werner, E. E., & Smith, R. S. (1977). *Kauai's children come of age*, Honolulu: University of Hawaii Press.

Werner, H. (1957). The concept of development from a comparative and organismic point of view. In D. Harris (Ed.), *The concept of development* (pp. 125–148). Minneapolis: University of Minnesota Press.

Wexler, M. (1975). Personality characteristics of marijuana users and nonusers in a suburban high school. *Cornell Journal of Social Relations, 10*, 267–288.

White, H. R., Johnson, V., & Garrison, C. G. (1985). Drug-crime nexus among adolescents and their peers. *Deviant Behavior, 6*, 183–204.

White, H. R., Johnson, V., & Horowitz, A. (1986). An application of three deviance theories of adolescent substance use. *International Journal of the Addictions, 21*, 347–366.

Wikler, A. (1948). Recent progress in research on the neurophysiological basis of morphine addiction. *American Journal of Psychiatry, 105*, 328–338.

Wikler, W. A., & Pescor, F. T. (1967). Classical conditioning of a morphine abstinence phenomenon, reinforcement of opioid drinking behavior and "relapse" in morphine addicted rats. *Psychopharmacologia, 10*, 255–284.

Wilkinson, D. A., & LeBreton, S. (1986). Early indicators of treatment outcome in multiple drug users. In W. R. Miller & N. Heather (Eds.), *Treating addictive behaviors: Processes of change* (pp. 239–261). New York: Plenum.

Wilks, J. (1986). The relative importance of parents and friends in adolescent decision making. *Journal of Youth and Adolescence, 15*, 323–325.

Williams, R., Ward, D., & Gray, L. (1985). The persistence of experimentally induced cognitive change. *Journal of Drug Education, 15*, 33–42.

Wilson, H. (1980). Parental supervision: A neglected aspect of delinquency. *British Journal of Criminology, 20*, 203–235.

Wilson, J. R., & Plomin, R. (1985). Individual differences in sensitivity and tolerance to alcohol. *Social Biology, 32*, 162–184.

Windle, M., & Miller-Tutzauer, C. (1991). Antecedents and correlates of alcohol, cocaine, and alcohol-cocaine abuse in early adulthood. *Journal of Drug Education, 21*, 133–148.

Winick, C. (1962). Maturing out of narcotic addiction. *Bulletin on Narcotics, 14*, 1–7.

Wise, R. A. (1985). Neural mechanisms of the reinforcing action of cocaine. *NIDA Research Monograph Series, 50*, 15–33.

Wise, R. A., & Bozarth, M. A. (1987). A psychomotor stimulant theory of addiction. *Psychological Review, 94*, 469–492.

Wolff, P. H. (1972). Ethnic differences in alcohol sensitivity. *Science, 175*, 449–450.

Woods, J. H., & Schuster, C. R. (1968). Reinforcement properties of morphine, cocaine, and SPA as a function of unit dose. *International Journal of the Addictions, 33*, 231–236.

Woods, J. H., Young, A. M., & Herling, S. (1982). Classification of narcotics on the basis of their reinforcing, discriminative, and antagonist effects in rhesus monkeys. *Federation Proceedings, 41*, 221–227.

Woody, G. E., & Blaine, J. (1979). Depression in narcotic addicts: Quite possibly more than a chance association. In R. L. Dupont, A. Goldstein, & J. O'Donnell (Eds.), *Handbook on drug abuse*. Washington, DC: U.S. Government Printing Office.

Woody, G. E., O'Brien, C. P., & Rickels, K. (1975). Depression and anxiety in heroin addicts: A placebo-controlled study of doxepin in combination with methadone. *American Journal of Psychiatry, 132*, 447–450.

Wright, M. H., & Obitz, F. W. (1984). Alcoholics' and nonalcoholics' attributions of control of future life events. *Journal of Studies on Alcohol, 45*, 138–143.

Wurmser, L. (1978). *The hidden dimension*. New York: Jason Aronson.

Yamaguchi, K., & Kandel, D. B. (1984). Patterns of drug use from adolescence to young adulthood: II. Sequences of progression. *American Journal of Public Health, 74*, 668–672.

Yochelson, S., & Samenow, S. E. (1976). *The criminal personality, Vol. I: A profile for change*. New York: Jason Aronson.

Young, A. M., & Hurling, S. (1986). Drugs as reinforcers: Studies in laboratory animals. In S. R. Goldberg & I. P. Stolerman (Eds.), *Behavioral analysis of drug dependence* (pp. 9–68). New York: Academic Press.

Zinberg, N. E., & Jacobson, R. C. (1976). The natural history of "chipping." *American Journal of Psychiatry. 33*, 37–40.

Zucker, R. A., & Baron, F. H. (1973). Parental behaviors associated with problem drinking and antisocial behavior among adolescent males. In M. E. Chafetz (Ed.), *Research on alcoholism: Clinical problems and special populations* (pp. 276–296). Washington, DC: U.S. Government Printing Office.

Zuckerman, M. (1979). *Sensation seeking: Beyond the optimal level of arousal*. Hillsdale, NJ: Erlbaum.

Index